A Catholic Eton?

Hilaire Belloc at the Oratory School, 1887.

A Catholic Eton?

Newman's Oratory School

Paul Shrimpton

GRACEWING

First published in 2005

Gracewing
2 Southern Avenue, Leominster
Herefordshire HR6 0QF

ISBN 0 85244 661 6

Typeset by
Action Publishing Technology Ltd, Gloucester, GL1 5SR

For Margaret

and for Charles, *in memoriam*

Contents

Illustrations and maps

The termly expenses are reproduced with permission of His Grace the Duke of Norfolk (Arundel Castle archive, A.1317). The library rules and fines are reproduced from *Extracts from a School Boy's Diary, 1864–65* (London: privately printed, 1887), Birmingham Oratory archive, N.L.D.2.1

Plates

Plates 1 and 3 are reproduced by courtesy of The College, Littlemore; Plates 5 and 13 by courtesy of the governors of the Oratory School Association; and Plates 6–9 and 14–24 by courtesy of the Fathers of the Birmingham Oratory. Plate 2 is reproduced from E. Bellasis's *Memorials of Mr Serjeant Bellasis, 1800–1873* (London: Burns & Oates, 1893); Plate 10 from the *Oratory School Magazine* 4 (November 1892), p. 8.

Preface

For several quite different reasons this book is not a standard school history. In the first place, it deals with a foundation only in the lifetime of its founder, leaving to others the task of bringing the story up to date. In the second place, the originality of the foundation (and the enormous difficulties the founders faced) can only be fully appreciated if the story of the beginnings is set against developments at the time, such as the changing nature of the public school system and the ongoing process of Catholic emancipation. As a consequence, this is no inward-looking school story, but a tale set in the full context of the times, and one which sheds light on various aspects of Victorian life. Thirdly, this is no standard school story because the Oratory School was no standard school; for its time it appeared an eclectic mix, and if it seems more familiar to modern eyes than to Victorian ones, this is probably because it was inspired by a man ahead of his times.

In completing this book I feel immensely privileged to have had the good fortune of being able to tell at length the story of the beginnings of the Oratory School under John Henry Newman. It was a story waiting to be told, and I was quite fortunate to stumble across the huge amount of archival material required for the purpose. In carrying out this pleasant task I hope I have been of service to all those in any way connected with the school; to those with interests in Cardinal Newman, and in particular to those like myself who are captivated by his ideas on education; and, not least, to those who admire the many other talented nineteenth-century converts, who tend to get forgotten.

Paul Shrimpton
Grandpont House, Oxford
2 May 2005

Acknowledgements

The idea of researching the origins of the Oratory School was suggested to me by Anthony Tyler back in 1988, and it was he who informed me of Tony Tinkel's translation of Willi Mohnen's doctorate on the subject. After reading this and Dr Andrew Nash's booklet, I was inspired to write an M.Ed. dissertation on Newman and the Oratory School. Sensing that there was much more to be discovered, I then enlisted on a research programme at the Institute of Education in London and seven years later, under the patient and expert guidance of Professor Richard Aldrich, I completed my doctoral thesis about the school. I could not have achieved this without the assistance of the late Gerard Tracey, who led me to the primary sources and gave me the breakthrough I needed to make my contribution to knowledge. But I am indebted to him for more than this, for I found his suggestions and uncanny 'feel' for Newman and the Oratory School invaluable: indeed conversing with him was like talking to someone who had actually known the venerable – now Venerable – John Henry personally.

I must also thank all the archivists and librarians whom I have dealt with, whether at Arundel Castle, the Bodleian Library Oxford, Cambridge University Library, Mount Street London (Jesuit archive), and the National University of Scotland, as well as the Birmingham Oratory, Littlemore and the Oratory School, as they have been thoroughly helpful and friendly. To these and other individuals who have helped me in any way, I wish to express my gratitude.

In recasting my thesis into book form, I am grateful for the guidance on structure I have received from Dr James Pereiro and above all for much editorial advice, as well as other suggestions, from Dr Peter Damian-Grint. Lastly I wish to thank Tom Longford for taking an interest in this project, and Jo Whale and rest of the Gracewing team for ensuring the final production of this book.

Naturally, I wish to thank the Fathers of the Birmingham Oratory for their kindness in granting me access to their archive and for permission to reproduce material from the collections held there.

Abbreviations

AW	*John Henry Newman: autobiograhical writings*
BOA	Birmingham Oratory archive
L&D	*Letters & Diaries of John Henry Newman*
OPM	*Oratory Parish Magazine*
OSA	Oratory School archive
OSM	*Oratory School Magazine*

The Oratory School and its surroundings, 1861

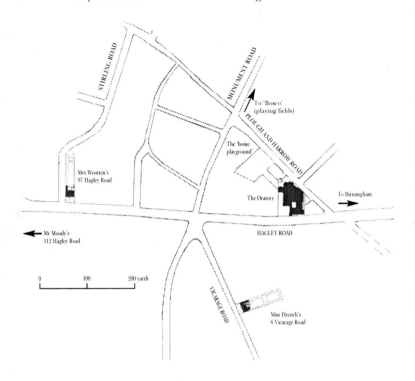

STIRLING ROAD

MONUMENT ROAD

PLOUGH AND HARROW ROAD

To 'Bosco'
(playing fields)

The 'home
playground'

Mrs Wootten's
97 Hagley Road

The Oratory

To Birmingham

Mr Moody's
112 Hagley Road

HAGLEY ROAD

0   100   200 yards

VICARAGE ROAD

Miss Ffrench's
6 Vicarage Road

This map is based on the 1855 Pigott Smith survey.

Expansion of the Oratory School, 1861–90

1. The Oratory Church
2. The Oratory House
3. The main schoolroom (opened in 1862)
4. The small schoolroom (opened in 1862); used as a school chapel (1869–73)
5. St Philip's dormitory, top floor (1862–)
6. St Joseph's dormitory, top floor (1865–80)
7. School chapel and tribune (opened in 1873)
8. Cloister
9. 67 and 68 Hagley Road (opened in 1861): first used as dame's house, then as dormitory; junior and senior libraries on ground floor replaced by new library in 1882

10. 21 Plough and Harrow Road (opened in 1862): accommodation and common room for masters
11. 22 Plough and Harrow Road (opened in 1862): used as dame's house (known as the 'brats' dormitory'); then after 1867 for Sixth Form Studies
12. Racquets court (set up in 1875)
13. New St Joseph's (opened in 1880)
14. Billiard room (opened in 1881)
15. 69 Hagley Road (acquired in 1872; used for accommodation, then as infirmary from 1890)
16. 70 and 71 Hagley Road (acquired in 1872; used for accommodation)
17. Fly-poles and parallel bars; replaced by a tennis court in 1881
18. The 'home playground'

This map is based on an Ordnance Survey original of 1887.

Introduction

'To my mind Eton, minus its wickedness, and plus the inculcation of the Catholic faith would be what I should best like to see'.[1] It was a sentiment many nineteenth-century converts to Catholicism shared with Sir John Simeon when confronted with the problem of where to educate their sons. The dilemma the Oxford Movement converts faced was that the Protestant public schools which most of them had attended were unacceptable for religious reasons, while the existing Catholic colleges were regarded as educationally unsuitable. It was not so much that the converts were unconvinced by academic standards at the Catholic colleges, as that they objected to other aspects: the 'Continental' influence in studies, customs and pastoral arrangements; the mixing of 'church' and lay boys in what were, effectively, junior seminaries; the close and continuous supervision of pupils; the impossibility of providing female care for young boys. This regime they considered as foreign and at odds with an upbringing in 'English virtues' and a spirit of freedom. When, in 1857, it became clear that Newman intended to retire from the rectorship of the Catholic University in Dublin, several convert friends approached him with a view to resolving their pressing need. Two years later, under Newman's patronage, a school was opened, close by the Birmingham Oratory: it came to be known as the Oratory School.

[1.] Simeon to Newman, 30 April 1857, BOA.

It was during the nineteenth century that that most English of educational institutions, the public school, emerged; at the heart of a thriving empire, old foundations were reformed and new ones begun, and there came into being what is called the public school system. With relatively few later additions to their number, and despite all the vicissitudes of the twentieth century, the public schools that gained pre-eminence in the Victorian age have retained their unofficial status and prestige. One of the lesser-known names in the litany of famous foundations, yet one of the most intriguing, is that of the Oratory School. It was unique in several respects: in being the first attempt to blend two distinct traditions of education, the Catholic Continental and the Anglican English; in being the first lay Catholic boarding school; and in being the first Catholic school in England to break out of the monopoly of direct control exercised by the bishops and religious orders.

These major innovations were seen as a challenge to the established pattern of Catholic education, and they were vehemently opposed by those wedded to the old order. The Oratory School was one of many new foundations that resulted from the growth of the Catholic Church in England as it emerged from three centuries of recusancy; and in this instance it was brought into being by the small but significant influx of converts in the wake of the Oxford Movement. The school's close association with leading 'Liberal Catholics' and prominent converts gave rise to virulent opposition from other Catholics for nearly a decade, and in the mid-1860s it was threatened with closure from Rome for flouting Church policy over 'mixed' (i.e. Catholic–Protestant) education. The situation was aggravated by the tensions that existed on the broader stage, as a result of the struggle within the Church worldwide between conservative and liberal tendencies, which came to a head in the 1860s. Besides being implicated in these more global controversies, the school had to withstand its fair share of local difficulties: a staff mutiny after only a couple of years that all but destroyed it, and the discovery afterwards that one of the masters was a thief and womaniser. Tracing the school's turbulent early history is thus a complex matter.

The central figure in the establishment of the Oratory School was the leading light of the Oxford Movement, John Henry

Newman. For his classic exposition of a liberal education in *The Idea of a University*, Newman is hailed as one of the greatest English writers on educational theory; by a happy coincidence the new foundation brought together this original mind with a unique educational opportunity. The origins of the school are all the more intriguing on account of the crucial part played by Catholic laymen, in an age when it was unheard of for the laity to take on such a task. Among these gifted laymen were the three most involved at the outset: two leading parliamentary barristers, Edward Bellasis and James Hope-Scott, and the distinguished scholar Lord Acton. No other school founded at the time could call on an active parental body of such a calibre as that of the Oratory School. The parental bodies behind the nineteenth-century proprietary schools (such as Cheltenham and Marlborough) were predominantly formed from the new middle classes, who were motivated by the noble desire to give their children access to the fuller education that had been, until then, the preserve of the professional and upper classes. The collaborators of this foundation, by contrast, were almost exclusively from the more privileged sectors of society; access to the best schools had been frustrated not by the depth of their pockets but by their reception into the Catholic Church.

The story of the foundation of the Oratory School, of interest in its own right, is also illuminating for the insights it gives into three areas of Victorian life. In the first place it serves as a useful tool for comparing the two educational traditions it intended to fuse together, since the foundation was in effect an attempt to select the best from each. Secondly, the story describes the effect of the injection into the Catholic body of a group of highly educated converts, and, as such, constitutes a social study. This in turn sheds light on a third area, the changing relation of the Catholic body to English society at large, from a state of isolation to one of gradual integration. It should be observed that the foundation was located precisely at the cutting edge of this development, and that while the immediate context was educational, the wider setting was the social and intellectual emancipation of Catholics.

The school story also contributes to studies of an eminent Victorian. Of all Newman's roles, it is surely that of schoolmaster which has been most overlooked; and yet for more than three decades he invested a large proportion of his time in nurturing the new establishment. This book describes how he went about the task of establishing and then overseeing the new school, and examines how practice at Edgbaston squared with the theory contained in his writings. It also illustrates Newman's understanding of the role of the laity, since the foundation provided an ideal setting for the application of his insights – above all in the working partnership he established with parents. Here Newman's line of action reflects a highly developed sense of the shared responsibility of laity and hierarchy in the task of education.

The school story is coloured by a number of recurring educational issues, many of which are as topical today as they were in Newman's age. The promoters of the Oratory School grappled with the problem of how to harness parental energy while avoiding interference with the day-to-day management of the school and limiting exposure to the full blast of market forces. Newman himself undertook the daunting task of answering the call for a new type of school, capable of meeting the needs of both converts and 'old Catholics': with limited resources available, he was expected to devise arrangements to secure the benefits of a public school education, yet without jeopardising the security of a Catholic upbringing. It was anticipated that the school's curriculum would reflect his notion of a liberal education and that pastoral arrangements would encapsulate his understanding of the delicate balance between enforcement of discipline and cultivation of trust; but all this had to achieved without neglecting the more prosaic demands of financial viability, workable structures, and (perhaps the most difficult) securing a staff capable of translating Newman's vision into reality. In observing how Newman and the promoters negotiated the difficulties they encountered, their attitude to the education of an elite becomes apparent.

A detailed study of the establishment of the Oratory School is long overdue, if only to resolve the conflicting accounts and interpretations of its chequered early existence. The confusion surrounding its foundation in 1859 and its major crisis of December 1861 (the so-called 'Darnell affair') can largely be attributed to insufficient use of evidence. Besides drawing upon the vast correspondence contained in Newman's *Letters and Diaries*, this book uses a further four hundred unpublished letters and other documents: these rich archival sources – mainly from the Birmingham Oratory – are indispensable for ascertaining the facts about the foundation process and discerning the motives of those involved. Much of the school-related material in the Birmingham Oratory archive originates from people well-disposed to Newman, but it also includes a good number of documents with an overtly wary or critical tone towards him; and by drawing upon the diaries, memoirs and biographies of masters, parents and others connected with the school, it is possible to round out the picture. As many of those involved were highly articulate, and committed to paper what later generations would tend to say on the telephone, the correspondence brings alive the drama of the events they lived through.

Although there does exist an extensive literature on Newman's educational theory, it is based predominantly on his educational *writings*. The danger of focusing exclusively on his literary output is that it can lead to consigning his theories to the realm of the quaint ideal, whereas they acquire a more convincing, dynamic quality when they are considered in the light of his educational practice. Seeing Newman in action, resolving the particular problems of the moment, supplies its own valuable lessons. For a man given to abstraction at the highest level, Newman had a remarkably hard-nosed practical judgement; he knew when and how to yield on non-essential principles, and on occasions abandoned an 'ideal' position for one contrary to what he endorsed in theory. To those unfamiliar with his ways, however, the apparent mismatch between utterances and actions can appear perplexing, even duplicitous.

The corpus of published material relating to the school in Newman's lifetime falls into three categories: biographies of Newman, histories of English education, and studies of the school itself. Coverage of school affairs in the four major lives of Newman – by Wilfrid Ward, Meriol Trevor, Ian Ker and Sheridan Gilley – is somewhat limited. The school is only briefly mentioned in Ward's early work, a triumph for its time (1912) but superseded fifty years later by Trevor's two-part opus. Trevor's biography provides the fullest coverage of school-related matters and uses a wealth of archival material; unfortunately, while her narrative is strong on detail, it is relatively weak on analysis, and its bias in analysing events solely from Newman's perspective is all too evident. Undoubtedly, the most authoritative biography is Ker's, which displays a mastery of the sources; despite giving the school less attention than Trevor does, he integrates his smaller number of facts into broader issues and patterns. It is usefully complemented by Gilley's shorter biography, which tells Newman's story in the full context of the times, though inevitably Gilley's placing of the school within wider developments comes at the price of over-simplification and loss of detail.

Although the vast literature documenting the development of public schools in the nineteenth century is littered with turgid and unscholarly school histories, often the product of unrestrained *pietàs*, there are several outstanding exceptions: some are studies of individual establishments, but there are also a number of excellent scholarly treatments of the system as a whole. There is, by contrast, a dearth of equivalent research on Catholic educational provision for the higher classes; histories of the individual establishments do exist, but they are generally anecdotal, descriptive, and parochial in outlook. The first attempt at an overview, A.S. Barnes's *The Catholic Schools of England* (1926), is a collection of nine separate school histories. H.O. Evennett's *The Catholic Schools of England and Wales*, which appeared two decades later, gives a broader description of the Catholic system but adopts the same piecemeal approach. Both these studies mention the fact that Newman responded to a call from Catholic parents, mainly converts, for a Catholic school along English public school lines, but they venture no further.

The first and longest of the histories of the Oratory School was compiled by its last Oratorian headmaster, Henry Tristram, and appeared in forty-eight consecutive numbers of the *Oratory Parish Magazine* between 1932 and 1935: it focuses on the school in Newman's time and provides interesting insights into the predicament of the converts and the school's early difficulties. (It is unfortunate that this work has been ignored by later researchers.) The next school history, contained in John Jackson's doctoral thesis, has suffered a similar fate, for no reference appears to have been made to it in subsequent Newman literature.[2] Jackson devoted nearly half his study to the school, with chapters on its foundation, the 'Darnell affair', and Newman's involvement thereafter. According to Jackson, Newman pretended to start a public school but instead founded a private school; not even his closest collaborators were privy to his intentions, and his secrecy and failure to clarify arrangements at the outset were the cause of the Darnell affair as well as other troubles. A very different conclusion was reached by A.J. Upton in his M.Ed. dissertation about Oscott College and the public school system.[3] In examining why the converts felt so dissatisfied with Catholic education, Upton argued that the Oratory School was in fact a full-blown public school; his lack of sympathy for the converts and his very restricted use of sources led him to view the foundation as the deed of upwardly mobile, class-conscious converts, whose values were those of upper-middle-class Victorian society. For Upton, old Catholics were bound together by their religion, whereas the 'social cement' for converts was class.

The only substantial piece of research which focuses exclusively on the school has been the doctoral thesis of Willi Mohnen. His stated aim was 'to illustrate the educational principles of Newman and of a small but influential section of Catholic parents, in order to achieve a clearer understanding of the efforts at emancipation of English Catholics in the educational sphere';[4] but the achievement of his goal is severely handicapped by his limited use of the sources at his disposal and his neglect of the educational context, particularly the

[2.] 'John Henry Newman: the origins and application of his educational ideas', Ph.D., 1968. The ASLIB catalogue identifies Leicester University as the institution where it was submitted, but the university library has no record of it and the copy at the Birmingham Oratory archive does not specify an institution.

[3.] 'Oscott College and Catholic education in the nineteenth century: a comparison with the English public school', M.Ed., Birmingham, 1981.

[4.] W.G. Mohnen, 'Voruniversitäre Erziehung bei John Henry Newman, dargestellt am Beispiel der Oratory School' ('Pre-university education in the eyes of John Henry Newman, as represented by the example of the Oratory School'), Ph.D., Cologne, 1978, trans. A. Tinkel (unpub.), p. 2.

public school tradition. Mohnen's failure to understand the outlook of other leading Catholic figures makes for an oversimplified context in which Newman is cast as a champion of freedom and his opponents as backward-looking authoritarians demanding unthinking obedience. More balanced is Andrew Nash's booklet *Newman's Idea of a School*, a first-rate work which is thematically well-developed and solidly based on evidence, though short. By stressing character formation at the school, Nash emphasises Newman's desire to produce educated Catholics capable of full participation in civil society.

What is in some ways the most scholarly research on the school comes from an unexpected quarter in that Alan McClelland, the foremost historian of nineteenth-century Catholic education, is generally hostile to Newman and has an open antipathy to private education. In several articles that deal with the school, he interprets events to promote his own views on Catholic society, the converts and Newman: significantly, he makes no use of the histories of the school and relies heavily on the biographies by Ward and Trevor.[5] As the school story unfolds, it will be necessary to challenge the views of McClelland, who portrays Newman as a prickly individual who lived his Christianity in a self-contained, privileged world, oblivious to the plight of his poorer co-religionists. One of the key claims advanced by McClelland is that Newman opened the school in answer to a call from the old Catholic aristocracy, who sought a socially exclusive education for their sons, and that they were joined in this aim by the converts. An equally ambitious claim about the foundation – but one very different from McClelland's – has been proposed by Joseph Altholz, the historian of the Liberal Catholic movement in England: he argues that the Liberal Catholics were the inspiration for the school and, indeed, that it can be regarded as its 'most lasting institutional accomplishment'.[6]

[5.] See especially V.A. McClelland, 'A Catholic Eton: by hook or by crook? John Henry Newman and the establishment of the Oratory School', *Aspects of Education* 22, 1980, pp. 3–17.

[6.] J.L. Altholz, *The Liberal Catholic Movement in England: the 'Rambler' and its Contributors, 1848–1864* (Montreal: Palm Publishers, 1962), p. 139.

Given that those investigating the school's origins have almost without exception failed to locate previous research, and have used the sources only sparingly if at all, it is hardly surprising that a very blurred picture emerges. The only serious attempt to place the Oratory School in the context of developments in education and society is McClelland's; but the conclusions he reaches conflict dramatically with the general consensus of other scholars: that the founding impetus derived principally from the converts, whose primary aim was to establish a school by merging two traditions. The school histories fail (mainly by omission) to identify the characteristics of the new institution – a surprising oversight, given the explicitly innovative aspirations of its founders. Only Jackson has taken up the challenge of identifying precisely what was entailed in this first experimental Catholic public school: what was originally envisaged in 1859, and how it was modified in response to events.

In attempting to tease out the true story of the beginnings of the Oratory School, this book also tries to shed light on the struggle for influence in Catholic boarding education between the laity, the secular clergy and the religious orders. As the story unfolds it will become clear how much Newman differed from his contemporaries in his ideas on education; and by the end of it the reader will be able to decide whether he deserves to be numbered alongside Arnold of Rugby and the other great nineteenth-century headmasters and school reformers.

Chapter 1

Background to the Foundation

Before looking at the origins of a foundation that was intended to merge two educational traditions, it is worth noting first how distinct these traditions were. In the published histories of each there is barely a reference to the existence of the other, a reflection of how little intermingling there was between the two social groups involved. A notable exception to this general pattern is C.R. Chichester's *Schools*, written in 1882. Setting out to undo the popular notion of the superiority of Protestant public schools, it begins by stressing the separateness of the two systems: the Catholic characterised by 'ceaseless surveillance', the Protestant by a 'deliberate abandonment' of boys outside lesson and study time. The former was conducive of a 'paternal system of government'; the latter led to antagonism between masters and boys, and rule by 'boy public opinion' – unless, exceptionally, a headmaster such as Dr Arnold of Rugby was at the helm. Chichester concluded that 'between the paternal solicitude of Stonyhurst and the total abandonment of Eton there is no advantageous mean' – a claim which implied that a Catholic public school, and *a fortiori* a 'Catholic Eton', was practically a contradiction in terms. His comparisons, however, relied on two very different types of evidence: a first-hand knowledge of one system, through his own schooling at Stonyhurst and visits to eight other Catholic institutions; and a spurious 'familiarity' with the other system, by means of his reading of two renowned schoolboy stories, *Tom Brown's Schooldays* and *Eric: or, Little by Little* (published in 1857 and

1858 respectively), supplemented by evidence from the reports of the Clarendon and Taunton Commissions (mostly the former, and mainly about Eton).[1] From this, he argued that Eton illustrated the pernicious consequences of a system which was 'choke-full of false principles'.[2]

Public school reform

It has been argued that there are few countries in the world where the concept 'school' is developed so amply and power-fully as it is in England, to the point of creating an institution ready to take on itself not just the education the mind, but the formation of the whole person.[3] This claim refers above all to a particular type of schooling, which by the middle of the nine-teenth century was in the process of developing into a highly-elaborated system with its own well-defined and pecu-liar characteristics. Despite its familiarity, the term 'public school' is notoriously hard to pin down; it came into usage early in the nineteenth century to denote schools with a national reputation, but its meaning was at first vague. In origin it described schools open to the general public, either because they were wholly or partly supported by public money, or because their endowments were originally provided for public benefit. By the 1860s, however, the majority of boys at the leading schools paid fees and came from the aristocracy or the gentry; the contradiction between ancient statutes and nineteenth-century reality was one of the elements which contributed to the ambiguity surrounding the term.[4]

[1.] The four-volume Clarendon Report (1864) inquired into the nine 'great' schools. The twenty-one volumes of the Taunton Report (1867–68) summarised findings on other secondary schools, includ-ing over seven hundred endowed grammar schools, as well as proprietary and private schools.

[2.] C.R. Chichester, *Schools* (London: Burns & Oates, 1882), pp. iii–iv, 38, 80.

[3.] J.R. de S. Honey, *Tom Brown's Universe: the Development of the Victorian Public School* (London: Millington, 1977), p. xiii.

[4.] C. Shrosbree, *Public Schools and Private Education: the Clarendon Commission 1861–1864 and the Public Schools Acts* (Manchester: Manchester University Press, 1988), pp. 11–12.

At the start of the nineteenth century there were three 'great' schools in England: Eton, Harrow and Westminster. By mid-century six other public schools with a national reputation could be identified: Winchester, Charterhouse, Rugby, Shrewsbury, St Paul's and Merchant Taylors' (the last two being day-schools). Their status was confirmed by the terms of reference of the Clarendon Commission, though by the end of the century the label 'public school' could be applied to a hundred or so institutions. Although there is no consensus among historians as to what precisely constituted a public school, all agree on the core characteristics enshrined in the 'Clarendon type': usually it designated a large boarding school in a rural setting that catered for sons of the upper classes; a great deal of liberty was permitted, self-governance was manifested in a prefect system, and classics was the main subject taught.

Before the reforms of the 1820s and 1830s, the public schools were brutal institutions where bullying was rife and living conditions primitive: the hardships were regarded by the schools' advocates as part of a toughening-up process, while a 'wholesome neglect' was assumed to foster self-reliance. Not a few parents were unconvinced of their merits, and until the public schools were noticeably improved many upper-class youths were educated under private tutors. Before reforming themselves, public schools trembled on the edge of anarchy: headmasters and their few assistants struggled to maintain control, despite resorting to flogging on a large scale, and rebellions requiring the use of armed force for their suppression were not unknown. The explanation for this parlous state of affairs lies in the fact that the ancient schools were citadels of 'boy power', where pupils' sacred liberties, confirmed by tradition, proved a serious obstacle to reform. Despite most of the teachers being clergymen, religion was either ignored or despised, and the master–pupil relationship was cold if not antagonistic.[5]

The two great reforming headmasters, Samuel Butler at

[5] The prevailing state of affairs, including the rebellions, is described at length in J. Chandos, *Boys Together: English Public Schools, 1800–1864* (London: Hutchinson, 1984).

Shrewsbury and Thomas Arnold at Rugby, managed to raise academic standards and restore discipline; significantly, both considered the training of character to be an essential part of the schoolmaster's task. Arnold's success lay in responding to the needs of the rising middle classes who were eager for the status accorded by a public school education but fearful of the depravity associated with it; he raised the moral tone of these 'nurseries of vice', as he called them, by assuming the chaplaincy himself and delivering the chapel sermons. A key to raising moral standards was his ability to transform the prefect system by using reliable boys as his moral agents and fellow-workers; he also enacted a ruthless policy of removing boys he regarded as unsuitable. The Arnoldian reforms, which transformed the public schools within a generation, arose from religious convictions (Broad Church in origin) and established a new order of priorities: first religion and morals, then gentlemanly conduct, and then intellectual matters.

By the 1850s the mood of the times called for a gentler regime and greater watchfulness. Flogging was reduced and master–pupil relations began to improve; the 'professionalisation' of games – the process by which a variety of disordered activities were replaced by compulsory organised team games – was just beginning; time outside lessons was becoming increasingly regimented and subject to elements of surveillance, thus eroding those most emblematic public school characteristics of independence and freedom. Nevertheless the public schools remained a world apart from the private schools, which were run for profit and typified by their closely supervised regime, the absence of a prefect system, and a wider, more modern curriculum. The idea of replacing public school prefects by a system of ushers as in private and foreign schools drew from Charles Vaughan, the headmaster of Harrow, the public remark that this would be ruinous of 'the great glory of an English public school – its free development of character, its social expansiveness, in short its *liberty*'.[6] This strength was recognised officially in the 1860s when, despite cataloguing the faults of the public schools, the Clarendon Commission praised

---

[6.] C. Vaughan, *A Letter to the Viscount Palmerston M.P. on the Monitorial System at Harrow School* (London: John Murray, 1853; 1854), p. 9.

them for the admirable qualities they instilled in boys:

> their capacity to govern others and control themselves,
> their aptitude for combining freedom with order, their
> public spirit, their vigour and manliness of character,
> their strong but not slavish respect for public opinion,
> their love of healthy sports and exercise. These schools
> have been the chief nurseries of our statesmen [...] and
> they have had perhaps the largest share in moulding the
> character of the English gentleman.[7]

The mid-century burst of school foundations in the United
Kingdom corresponded to a surge in demand for boarding
education, made possible by the new prosperity and growth of
the professional and industrial classes. Many of the new schools
catered for sons of particular professional groups: Cheltenham
(1841) for colonial officers, both civil and military;
Marlborough (1843) for Anglican clergy; Epsom (1853) for
doctors. Others were aimed at particular social levels, such as
the three grades of Nathaniel Woodard's schools which were
originally intended for three tiers of the middle classes:
Lancing (1848) for gentlemen of limited means,
Hurstpierpoint (1849) for tradesmen and farmers, Ardingly
(1858) for small tradesmen. Most of the new foundations were
in some measure the product of religious impulse, and several
were directly inspired by the Oxford Movement, such as the
schools begun by Woodard and St Columba's (1843) and
Radley (1847), both set up by William Sewell. But whatever
particular characteristics schools possessed at the outset, they
were invariably modified early on by market pressures or internal crises. Most new schools struggled at first for their
existence, as well as a distinctive identity. Much depended on
how the initial capital was raised: some, like Radley and
Bradfield (1850), relied on the founder's wealth; others, such
as Cheltenham, Marlborough and Rossall (1844), began as
non-profit-making companies on the joint-stock or proprietary
principle. In Woodard's case the funds were raised by what
Gladstone termed 'the machinery of philanthropic agitation':

[7.] Clarendon Report I, p. 56.

pamphlets, circulars, events, subscriptions and the like. Whatever their financial arrangements or idiosyncrasies, during the 1860s all the recent foundations, as well as most of the older ones, began to conform to what became a recognised 'type' – the public school.

By investigating nine ancient endowed grammar schools or collegiate foundations, the Clarendon Commission formally recognised their claim to a pre-eminent status, thereby (unwittingly) endorsing a new hierarchical system. Although the term 'public school' referred to their common characteristics, it remained imprecise and, moreover, proved to be capable of undergoing change. Day schools, for example, were not generally designated as public schools, even though two Clarendon schools were; and the apparent precondition of being an ancient foundation was almost immediately relaxed, as the Commission made special reference to four recent foundations: Cheltenham, Marlborough, Rossall and Wellington. Thus the way was paved for a system that would grow by admitting applicants of proven worth, whether of ancient lineage or modern origin.

English Catholics, old and new

The stark separateness of Anglican and Catholic educational traditions that C.R. Chichester portrayed was a consequence of vastly different fortunes and developments since the Reformation. In 1850 Catholics formed three and a half per cent of the population in England, and could be broadly divided into three social groupings: the old Catholics, the remnant of those who had survived penal times, dominated by a titled aristocracy; the Irish Catholics, who mainly lived in urban poverty; and the converts issuing from the Oxford Movement, most of whom were highly educated and cultured. A few figures are sufficient to convey the extent of the imbalance between the groups. Between 1770 and 1850 the number of Catholics in England and Wales rose tenfold to about 600,000, but of these only 25,000 were old Catholics; the main expansion occurred in the decade after the 1841 famine, when about half a million Irish Catholics poured into England. The smallest of the three groups was the Oxford Movement converts, who in mid-century numbered less than 2000.

The emancipation and social integration of Catholics into English society was a painfully slow process. It was during the eighteenth century that, as the application of the penal laws was gradually relaxed, Catholics began to emerge from an under-class whose civil freedoms had been severely curtailed. The first Catholic Relief Act of 1778 enabled Catholics to purchase and inherit land legally; in 1791 Catholics were permitted to worship publicly and to set up credal schools, provided they were not seminaries or schools run by religious orders. Finally, in 1829 the Act of Catholic Emancipation made wide-ranging concessions, by granting the exercise of all civil rights to Catholics and opening up most positions under the Crown to them. These changes enabled the Catholic Church to restructure itself and meet the needs of its growing flock. Until the restoration of the Catholic hierarchy in 1850, the Vicars Apostolic had exercised what ecclesiastical control they could in their Districts (four from 1588, eight from 1840). Technically speaking, until 1908 the Catholic Church in England was mission territory and came under the Sacred Congregation for the Propagation of the Faith (Propaganda Fide), and thus the ordinary prescriptions of canon law did not fully apply. These anomalous conditions, in which irregular ecclesiastical arrangements were common, made it easier in some respects to set up a new type of school. At the same time tensions arose within the Catholic body as a result of its rapid growth and lack of homogeneity, and these were manifested in disputes between English Catholic leaders which frequently had to be resolved in Rome. Tensions were also created by the whole question of the repeal of the penal laws, since a major concern of the higher clergy was the re-establishment of ecclesiastical order and the reimposition of due clerical control, whereas lay leaders were on the whole more preoccupied with gaining civil concessions. In the 1780s a group of prominent laymen, styling themselves the 'Catholic Committee', fought a long and acrimonious dispute with the bishops over their authority to act on behalf of the Catholic body. Similar though less divisive episodes occurred around 1829 and 1850, and helped create in ecclesiastical circles a climate of extreme caution, even suspicion, towards lay initiatives.

The mid-century Established Church had been challenged from within by the Tractarian or Oxford Movement, which had begun in 1833 with the publication of the first of the *Tracts for the Times*. These *Tracts*, written by Newman and his Oxford associates, asserted the principles of apostolic succession and spiritual independence of church from state, and were intended to reform the Established Church – which they viewed as one of the three branches of the one true Church – and defend it against liberalism. In reviving interest in the Church Fathers and writing about Catholic practices on the European mainland, the Movement inspired changes that began to reverse some of those made at the Reformation. One unintended effect was the exodus to Rome of many of the Movement's strongest supporters.

Although the converts were by far the smallest group, the fact that many came from the heart of the English Establishment meant that their impact on the Catholic Church was out of all proportion to their numbers. It is not difficult to understand why, when one consults W.G. Gorman's *Converts to Rome*, which provides a breakdown of the professions and status of about 2000 of them. They include 572 clergymen; 29 peers and 53 peeresses, 432 other members of the nobility and 42 baronets; 92 from the medical and 192 from the legal professions; 306 army and 64 naval officers; 39 from the diplomatic service; and 470 authors, poets and journalists. Some 586 were educated at Oxford and 346 at Cambridge.[8] Given their background it is easy to appreciate how the converts were able to bring fresh light to old problems; but in opening up Catholic educational practice to public debate and scrutiny, they created tensions which were to have a direct bearing on the Oratory School.

For a while, relations between old Catholics and converts were strained: indeed, the antipathy between them has been described as one of the leading features of English Catholicism in the nineteenth century.[9] Distrust of the converts stemmed from an inability of some old Catholics to comprehend the

[8] W.G. Gorman, *Converts to Rome* (London: Sands & Co., 1910), pp. xiii–xv.
[9] E. Norman, *The English Catholic Church in the Nineteenth Century* (Oxford: Clarendon Press, 1984), p. 211.

genuineness of the conversions. Some understandable resentment was felt, besides, by those who had borne 'the day's burden and the heat' at the favour and attention bestowed on converts by church leaders such as Nicholas Wiseman, who hoped that their arrival heralded England's reconversion. Their optimism was not shared by the Catholic press, which gave the converts a cool reception and was suspicious of, and sometimes openly hostile to, them.

Relationships were not improved by the dismissiveness of converts towards the educational and cultural achievements of old Catholics. This view was openly articulated in *The Rambler*, a journal which was essentially an organ of lay Oxford converts. *The Rambler* was founded in 1848 by John More Capes, a product of Westminster School and Balliol College Oxford, who like other converts soon experienced the cultural limitations of Catholics and their isolation from intellectual and public life in England. He hoped *The Rambler* would 'serve to raise the level of culture of the English Catholics and, by removing the reproach of intellectual backwardness, to enable them to exert their influence on other Englishmen';[10] in particular he wished to see educational standards at the colleges raised, with greater financial support from the laity. In these and similar examples of their zeal to remedy the shortcomings they saw, the converts frequently provoked cradle Catholics by their insensitivity and shocked them by their lack of inhibition, which reflected their different educational background, with its greater emphasis on critical analysis and open debate. Orestes Brownson, an influential convert in North America, commented that the unfamiliar 'choice of terms' and prose style of Anglican converts like Capes left cradle Catholics 'perpetually in doubt whether their thought is sound or heretical'.[11]

The foundation of the Oratory School was, as McClelland has observed, 'part and parcel of the continuum of the debate about the nature of freedom and authority in education'.[12] Its

---

[10.] Altholz, *Liberal Catholic Movement*, p. 9.

[11.] O. Brownson, 'Capes's four years' experience', *Brownson's Quarterly Review* 20, July 1850, p. 3.

[12.] V.A. McClelland, 'Authority and freedom: John Henry Newman and the formation of youth', *History and Education: Essays Presented to Peter Gordon*, ed. R. Aldrich (London: Woburn Press, 1996), p. 71.

establishment occurred at a time when the resolution of the
rival claims of ecclesiastical authority and intellectual freedom
within the universal Church was exercising Catholic minds.
The collision of two opposing tendencies – Ultramontane and
Liberal Catholic – led to friction between ecclesiastical authority and lay liberal thought. The situation was aggravated by the
process of centralisation which was taking place within the
Church under Pius IX, and the clash of religious and secular
ideas. To Liberal Catholics, the Ultramontane tendency
denoted a Church in a state of siege, in opposition to and
isolated from the prevailing spirit of the age; by Ultramontane
reckoning, the Liberal Catholics had imbibed too much of the
rationalism of the times and lacked a Catholic spirit.

The Liberal Catholic movement has been described as 'an
attempt to bridge the gap between the doctrines of the Roman
Catholic Church and the dominant secular principles of the
age. [...] it was an intellectual liberalism, characterised by an
emphasis upon the legitimacy and value of intellectual sources
independent of the authority of the Church'.[13] It had developed in France, first under Lamennais and then under
Montalembert, but by mid-century the leadership had passed
to the Germans, with Ignaz von Döllinger of Munich becoming
the movement's most distinguished scholar. The influence of
Liberal Catholicism in England was muted, as it lasted little
more than a decade and was confined mainly to the converts –
but their close association with the Oratory School had a
profound effect on its fortunes. By 1857 *The Rambler*, now
under the direction of Richard Simpson and Sir John (later,
Lord) Acton, had become the movement's mouthpiece in
England. Simpson, an Oxford convert, was an able polymath;
intellectually pugnacious and with an instinct for sensitive
subjects, he employed his sharp wit fearlessly. Acton, although
of old Catholic stock, had a thoroughly cosmopolitan background which enabled him to identify with the Liberal Catholic
converts. He had studied as a private pupil under Döllinger in
Munich, where he laid the foundations for his immense learning and developed his passionate devotion to liberty of
conscience and religious toleration. In 1857 he decided to

[13.] Altholz, *Liberal Catholic Movement*, p. 1.

settle in England, with ambitious aspirations for raising the cultural and political thought of Catholics; like Capes he hoped that a concentration of the limited intellectual resources in the Catholic body would enable it to give Catholics an influence on national life.

Newman had long sympathised with *The Rambler*, especially its abiding aim of meeting the intellectual challenges of the day and fostering an educated laity: nevertheless he sought to soften its wayward tendencies and 'indefensible' literary style – 'its method, its tone, and its mode of saying things'.[14] But the price he paid for attempting to reason with those connected with *The Rambler* (and its successor, the *Home and Foreign Review*) was that they frequently invoked Newman's authority and sheltered under his name. Insofar as Newman completely rejected liberalism in religion, their claim on him was entirely false; however, in matters concerning freedom of intellectual enquiry Newman argued against a narrow circumscription by ecclesiastical authority, and therefore could be counted with them. The result was that many in the hierarchy and elsewhere suspected that Newman had never really espoused Catholic principles and attitudes; and as his thoughts were couched in a form and language unfamiliar to cradle Catholics, his writings were frequently suspected of being tainted with heresy. Newman's name was thus a mixed blessing for the new school.

The Catholic educational system

The considerable cultural gap that existed between old Catholics and their Anglican counterparts was largely the result of the former's restricted educational possibilities. Until the 1791 Relief Act, Catholic schools were not permitted in England, although there were in fact dozens of short-lived and precarious (and illegal) establishments on English soil.[15]

---

14. Newman to Monsell, 14 November 1862, *L&D* XX, p. 354.
15. Two which are worthy of note, both foundations of Bishop Challoner, emerged in the mid-eighteenth century and functioned as preparatory boarding schools for the colleges overseas: Sedgley Park in Staffordshire and Standon Lordship in Hertfordshire (later absorbed into Old Hall Academy).

Furthermore, Catholics were forbidden to send their children to the colleges[16] established abroad for Englishmen, several of which had long served the double purpose of educating both seminarians (junior and senior) and the sons of the Catholic gentry. They comprised the Jesuit college at St Omer (later at Bruges, and then Liège); the Benedictine colleges of St Gregory's, Douai and St Lawrence's, Dieulouard; a Dominican college at Bornhem; and the English College for the secular clergy at Douai. Each had its clientele of families in England; but despite catering solely for English youths, the colleges had characteristics that reflected their development in a Catholic Continental tradition from which England had split after the Reformation.

Initially the Catholic Committee lobbied for changes in the studies at the colleges abroad. Later they proposed that a school be established in England to provide an education 'proper for those who are destined for civil or commercial life', as the colleges abroad were inappropriate;[17] and a letter was circulated to gather support for the addition of modern languages to the core classical curriculum and for a higher prominence to be given to mathematics, particularly in its applications to business. The proposal was viewed with apprehension by most of the clergy and many of the gentry, and as a threat to the colleges by those with strong ties of loyalty to them. It was thought that the scheme would lead to a drop in numbers for the priesthood and precipitate the demise of the colleges; and if the colleges closed, all would be jeopardised if the religious situation worsened in England and the proposed new school was also forced to close. A public letter to the Committee expressed an additional concern:

the students in our foreign Colleges are placed at a

[16.] In the nineteenth century 'college' was the term used for institutions attached to religious communities or seminaries, and 'school' for those without such links. The term 'secular college' (or 'ecclesiastical college') was used to denote one run by the secular clergy, while 'religious college' denoted one run by a religious order.

[17.] Address of the Catholic Committee, May 1787, B. Ward, *Dawn of the Catholic Revival in England* II (London: Longman, Green & Co., 1909), p. 263.

distance from objects of dissipation and bad example, so much complained of in the public schools of this country, and we deem it a matter of extreme difficulty to guard against this objection in any extensive plan of education proposed to be set on foot in England.[18]

These reservations and fears, together with the potential competition for the colleges, forced the Committee to drop its plans; and seventy years later these same fears were still held strongly enough to be major obstacles to the beginning of the Oratory School.

Despite the prevailing mentality, fundamental changes were forced by external events in 1793, when the Revolutionary authorities in France seized Church property and shut down the colleges. The abandonment of the colleges and the resettlement in England of pupils, students and teachers provided the opportunity for wholesale change to the Catholic system of education, and within three years a new order was established which was to remain unchallenged until the arrival of the converts half a century later. In this brief foundational period there was intense rivalry in the struggle for the control of education for the higher reaches of Catholic society – between the Vicars Apostolic themselves, and between them, the religious orders, and the laity; these divisions lasted throughout the next century and rendered futile the possibility of any co-ordinated policy for the education of this social group.

Among the many schemes and counter-schemes proposed, the views of John Milner, the future Bishop of the Midland District, deserve a mention since they show that structural flaws were recognised within the system of Catholic education, and that a remedy was at hand. Milner argued against the coexistence of a school and a seminary within the same college, and in favour of the establishment of a good grammar school. He recognised that 'a different kind of discipline, of education and of superiors is requisite for that College where our young men of family are to be instructed, and that Seminary where our priests are to be formed'. In recommending a plan that was

---

[18.] Letter to the Committee of English Catholics, n.d., B. Ward, *Dawn* I, p. 121.

suitable to the gentry, Milner also hoped to prevent the estab-lishment of a lay-sponsored school which would, he felt, do 'irreparable mischief' because of what he saw as Gallican tendencies among the lay leaders of the aristocracy. He also warned that unless a good classical school was established, 'with masters of first-rate talents', the religious orders 'will have three parts in four of the Gentry to educate' – a prediction that proved to be remarkably accurate.[19]

Reacting to the upheavals across the English Channel in 1793, the Northern and Southern Districts began collaborating on the establishment of a single secular college. At the same time the Catholic Committee's successor, the Cisalpine Club, began planning a very different kind of school: a public school with a governing body composed entirely of Catholic noblemen and gentlemen. But as chance would have it, Bishop Thomas Talbot of the Midland District selected as head of *his* college the very same priest the Cisalpines had wanted for *their* school; in the absence of a suitable alternative, a compromise was reached and Oscott College was established in Birmingham in 1794 for 'church' and lay boys under joint management. The North–South plan for a single secular college was abandoned when the Bishop of the Southern District pressed ahead with the absorption of pupils and staff from Douai into Old Hall Academy, renamed St Edmund's, at Ware, Hertfordshire. A similar college, called St Cuthbert's, was founded (the same year) at Crook Hall, near Durham; it derived purely from Douai and, like Oscott and Ware, inherited its characteristics – including the old rules.

Significantly, in the reorganisation of the 1790s Milner's plea for the separation of church and lay boys was lost, together with his lesser request for the separation of boys from older students of philosophy and theology. Consequently, the custom of educating lay and ecclesiastical pupils together – which had arisen out of necessity in the overseas colleges – was perpetuated. However, it should be borne in mind that an element of necessity remained, as it is doubtful that public opinion of the time would have tolerated the establishment of a

---

[19.] Milner to Douglass, 14 February 1784; 30 March 1785, B. Ward, *Dawn* II, pp. 102, 106.

'pure' seminary. At the secular colleges, the arrangement was reinforced by financial convenience: fees from the lay boys helped support the church boys; and costs were reduced by employing students in theology as teachers and ushers. But what the arrangement gained in financial terms it lost in suitability: an Italian missionary priest working in England reported to Rome that the colleges were 'anything but seminaries', whereas a convert who taught at one remarked that the 'lay element is absolutely subjugated to the sacerdotal'.[20] In the 1850s the studies, rules, discipline and pious practices at the secular colleges were essentially those of Douai – that is, an ecclesiastical college. Spiritual exercises included daily prayer, Mass, visits to the Blessed Sacrament after meals, spiritual reading during meals (which were had in silence), the Rosary and night prayers, as well as Benedictions and frequent Confession. Moreover, the inherited characteristics of the overseas colleges inevitably perpetuated foreign customs and a Continental slant to studies. Given all this, it is no surprise that public school converts should have sought an alternative to collegiate education.

Like the secular clergy, the religious orders were also forced to migrate, and they too used the opportunity to resettle in England. With exiles from Liège, the Jesuits opened a college in 1794 at Stonyhurst Hall, in Lancashire, which Thomas Weld (an old boy from their college at Bruges) had given them. It operated according to the Jesuit tradition, using the *ratio studiorum*,[21] and ushers were entrusted with the task of keeping the boys under their eyes at all times, as well as administering punishments. The system of 'surveillance' applied to the playground, the chapel, the wash-rooms and above all the

---

[20.] C. Leetham, *Luigi Gentili: a Sower for the Second Spring* (London: Burns & Oates, 1965), p. 286; J.M. Capes, *To Rome and Back* (London: Smith, Elder & Co., 1873), p. 229.

[21.] The *ratio studiorum*, the Jesuit scheme of studies devised in the late sixteenth century, gave comprehensive instructions for Jesuit colleges and schools: choice of text books, arrangements for the arts courses, advice on how to stimulate students, rules to be followed in classes and exams, even when and how to distribute prizes and awards. Its influence was also felt in non-Jesuit establishments, including Douai.

dormitories, where an usher remained on duty all night: opponents of the system called it 'espionage'. The Benedictine exiles took longer to establish themselves. Those from Douai settled initially at Acton Burnell on property loaned by an old boy, moving to Downside in 1813; those from Dieulouard finally settled at Ampleforth in 1806.

One manifestation of the strong rivalry between the new foundations was the desire for grand buildings, a surprisingly common characteristic given the poverty of material resources among Catholics – not to mention the uncertainty over legal protection of endowments and the loss of all property and goods on leaving foreign shores. It led Newman to remark upon the Catholic tendency to lay money out on *'showy* works'.[22] Consolidation in bricks and mortar gave a new permanence to the colleges, while architectural designs were chosen to give substance to claims paraded in their prospectuses that they were the true descendants of the medieval foundations at Oxford and Cambridge. Fine new buildings were opened at St Edmund's, Ware in 1799, to which a Pugin chapel was added in 1853. St Cuthbert's moved to new buildings at Ushaw, grander than those of Ware, in 1808; a later series of magnificent buildings imitating University College, Oxford included a museum and a Pugin chapel. Oscott, meanwhile, moved to a new site in 1838 with buildings erected on the plan of Wadham College, Oxford, including a Pugin quadrangle, while Stonyhurst's chapel was modelled on that of King's College, Cambridge. The buildings added to the fine manor house at Downside were so splendid that they attracted comment in Parliament – and that was before the Pugin additions arrived.

The loyalty of old boys to their *alma mater* facilitated the refounding of the colleges and confirmed their growth in numbers as well as bequests. The pre-eminence of St Omer – in tradition, organisation and size – among the overseas colleges gave the Jesuits an early advantage at Stonyhurst. In 1815 Weld gave them more land, on this occasion for a junior school: by then the college had grown to over two hundred boys. But after its flying start, numbers fell and by 1829 they

[22.] Newman to Capes, 7 December 1848, *L&D* XII, p. 366.

had dropped to around one hundred. Oscott's progress was slower since it began without a traditional clientele, and in 1808, faced with low numbers (just seven church and forty lay boys) and mounting debts, the lay governors decided to retire from the management and hand the college over to Bishop Milner. But during the 1840s, under the presidency of Wiseman, Oscott witnessed a remarkable turnaround and established itself as the preferred college for the Catholic upper classes. Wiseman's aspiration for a 'Catholic Eton' led to extensive concessions to 'high' tastes; the drawback was that conditions to the liking of the upper classes were ill-suited for the education of ecclesiastical students.

Of the other foundations before the Oratory School, only one succeeded in breaking into the circle of colleges supplying the needs of the upper classes. Unable to force Downside to become a secular college, Bishop Baines of the Western District founded Prior Park, near Bath, in 1830. It consisted of two colleges in one, St Peter's for schoolboys and St Paul's for older students, on either side of a splendid mansion set in two hundred acres. Numbers at Ampleforth under his presidency had risen from twenty to eighty; now he poached thirty of their best boys for his own grand scheme. Despite the initial numbers and an attractive setting, the project struggled to get going; on Baines's death in 1843 his establishment was only half-full and there were colossal debts amounting to £40,000. It finally closed in 1856, three years before the Oratory School opened.[23]

Although it was universally acknowledged that the main strength of the collegiate system was that it provided security in religion, it was also clear to many that this was purchased at the expense of preparation for life 'in the world'. This glaring shortcoming was one reason why a radically new foundation – the Oratory School – was attempted. Yet the attempt was no simple matter, for the developments described in this chapter highlight the difficulty of challenging an educational system characterised by intense competitiveness, dependency on traditional family loyalties, and the proclamation of permanence

[23.] J. Cashman, 'Old Prior Park: the final years, 1843–1856', *Recusant History* 23, 1996, pp. 79–106.

and status through grandiose architecture. It is easy to see why the laity acquiesced in a system under clerical and religious control, for the difficulties involved in setting up a lay school were formidable: the problem of guaranteeing religious character; financial handicaps in competing with a system that used student teachers; and the tarnished reputation of lay action. Furthermore, any challenge to the collegiate system could be perceived as a threat to the establishments nurturing those aspiring to ecclesiastical or religious life, and hence a danger to ecclesial life as a whole.

The picture of Catholic education would not be complete without some reference to provision at the tertiary level. The 'university question' – the absence of a university in England that Catholics could safely attend – vexed Catholics for much of the nineteenth century. Numerous attempts, both by individuals and by the hierarchy, were made to solve the problem, but these either fell short of providing a satisfactory answer or else came to grief. In the absence of university education, the Catholic colleges attempted to retain lay boys for higher studies by allowing them to follow the first two years of seminary training (the philosophy course); but few parents were able to afford what amounted to an aristocratic finishing school. Before the universities were opened up to Catholics, the question had been one of expediency: how best to cater for the small number in pursuit of higher education. When the barriers preventing Catholics attending universities were removed in 1854, the question of 'mixed' education became more troublesome: under what conditions was it permissible for Catholics to attend institutions of higher education that were either Protestant or non-denominational?

In 1835 Wiseman, then rector of the English College in Rome, visited England with a view to founding a Catholic university, bringing with him the promise of a papal charter for one. He visited Prior Park to discuss the plan with Baines, but it proceeded no further on account of fundamental disagreements: Wiseman envisaged the university as a centre of Catholic learning, culture and research, whereas Baines's vision was far narrower; though his scheme anticipated the admission of laymen, it still went little further than a seminary training. Later, when Wiseman was president of Oscott, he entertained hopes that Oscott itself might evolve into a university – but again without result. The truth of the matter was that arrangements for higher studies at the colleges were not really the answer: until they could get degrees, there could be no admission of Catholics into the professions on equal terms with Anglicans. This became a source of frustration to the gentry once career prospects were opened up in 1829. A limited solution was provided when the University of London gained its charter, enabling it to act as an examining body for teaching institutions that wished to affiliate. Among the first wave of institutions to do so, in 1840, were six Catholic colleges: Downside, Oscott, Prior Park, Stonyhurst and Ushaw and Ware. The exams provided a welcome stimulus and led to substantial reorganisation as studies were realigned to coincide with the Matriculation and B.A. syllabuses. At Stonyhurst the class-master system (in which a class was taught by the same master as it moved up the college) was abandoned for specialist teachers. Reforms at Ushaw were more extensive. Out went the old nomenclature, flogging and the class-master system; in came a tutor system, prizes, academic specialists, new books and new courses. But in both cases the reforms were short-lived. At Ushaw a revolt by students at the abandonment of 'Douai traditions' reversed most of the changes, while at Stonyhurst the class-master system was reinstated.[24]

One feature of the London University exams was that they were essentially non-classical and non-literary, and this lessened their appeal to the Catholic colleges: the dearth of aristocratic names on the degree lists indicates how unattractive the option was for this social group. Oscott, the college with the greatest proportion of upper-class boys, had the least contact with London; instead many boys ignored the exams and passed directly into the army, navy or law. But there were other reasons why the colleges were ambivalent about the London exams – not least a reluctance to disrupt their established patterns of studies, as preparation for an exam covering many disciplines was considered incompatible with a deep

[24.] V.A. McClelland, *English Roman Catholics and Higher Education, 1830–1903* (Oxford: Clarendon Press, 1973), pp. 33–38, 48–53.

study of the classical languages. The greater specialisation in the final B.A. exam and, after 1859, the Intermediate exam suited them better.

Fresh approaches to education

Among the converts it was generally accepted that the Catholic laity were less well educated than their Protestant counter-parts. In the pages of *The Rambler*, Capes laid the blame on the system of shared education, the 'practical jumble of the secular and ecclesiastical systems' which had arisen through historical accidents and left Catholics in the mid-nineteenth century without 'a single purely ecclesiastical, or purely secular' establishment in Great Britain; he suggested that the first step towards reform should be the system's eradication. Capes also identified three reasons why teaching at the colleges suffered: 'the want of a race of competent professors and teachers; the want of funds to support such instructors, if they existed; and the wretched apathy of the Catholic laity on the subject of education'.[25] (His criticisms were based on personal knowledge of Prior Park, where he had taught.)

Old Catholics reacted with mixed feelings to such public airing of the shortcomings of educational provision. While they may have taken heart at the prospect of reform, they found the criticisms of the colleges painful, even if not impertinent; one bishop protested strongly on behalf of collegiate education by objecting to public discussion of such 'delicate subjects which depend entirely on Church authority'.[26] Capes replied that the inferiority of Catholic education was an indisputable fact, attested to by the absence of English Catholics in almost every field of learning. And he blamed the wealthy laity for throwing away money on buildings instead of funding endowments for teachers and scholarships. The money that had been lavished on collegiate buildings, he calculated, would have been sufficient to endow at least two Catholic colleges on the scale of

[25] 'Catholic and Protestant collegiate education', *The Rambler*, December 1848, p. 236.
[26] Ullathorne to the editor, *The Tablet*, 9 December 1848, p. 787.

those at Oxford or Cambridge.[27] Frederick Oakeley, a former undergraduate of Christ Church Oxford and a Fellow and chaplain of Balliol, now a convert studying for the priesthood at Ware, supplied a crucial insight to the debate:

> the difference between the existing English Catholic idea of education and that to which we [converts] were accustomed at Oxford is [...] a fundamental one; the one making the formation of [mental] *character* its great aim, the other, the storing of the mind with a certain amount of valuable facts. Hence *our* requirements seem to Catholics 'limited' and *their* intellectual character and habits seem to us shallow and desultory. [28]

While defending collegiate education, he admitted that it was faulty in making too little allowance for the distinctions of individual character, both moral and intellectual.

Another significant contribution came from the outspoken intellectual William George Ward, who was destined to become the most vocal and articulate voice of Ultramontanism over the next three decades. By vigorously opposing the educational ideas of many of his fellow converts, he influenced Catholic public opinion against Protestant models of education, and therefore against the Oratory School. Many Catholics were astounded at his appointment to teach philosophy and theology at Ware, since he was not only a layman, but a married one – though in academic terms he was eminently fitted for the post. Before converting to Catholicism with his wife and resigning his fellowship at Balliol, he had been condemned by the Oxford Convocation for his *Ideal of the Christian Church* and stripped of his degrees. Entering the debate in 1849, Ward publicly dismissed the notion of a convert conspiracy against old Catholics: the converts, he said, spoke not from an external standpoint but 'precisely *because* we feel ourselves as fully part and parcel of the existing system' as the old Catholics. It was an indubitable fact that 'Protestant lay education is superior to

[27.] 'The duties of journalists: Catholic and Protestant education', *The Rambler*, January 1849, p. 330.
[28.] Oakeley to the editor, *The Rambler*, January 1849, p. 373.

ours',[29] and that there was a lack of appropriate education and training for future leaders, for those entering professions or other intellectual occupations, and for those suited to teaching secular subjects at the colleges.

Ward maintained that the London exams contributed to the lack of real scholarship at the colleges; others, such as Capes and Newman, thought that the arrangement barely constituted a university education, since it separated learning from religion. Newman privately encouraged and reassured Capes in his efforts to stimulate debate; and while cautioning him to avoid even the appearance of hostility to old Catholics, admitted that it was not possible 'to do good without giving offence and incurring criticism'. Newman's only reservation was that Capes had not 'brought out *enough* that the stinginess of the laity is at the bottom of it'.[30] However, it was Capes who went to the heart of the matter and pinpointed the real weaknesses of collegiate education: the diversity of interests (school, noviciate or seminary, and mini-university), the duplication of resources (with no fewer than seven institutions catering for under 900 students), and the heterogeneous composition of the student body (the middle-class, the aristocratic and the clerical all educated together). He suggested the colleges subordinate their individual interests to the common good by agreeing to establish a single institution.

Newman's influence on the debate about Catholic education begins around 1847, when the Pope established the first Oratory of St Philip Neri in England, at Birmingham, with Newman as its superior. Significantly, at Newman's request, the Pope's Brief of Institution granted explicit permission for the Oratorians to run a school for boys, in case of necessity. And, on the Pope's initiative, it added that the Oratory should work especially 'among those in the higher ranks, the more learned and generally among the more educated'.[31] This additional

---

[29.] W.G. Ward to the editor, *The Rambler*, February 1849, pp. 446, 449.
[30.] Newman to Capes, 7 December 1848, *L&D* XII, p. 366.
[31.] *Newman the Oratorian: His Unpublished Oratorian Papers*, ed. P. Murray (Dublin: Gill & Macmillan, 1969), p. 426. Searching for a way of combining the advantages of the religious life with the secular priesthood, Newman choose the Rule of the Oratory of St Philip Neri, established in the sixteenth century. The Oratorian Rule

phrase was to guide Newman in his educational ventures.

Soon after Newman returned from Rome, the Oratorians inherited a property called St Wilfrid's near Cheadle in Cheshire. Unable to dispose of the property, Newman devised two educational schemes for its support. His first idea was to start what he called an 'Eton of the Oratory', from which he hoped future Oratorian vocations would come, though he was unsure whether 'it would take the formal shape of a Seminary, school, noviceship or College'; when the draft prospectus appeared, it was advertised as offering a classical education 'conducted on the system pursued at the Universities and public schools' for boys aged eight upwards.[32] The plan was not pursued, nor was an equally ambitious one which also aimed at meeting a recognised need: providing something 'for Catholic lay students, when they have completed the ordinary school course, which should be to them what Oxford and Cambridge are to Protestant boys from Eton and Harrow'. The prospectus for the New College at St Wilfrid's (or Cotton College, as it was otherwise called) gave prominence to ancient, classical and modern languages, as well as mathematics and general literature, and listed nine staff, all converts from Oxford and Cambridge and all but one Oratorians.[33] Although it was to be established by both the London and Birmingham Oratories, Newman envisaged that if it prospered it would become independent of them; but the plan petered out because of the reluctance of the London Oratory to back it. Even after St Wilfrid's was taken off the Oratory's hands, there was a third attempt at an educational venture when Newman invited a married convert to begin a school in the houses adjacent to the Birmingham Oratory; but this scheme, like the other two, never left the drawing-board. Even though none of them prospered, the Oratory addressed the educational needs of some convert families during the 1850s by taking in a few boys and providing tuition for them.

---

enables priests to undertake parochial duties in large towns and cities, while benefiting from community life, and can be adapted to particular circumstances and local needs in order that each Oratory house, which is independent, can develop its own style.

[32.] Newman to Faber, 10 May 1849, *L&D* XIII, pp. 143, 421n.
[33.] W. Buscot, *The History of Cotton College* (London: Burns, Oates & Washbourne, 1940), pp. 238–42.

Although all three schemes were, in a sense, forerunners of the one that came to fruition in 1859, they were sideshows in comparison with the project of starting a university across the Irish Sea. In 1845 the British government established the secular Queen's Colleges at Belfast, Cork and Galway to provide an alternative to Trinity College Dublin, where some religious tests were still in force. Rome forbade the Irish bishops to take part, as the scheme countenanced mixed education, and urged them to establish a Catholic university on the model of Louvain, which had been set up successfully by the Belgian bishops in 1834. In 1851 Archbishop Cullen, on behalf of the Irish episcopacy, invited Newman – 'fitted beyond all others [...] to mould into shape, to govern, and give character to the future University' – to be the first rector.[34] It was to be Newman's biggest educational project, and though the story of its difficult beginnings is too long to recount here, it is useful to identify a few of its salient characteristics for the purposes of understanding the later school foundation. In the process of setting up the university, four collegiate houses were established; in the one Newman ran personally great liberty was granted, reflecting his view that discipline at university, being a preparation for life beyond, should be characterised by 'a certain tenderness, or even laxity of rule'. He expanded on these views in his first university report where he laid down the 'guiding principle [...] that the young for the most part cannot be driven, but [...] are open to persuasion, and to the influence of kindness and personal attachment'; they were to be guided by 'indirect contrivances rather than by authoritative enactments and naked prohibitions.'[35]

Fundamental differences of view between Newman and the Irish bishops (including Cullen) gave rise to innumerable problems. Newman wanted the university to provide a general liberal education; the bishops wanted training for the professions. Newman wanted a collegiate structure, like Oxford (and, incidentally, Louvain); the bishops opposed him. Newman appointed men according to his vision, typically Oxford

[34.] 'Report of the Committee of the Catholic University', McClelland, *English Roman Catholics*, p. 98.
[35.] 'Report for the year 1854/55', *My Campaign in Ireland*, ed. W. Neville (Aberdeen: A. King & Co.), 1896, pp. 36, 38.

converts; the bishops wanted more priests and more Irishmen. Newman intended the university to be mainly a lay institution, and wanted its finances to be in lay hands; the bishops refused to relinquish financial control. Newman hoped to attract English Catholics in considerable numbers; the bishops wanted it primarily for Irishmen. And Newman scandalised the bishops by having a cricket field laid out, and allowing billiards, smoking and hunting.[36] Various other considerations, together with the hindrances and frustrations he experienced at Dublin, contributed to Newman's decision to resign the rectorship in 1857 at the end of his three-year 'loan' from the Birmingham Oratory: the lack of English support for it, either in finance or in students; the conflicting requirements of the rectorship (as understood by Cullen) with his duties as provost of the Oratory, which needed his presence and guiding hand; and his conviction that 'really I may be *wanted* in England'.[37] While Newman's resignation from the university was interpreted by some as an admission of failure, the experience proved invaluable for future educational ventures. Working with the Irish hierarchy had provided him with crucial insights into the mentality prevailing among the higher clergy, while contact with the Catholic laity had warned him of its apathy and reluctance to give financial support for educational endeavours. He would encounter these traits again in the days ahead.

[36.] Norman, *English Catholic Church*, pp. 322–25.
[37.] Newman to St John, 7 May 1857, *L&D* XVIII, p. 30.

Chapter 2

A 'Great Catholic Desideratum'

First soundings

All foundational periods have their particular phases, reflecting the uneven passage from idea to reality, and that of the Oratory School was no exception. Between the first sketch of the plan in January 1857 and the first intake of boys in May 1859, periods of frantic activity alternated with others of apparent passivity; though it may not have seemed so at the time, each of these phases served a purpose. The idea of founding a Catholic public school cannot be attributed to a remarkable insight by any one individual, since the want of one was patent to most of Newman's convert friends who had sons to educate. Initially, independently of each other, several of them turned to him for advice on how they might resolve their need. The first to do so was one of his most devoted friends, John Hungerford Pollen, formerly a Fellow and Senior Proctor at Oxford, and at the time Professor of Fine Arts at the Catholic University in Dublin. The detailed nature of Newman's response suggests that he had long anticipated the approach: he advised Pollen that those 'interested in a Catholic Eton should form themselves into a quasi trust with a certain sum of money at their disposal'; that they should keep a low profile on account of the '*personal* interests and jealousies of the existing Catholic Schools', which would become less formidable with the passage of time; that they should start with little boys, and after about five years decide on the question of a public school;

that if Pollen could gather three or four trustees, 'enough for
the experiment', they could approach the Oratory without
either side committing itself; and that, if both sides were agree-
able, the quasi-trustees could take a nearby house and field,
and install Mrs Wootten (a widowed friend of Newman who
lived near the Oratory) as 'Guardian of the children'.[1] By
chance, their discussion coincided with Newman's concern
about the Oratorian priest Nicholas Darnell, who had recently
been ill with pleurisy; he had just returned to the Oratory after
two months' convalescence and was 'anxious for indoor
employment, preferably teaching boys Classics and having
charge of them'.[2]

The note of caution sounded by Newman might well have
surprised Pollen, but it had its history. Four years previously
Newman had warned a convert friend who wanted to open a
boys' school at Clifton about the difficulties he would face.
Catholics were 'so used to absurdly low prices', Newman told
him, that they would balk at proper fees, while parents were 'so
wonderfully capricious' they were reluctant to commit themselves. Moreover, the project would involve a considerable
outlay at the beginning and run at a loss for a while. There was
yet another 'great difficulty' which lay in challenging 'the
Catholic monopoly – either *you* cannot succeed, or the *Colleges*
cannot'.

> This will hinder your getting the *names* of people as
> patrons of your undertaking, who in their hearts feel how
> much good you would be doing and would rejoice in your
> scheme for its own sake – but they will say I cannot come
> into a project which will *break* this or that diocese.

Nevertheless, Newman thought that there might be sufficient
people who '*feel* the desideratum' to help establish it, and even
share in the financial risk;[3] but with such slender hopes and so
many obstacles the plan was abandoned.

In April 1857, just days after notifying the Irish bishops of

---

[1.] Newman to Pollen, 28 January 1857, *L&D* XVII, p. 511.
[2.] Flanagan to Newman (editor's abstract), December 1856, *L&D* XVII, p. 479n.
[3.] Newman to Thompson, 12 June 1853, *L&D* XV, pp. 379–80.

his intention to resign the rectorship of the Catholic University the following November, Newman decided to test the school idea on Sir John Simeon, whom he had suggested to Pollen as a possible trustee. Simeon had been a Liberal MP until he resigned when he and his wife became Catholics, and his London house was a rendezvous for literary and political society. Newman confided in Simeon that, 'having set the University off', he thought he might be 'instrumental also, in setting off another great Catholic desideratum, a public school'. He had in mind a 'very modest beginning' at the Oratory, with boys about nine years old under the care of a lady, and Darnell as headmaster. After four or five years, when they were of public school age, a change of plan would occur and the Oratory might then retire from the scheme. But Newman resisted fleshing out the idea any further, as he was unsure 'whether others will think such a project possible', and he insisted: 'You will be more able than I am to decide both on the idea itself and on the mode of carrying it out.'[4] He added that the Oratory had no wish to be involved in the financial arrangements or to receive any remuneration.

It is worth pausing to assess the letter. The outline of the ambitious plan was not conveyed with gushing enthusiasm in order to gain support; it was a tersely-worded communication which anticipated great difficulties – especially those of attracting a sufficient number of boys and contending with opposition – and invited the recipient to take up the challenge. There was no hint of enlisting support for an already elaborated plan; it was an invitation to tackle a project together. It was for Simeon and others to fill out the idea and to decide on the *modus operandi*.

Expressing his longing for this 'great Catholic desideratum', Simeon maintained in his reply that it was 'impossible for the Catholic body in England to elevate themselves into intellectual equality with their fellow Citizens' unless something was done to improve their education; until then, it was 'vain and childish for us to complain of and grumble at the inferiority of our social position', and still more childish to try to make up for this deficiency 'by a system of self exclusion'. The mere acces-

---

4. Newman to Simeon, 17 April 1857, *L&D* XVIII, pp. 16–17.

sion of numbers which the converts were bringing to the Catholic body would have no effect, unless they (the converts) were 'ready and able to do something to meet this state of things'. In fact, the effect would be prejudicial, in merely supplying more instances to illustrate 'the popular theory of Catholic inferiority'. The prospect of a new school was a great consolation to him on another score, as it would enable his boys to 'receive a training which might fit them to take their place hereafter in active life on a par with other educated Englishmen'. Simeon proceeded to enumerate what he considered to be the defects of the collegiate system: 'Want of Manliness,[5] want of completeness, want of definite purpose; and consequent want of influence on the future pursuits and character of the man'. Against these defects, he acknowledged its considerable strengths, above all 'the inculcation of purity, and the consequent production of a high moral standard'. However, this was 'apparently purchased at the expense of many valuable qualities of manliness, energy and readiness to face the world'. Simeon's ideal was eloquently summed up: 'To my mind Eton, minus its wickedness, and plus the inculcation of the Catholic faith would be what I should best like to see'.[6]

Like other converts, Simeon wrestled with the problem of maintaining his Englishness at a time when the Catholic Church was regarded by the majority of his countrymen as intrinsically and irredeemably foreign. He recognised his over-sensitivity, but confessed he distrusted 'the disposition to denationalize the English Catholic, and to set up as a model for his imitation, some foreign type' – a type which he regarded as 'in every way inferior'. The 'Convert element' had much to answer for in this respect, and it was on this account that Simeon felt some uneasiness at the involvement of the Oratory in Newman's proposal, for he incorrectly assumed that the Italianate leanings of the London Oratory also typified the Birmingham Oratory. He felt uneasy about his boys being

[5.] The concept of 'manliness' encapsulated the essential boyhood ideal which a public school education was supposed to foster. By early exposure to difficulties and hardships, self-reliance and character were cultivated – though not brains, for manliness coexisted happily with anti-intellectualism.

[6.] Simeon to Newman, 30 April 1857, BOA.

'encouraged to throw overboard their distinctive English character'; nevertheless he was prepared to dismiss such fears if Newman's was to be 'the presiding head, and the guiding hand'. Simeon agreed that the scheme would run up against opposition; the 'attachment of many of the old Catholics for the particular Seminaries in which they have been educated' was thoroughly bigoted, and since this was particularly strong 'among the Oscott men' it was not possible to do much with them, yet without them the idea of a large public school seemed impossible.[7] It was an obstacle he could not see his way round. The prospect of competing with Oscott was daunting on two counts: its proximity, five miles from the Oratory; and its popularity among the upper classes, as the great majority of its boys (unlike those of Ushaw and Ware) were lay pupils.

Not only was Newman taken aback by the references to the supposed un-Englishness of the Oratory, but he considered Simeon's response 'so little encouraging, that we have dropped the subject'.[8] All correspondence about a prospective school ceased, except for a separate exchange of letters with Richard Ward, an Oxford convert who had become a priest and who had previously discussed the plan with Newman. After receiving Simeon's letter, Newman wrote to Ward to emphasise the need for the utmost discretion, above all in connecting his name with the plan. Ward revealed that he had already confided in his brother, Francis, also a convert, who had shown great interest and compiled a list of those likely to support the scheme. Because of the 'peculiar difficulties' involved, Richard pointed out that the first question everyone would ask was: 'Who could be found to carry the plan through?' He asked Newman to allow Francis to tell his friends 'confidentially, that he had reason to think you would give such a plan your formal consideration if it were brought before you';[9] and he explained that his brother had volunteered to send Newman his list before approaching those on it, and to say as much or as little as Newman wished. Newman's reply does not seem to have survived but, judging by the absence of any further activity, it

7. Simeon to Newman, 30 April 1857, BOA.
8. Newman to Bellasis, 28 October 1857, *L&D* XVIII, p. 153.
9. R. Ward to Newman, 9 May 1857, BOA.

may be assumed that it was at least cautious, if not broadly negative.

Newman's convert friends faced a problem. The solution – the establishment of a school matching the great public schools but informed with, and imbued by, the Catholic faith and morals – seemed straightforward, but they were searching for the means to bring it about. Newman was in a position to offer them more than advice, and indeed was open to the possibility of collaborating with them. The offer to begin at the Oratory was an attractive proposition on several counts: Newman could oversee the foundation, Darnell had the makings of a head-master, and Mrs Wootten was available to care for the young boys. Moreover, the location of the Oratory on the outskirts of Birmingham was not inappropriate for a small boys' school, as the neighbourhood was semi-rural and covered with trees and gardens. Ultimately, however, the site had to be in the country-side as that was the proper setting for a public school, though this implied that the connection with the Oratory would only be temporary, as the Oratorian Rule stipulated that the Oratory must be city-based.

Bellasis takes the initiative

In October 1857 Newman was approached by Edward Bellasis, who was searching for a suitable preparatory school for his eldest son, aged seven. It was after reading the *Tracts* and Newman's sermons two decades earlier that Bellasis had visited Oxford and there began what Newman described as 'a long, equable, sunny friendship'. Unlike his father and brothers, Bellasis was not an Oxford man, but he was soon accepted by the Tractarians and corresponded on a range of religious topics. He pointed out that, for those like himself who had chil-dren to educate, the confusion in Anglican teaching and the absence of clear authority were a recipe for doubt and indiffer-ence; and these concerns contributed to his conversion in 1850.[10] Thereafter he was always at Newman's side, advising,

[10] For further details see *Memorials of Mr Serjeant Bellasis, 1800–1873* (London: Burns & Oates, 1893; 1895), written by Bellasis's second son Edward.

encouraging and helping him in every way he could. Many of the converts, particularly those in holy orders, struggled to make a living after their conversions, but there were a handful like Bellasis who flourished in their professions despite becoming Catholics. After being called to the Bar, Bellasis practised in the Court of Chancery and in 1844 was introduced as Serjeant-at-Law in the House of Lords. His professional work was mainly related to the expansion of the railways, and it brought him into contact with the great civil engineers of the time, who like others valued his calmness, courtesy and eye for detail.

Bellasis's enquiry at the London Oratory as to whether the Congregation planned a school had been met with such a negative response that he had turned his thoughts elsewhere. Since then he had met Pollen, who had encouraged him to contact Newman. Bellasis was told that the plan would require a considerable outlay; that the Oratory was unable to help financially; and that, once the school was set up, the Oratory would gradually relinquish control to avoid interfering with the interests of existing schools. Newman declared: 'We will try to carry out any thing which others originate, but this is all we can promise, should our aid be desirable.'[11] The response may appear lukewarm, but it reflected Newman's view that the responsibility for educating children lay in the first instance with their parents; his caution also stemmed from a concern to identify suitable works for the Oratory to engage in. Bellasis returned to the charge and, while heeding Newman's request not to air the scheme publicly, replied that he would sound out others about the possibility of providing the support asked for.

The first four months of 1858 were busy ones. Bellasis's soundings resulted in a growing awareness among a group of influential Catholics of their common responsibility for educating their children, and this in turn led to addressing their common need. In January, two converts called on Newman to discuss the scheme: Thomas Allies, an Oxford graduate and Fellow who had taught history at the Catholic University, and Francis Ward. To Newman, Allies stated his concern robustly: 'without mincing words, there is not I suppose a convert of Oxford or Cambridge who is not forced into a feeling made up

---

[11.] Newman to Bellasis, 28 October 1857, *L&D* XVIII, p. 153.

of despair and disgust at the condition of scientific [i.e. first-rate] teaching among us, compared with that existing in the best Protestant schools'. He brushed aside the difficulties in bullish mood: 'We know well enough the number and the weight of those who will be ready to thwart such a design, but if this school be the greatest want we have, ought it not to be attempted?'[12] Newman reminded Allies of the difficulty of acting against Oscott, and suggested they try to win over the bishop and the 'Oscott people' by ensuring the fees were sufficiently higher than Oscott's to preclude competition. By declaring that he would not launch into a scheme he could not see his way through, Newman showed he was wary of moving too quickly and displacing the initiative and know-how that parents could provide.

As the plan moved gradually into the public domain, Newman decided to broach the topic with his bishop, William Ullathorne, only to find that he already knew of the scheme from his secretary, Edgar Estcourt, who had just met Bellasis. Estcourt and Bellasis had previously known each other as Anglicans, and exchanged views on education. Now Bellasis explained that he and others were concerned about the education of their sons; they were dissatisfied with arrangements at the colleges, where the majority of the masters were *in statu pupillari* and church and lay boys were mixed together, and he revealed the plan afoot for remedying the situation. He admitted, however, that fundamental difficulties were unresolved – in particular the question of guaranteeing the school's religious dimension. Bellasis was convinced that the school should not be in lay hands but under some ecclesiastical body, and explained that he had approached several parties, including Newman. In response Estcourt suggested that Bellasis should investigate whether, by solving the financial issue and reducing the proportion of ecclesiastical student–teachers, one of the colleges could not meet parents' wishes by separating church and lay boys. Any new school ought to be in ecclesiastical hands, he thought, but neither the Jesuits nor the Oratorians were the ones to carry it out successfully.

Estcourt then alerted Ullathorne to what he considered to be

[12.] Allies to Newman, 7 January 1858, BOA.

an imminent crisis. The plan for 'an education of a higher character' and with good discipline promised to be a very formidable rival to the colleges; the higher fees would not be sufficient to prevent the idea catching on with other families, for it was clear that 'these parties are determined that something shall be done'.[13] Estcourt considered that urgent action was required to meet their valid objections to the colleges. Since there were insufficient priests to fill more teaching posts, he wondered if lay or even married men might be considered as tutors – if not for church boys, then at least for the lay boys. And to deal with the main difficulty, finances, he proposed they adapt the scheme used at the new proprietary schools.

Though Ullathorne was of old Catholic Yorkshire stock, he occupied a middle ground between old Catholic values, Roman influences and the converts. He looked sympathetically on the new initiative and even welcomed the school plan – 'purely secular as to students, yet under clerical management' – as it would lead to the separation of schools from seminaries: 'It would be just that wedge in the present system that is wanted.' Any attempt to graft the scheme onto Oscott, as Estcourt suggested, 'would rivet on us the very system we want to get rid of'. As the existing colleges were full to overflowing, Ullathorne considered there was room for another, though he realised it would take time to win over the old Catholic families. It ought to employ converts – but not for all the posts, since 'the moral management would require good Catholic experience, otherwise it will fail'. Far from disapproving of the scheme, Ullathorne told his secretary, 'I should be the first to say to Dr Newman [...] you need have no fear of interfering with us'.[14] Ullathorne anticipated it would be a long time before the venture affected the colleges, and that by then they would be ready for the competition. Nevertheless, his stance was courageous since, of the three secular colleges, Oscott (the college in his own diocese) was undoubtedly the one least able to survive without lay boys.

[13.] Estcourt to Ullathorne, 22 January 1858, BOA.
[14.] Ullathorne to Estcourt, 24 January 1858, BOA.

The promoters meet

The upshot of these deliberations was the first of several promoters' meetings organised by Bellasis in his Westminster chambers; the purpose was to consider 'a direct personal application to be made to Dr Newman respecting the establishment by him of an Upper Class Lay Catholic Boys' School in England'.[15] Besides Allies, Bellasis and Francis Ward, four others were present on 29 January 1858: Frederick Capes, William Dodsworth, Richard Macmullen, and Francis Wegg-Prosser. The only one without an Oxbridge background was Capes, who had been educated at King's College London, yet it was he who saw the venture through to completion and sent two sons. Like his brother, the founder of *The Rambler*, he had made a large financial sacrifice on becoming a Catholic.

The seven converts agreed that Bellasis should petition Newman to start the scheme and 'move it into maturity', on the assurance he was given the financial backing. They agreed the substance of a letter to Newman: that all thought the school necessary; that the plan ought to be formed 'not upon the accidental views which a variety of persons might take but upon the mature deliberation of some one mind'; that Newman's connection with the Catholic University, and interest 'in the earlier education of youth' pointed him out as the one to whom they should apply; and that they desired a lay school which combined 'a vigorous intellectual training' with a 'thoroughly Catholic atmosphere'. If Newman agreed to undertake the project, the promoters wished to know three things: the initial capital required, the minimum number of boys to begin with, and the annual fees. Discussion then focused on how to raise the initial sum, and they considered a plan that had been proposed which argued for a starting fund of £1000–£2000.

The originator of the plan was James Hope-Scott, a wealthy and prominent parliamentary barrister who was destined to play a major role in the setting up of the school. After an education at Eton and Christ Church Oxford, Hope (as he was called originally) had become a Fellow of Merton College, and

---

[15.] Bellasis, *A Contribution towards Oratory School Annals: the Year 1858* (London: privately printed, 1887), p. 1, BOA.

by 1837 a committed Tractarian. A year later he met Newman and began a friendship, which 'rapidly assumed a very intimate and confidential character, and was indeed *the* great friendship of Mr Hope's life'.[16] Hope married a grand-daughter of Walter Scott, and on the death of his brother-in-law inherited Abbotsford and assumed the name Hope-Scott. In 1851 he was received into the Catholic Church, and followed soon afterwards by his wife and other relations. Electing to work at the Parliamentary Bar on legislation for railways, he became standing counsel to nearly every railway system in the country and for a decade was unrivalled in reputation. He was greatly admired for his courtesy, his eloquence, his clarity of thought and memory for detail, Gladstone describing him as 'the most winning person of his day'.[17] Hope-Scott spent most of his considerable patrimony supporting organisations more or less in the service of religion, and undertook the guardianship of numerous children of friends and relations. He was liberal too with his advice, which was so highly valued that the expression 'ask Hope' became proverbial in Catholic circles. He became Newman's chief adviser, managed his defence in the libel action *Achilli* v. *Newman*, helped negotiate his appointment as Rector of the Catholic University, and assisted him in setting it up. Now, in January 1858, he was willing to advise on another Catholic enterprise.

At the promoters' first meeting the consensus about fees was that they should not be too high, no higher than £70 per annum, and that they should be determined 'not by reference to what is paid at existing schools, but by what may prove to be required for its effectual support'.[18] (At Oscott, fees for lay boys were 50 guineas for those under fifteen, and 55 guineas for those above.) Dodsworth provided confirmation that the colleges were over-subscribed, relating that the previous year some forty boys had been turned away from Downside, where he had a son. The promoters also received news of

---

[16.] R. Ornsby, *Memoirs of James Robert Hope-Scott* I (London: John Murray, 1884), p. 172.
[17.] Entry for Hope-Scott in the old *Dictionary of National Biography*.
[18.] Bellasis (on behalf of the promoters) to Newman, 30 January 1858, BOA.

Ullathorne's positive reaction to the plan, which they considered an unexpected bonus.

Newman now began to focus on practical problems, such as how to reconcile the access and availability of Mrs Wootten to the boys with Darnell's responsibility for them, given that priest and dame could not live together, and the wisdom of converting a local house. To resolve these difficulties, he formulated a proposal which had the status of a suggestion offered by him to both parties (the promoters and the Oratorians). His proposal entailed taking boys at £70 per annum, some of the Oratory Fathers engaging in the scheme for up to twenty years, and having an advance of £2000 for preparations. He suggested using the top storey of the Oratory House, which could take up to fifty boys, despite the considerable inconvenience to the Oratorians, and the adjoining playground and ball-court. Land alongside the House could be used for a new school building, which would be ready by December if works began at once; the alternative was to rent a house nearby. The Oratory would receive a fair remuneration for accommodation offered, interest on all money invested in the school, and £50 per annum for the headmaster. Newman's assumption was 'that I am to have the whole management of the undertaking'.[19]

To the promoters, at their second meeting (on 3 February), the proposed location of the school seemed to suggest that the whole Oratory was intending to drop other concerns and become schoolmasters, and this provoked disagreement. Strenuous objections were raised to any connection with a religious order, particularly by Macmullen, who assumed that this meant the masters would be unpaid and therefore Oratorians. The promoters agreed that Newman's involvement was crucial for creating confidence in the infant establishment. But attaching the school to the Oratory was another matter: it was likely to 'create great jealousy and dissatisfaction' and 'would tend sooner or later to confine the selection of teachers to that body and so cramp the advance of the school' – 'what was wanted was an "independent school"'. Evidently Newman's proposal frustrated their aspirations for a public school by introducing

19. Newman to Bellasis, 2 February 1858, *L&D* XVIII, p. 244.

unnecessary constraints. At the same time, however, they had to decide how the religious character of the school was to be guaranteed. Bellasis argued that, 'as all existing Catholic schools of any note were connected either with Episcopal seminaries or religious bodies, an attempt, and that by converts, to establish a school independent of some known Ecclesiastical or religious foundation would create distrust'. There would be no security for proper religious training if the school had to rely on such unoccupied priests as the bishop might be able to spare from his own clergy. The connection with the Oratory was a natural one, and 'would create that confidence in the religious element which an independent school might not have'. But the others took a different view: they wanted Newman to establish a school entirely under his personal control, for as long as he thought necessary, and then to create 'a trust for its continuance'.[20] A letter summarising all these doubts was prepared but not sent, pending reconsideration, and the meeting adjourned.

From the outset Bellasis was accepted by the promoters as their natural leader, and at no time during the foundational period does he appear to have lost their confidence. In these early stages he became a special focus for the interchange of aspirations, impressions and fears in the attempt to formulate a response to Newman's offer. Having an overview of their ideas, he was effectively entrusted with the task of securing the best deal for them, consequently his objections were duly heeded and the adjournment granted. In fact, most of the parents with whom Bellasis had spoken considered the school's connection with a religious body as essential and were, as he put it, 'disinclined to the idea of an independent school'.[21]

It was at this stage that the promoters were joined by the distinguished old Catholic Sir John Acton. Having heard of developments through Darnell, Acton was invited to join the dinner organised to talk over the plan because Bellasis felt 'there are many interests to be considered besides our own'[22]

[20]. Bellasis to Newman, 5 February 1858, BOA.
[21]. Bellasis, memorandum: statement of the Darnell trouble, n.d., BOA.
[22]. Bellasis to Acton, 1 February 1858, Cambridge University Library, Add. MS 8119(1)/B68.

and was eager to hear his views. Acton's imagination was fired by the project, which he considered as a 'necessary appendix to the [hoped-for Catholic] university and to the project of a regular separate seminary for our ecclesiastical students; and it will be a great step towards emancipating Catholic lay education from protestant influence on the one hand and from the defects of our Colleges on the other'. He only wished he had a young son to offer, though he was able to supply the valuable information that the Jesuits were contemplating a school of their own near London. As the first cradle Catholic to join the promoters, and having been recently educated at Oscott, Acton's views were bound to be given a special hearing; he described how he and his contemporaries were like 'specimens of the monstrous deficiency of the best education which is now accessible to Catholic lay boys in England'.[23] He anticipated that the real difficulties would not be of a material kind, but those arising 'from the variety and division of opinions which at present characterise the Catholic body':

> a lurking jealousy of converts, a more bold and rampant aversion to whatever is connected with the Dublin university, objections to the Oratorians, objections from some of the Oratorians themselves against everything that Newman does, and especially against such a presumed departure from the principles of the order, some annoyances, at first, from the existing colleges, etc. etc. all which I trust will not stand in the way of a successful beginning and a gradual progress which will be none the worse if it is slow at first.[24]

This was an astonishingly accurate catalogue of the difficulties that lay ahead, yet Acton simply brushed them aside with the expectancy that they would all be overcome. Nevertheless he realised that a foundation that would have such far-reaching consequences – reforming the whole collegiate system, and paving the way for the establishment of a Catholic university in England – was likely to arouse much opposition.

[23.] Acton to Bellasis, 2 February 1858, BOA.
[24.] *Ibid.*

Before their next meeting the promoters were informed by Francis Ward (after a chance conversation with Ambrose St John, Newman's right-hand man at the Oratory) that Newman had been considering the plan primarily from the Oratory's point of view: not what was best in the abstract, but what would be best for the Oratory if it was approached. The plan was consistent with the Oratorians' work, Ward was told, but would remain one among several; except for two Fathers, none was addicted to teaching or qualified to govern the school, yet it had the advantage of connecting them with those they were charged to work with, as well as helping them fill vacant rooms. The promoters, on the other hand, should view it from a different perspective and consider whether the Oratory's proposition suited their needs. The clarification had its effect, and at their next meeting on 6 February the promoters agreed to withhold the joint letter describing their doubts. Despite lingering reservations, they also decided that Bellasis and Acton should visit Newman to talk over the plan, and discussed the wider contribution it would make by raising Catholic educational standards and preparing the ground for a Catholic university. Apart from Acton, the other new recruit at their meeting was Henry Wilberforce, the youngest son of the philanthropist. He had been tutored by Newman at Oriel College Oxford and had resigned from a rich living to become a Catholic with his wife and children.

On account of the divergence of views among the promoters, Bellasis decided to consult Hope-Scott, whom he had kept up to date with developments. Hope-Scott's considered opinion was that Newman's plan was the best, except for one detail: Newman's suggestion that the 'Gentlemen in London' have the power to 'nominate' boys, so as to avoid finding himself in a difficult position as regards local Birmingham boys. Hope-Scott thought that, since Newman ought to have the power to expel, so he ought to have the sole power to admit. Regarding doubts about accepting boys 'of inferior rank or manners', Hope-Scott pointed out that the English public schools were open to all who could pay. A mixture of classes was advantageous, though he conceded that Birmingham 'might pour an inconvenient number into the school'. To offset this risk he recommended the standard remedy: to insist that those who lived within two or three miles be admitted only as day-boys. Hope-Scott proceeded to emphasise two points: '1st that Newman's independence must be complete, 2nd that to have a good public school it must be in the true sense *public*'. Against the latter, it could be argued that the expense of a public school put a check on too great an admixture of classes, yet this was not the case, he felt, with schools like Rugby. Though the new school would, for a while, be too small to bear a mixture of classes safely, he insisted that if the aim really was to have a public school then it should be professed from the first: any class limitation would meet with ill-will. The plan was already exposed to 'another cause of *jealousy*' due to 'the movement being one of Converts, and of Converts dissatisfied with the old Catholic Schools'. In his opinion, any exclusiveness in the nominations would, quite rightly, add to the arguments against the plan.[25]

It is significant that Hope-Scott, like the other promoters, rejected the proprietary or joint-stock principle which had funded canal and railway construction. The system had been used in the 1840s to establish secondary schools by raising funds from a large number of subscribers or shareholders, each of whom had the right to nominate a pupil; the subscribers elected the directors, who appointed the masters and a Visitor and drew up an annual report. The directors had a veto on admissions and on the transfer of shares; it was exercised at Cheltenham College to bar the sons of shopkeepers, and at Clifton College against sons of local tradesmen. Due to the problems caused by the dispersal of power, the successful proprietary schools were restructured in the 1850s and early 1860s. Despite the early success of such schools, Richard Ward considered it 'of the utmost importance that the promoters [of the Oratory School] should have absolutely nothing to do with any part of the management – in fact should simply raise the necessary funds, send their children, and rather take their chance for the rest'![26] Hope-Scott argued that the creation of a committee to control school admissions would result in it thinking it had more power than was safe or desirable: the

[25.] Hope-Scott to Bellasis, 7 February 1858, BOA.
[26.] R. Ward to Newman, 9 May 1857, BOA.

committee would inevitably be comprised of subscribers, and 'the proprietary element would thus insensibly come in'. He thought it ought to be made clear at the outset that those subscribing should have no extra rights over other parents: if a subscriber were to think himself hard done by when his son was refused admission or removed, then 'the discipline of the school is at an end'.[27]

In accordance with the promoters' decision, Bellasis and Acton travelled to Birmingham to discuss Newman's offer with him. There was full agreement between them, except that the two promoters considered that the next move was to collect names to back Newman, while Newman wanted the cardinal and the president of Oscott to be informed and won over first. Newman also explained the crucial distinction between the different ways in which he could be involved: he could 'advise abstractedly', but when it came to action he must act as an Oratorian. Thus he could say, in the abstract, that *his* proposal – for the school to begin under the care of the Oratory 'till it has gained such strength and consistency as will enable it to dispense with such protection' – seemed the best possible. However, as an Oratorian he had to declare that the Oratory would be unable to supply masters and ushers:[28] it could only give general 'superintendence, a Father prefect [i.e. headmaster] for a time, and spiritual care'. The closer the school was, the greater the service the Oratory could be to it: hence the suggestion that it be placed on Oratory ground. However, once it had increased above a certain size it could no longer continue under the Oratory, as space was limited. The scheme, in fact, was to be like other Oratorian ones, with a Father or two giving a certain amount of time, since Newman (still thinking as an Oratorian) considered that 'it was as little out of the way to take charge of a rich school than of a poor, and that this plan might be entered into by the Oratory, if Reformatories might, and ragged schools, and guilds'.[29]

Before leaving Birmingham, Acton and Bellasis showed

---

27. Hope-Scott to Bellasis, 7 February 1858, BOA.
28. Newman, memorandum (given to Acton and Bellasis), 8 February 1858, BOA.
29. Newman, memorandum, 9 February 1858, *L&D* XVIII, p. 251.

Darnell and St John the letter the promoters had intended to send expressing their reservations over Newman's offer. Inevitably, Newman came to hear of the letter after their departure, and it caused him acute anxiety about what should be his next move. He surmised that, if the promoters had only been won over during their last meeting, there was no guarantee they would not change their minds again; and he would be left with 'all the responsibility and odium',[30] as well as other consequences: the perception by others that he was bent on filling rooms at the Oratory to provide income; gossip from the London Oratory; and explanations that might be required of him at Rome.

After mulling over the matter, Newman decided to withdraw his proposal and the indirect promise to present it to the Oratorians. Assuring Bellasis of his entire readiness to cooperate, he explained in a sensitively-worded letter, which reflected his keen awareness of the imbalance in commitment of the interested parties: 'I am afraid of going too fast in a delicate matter'.[31] But at their next meeting, on 10 February, the promoters verified that their assent to Newman's initial proposal had been wholehearted once the connection with the Oratory had been fully appreciated; and they acknowledged Newman's hesitation over asking the Oratorians to commit themselves to a plan for people less anxious than anticipated. Without making further use of Newman's original offer, and leaving unresolved the question of the school's relationship with the Oratory, they decided to go ahead with their original plan to gather more support before communicating with the bishops, and drew up a list of important Catholics to contact. Of the nine who were supposed to do the asking, three had not attended any of the promoters' meetings: Hope-Scott, Henry Manning (the future cardinal), and Edward Badeley, a lawyer who an intimate friend of Bellasis, Hope-Scott and Newman; and one, Daniel Rock (former chaplain to Lord Shrewsbury), had attended only the meeting of 10 February. More significantly, all but two – Acton and Rock – were converts. In fact, up to this point the plan had been dominated by converts: the

---

[30.] Newman, memorandum, 9 February 1858, *L&D* XVIII, p. 251.
[31.] Newman to Bellasis, 9 February 1858, *L&D* XVIII, p. 251.

six promoters who had initially approached Newman were all converts, and only two – the same two – of the ten who had attended the promoters' meetings were cradle Catholics. Now the intention was to widen the base by asking prominent Catholics – eleven converts and ten old Catholics – to give public support.

Reassured by the promoters' reaction, Newman changed his proposal from a 'suggested plan at present withdrawn' to one that could now be made use of. However, his amended proposal was weakened by his growing doubts about gaining the unanimous consent of the Oratorians, since the prospect of the Oratory being invaded by a school for small boys was 'a matter so nearly affecting the comfort of individuals'. Newman again urged Bellasis to get others to consider '*what they propose to themselves to gain*, over existing schools – else, the door is left open to much disappointment'.[32] It was common-sense advice: before taking up his plan, it was essential that the promoters should consider the alternatives. Once Newman had tempered the initial excitement, the initiative was again put back into the hands of his friends.

In response to Newman's exhortation that the promoters examine their motives, Bellasis noted down:

Bellasis's four reasons [for a new school]
1. care of their persons
2. intellectual culture
3. select class of boys
4. division of eccles^l and lay, and thereby better masters.

The reasons were interconnected, but hinged on the separation of lay and church boys: once that was achieved, the other advantages would follow. Bellasis also jotted down four 'hypothetical causes' for securing intellectual culture:

1. getting by heart and learning Latin verses
2. keeping to nothing but Latin and Greek
3. but good teachers
4. trad^l teaching. [33]

[32] Newman to Bellasis, 12 February 1858, *L&D* XVIII, pp. 252–53.
[33] Bellasis, memorandum, 12 February 1858, BOA.

As Bellasis recorded, the promoters did not intend to fault the colleges on religious matters or the kindness with which the boys in them were treated; nevertheless, they had obvious deficiencies:

> (1) that the classical instruction might be improved and made more conformable in degree to that of the highest Protestant schools;
> (2) that in the existing schools there was too great an admixture of classes, many of the scholars coming from homely dwellings, bringing with them provincialisms, not to say vulgarities, which were, perhaps, in great measure, got rid of by associating with their school-fellows, but at the cost of leaving a portion of them behind;
> (3) that the charge for education was not sufficient to ensure really competent masters, who were, in general, divines, themselves in course of education, and only temporarily occupied as teachers, having in many cases no taste for teaching, and, if possessed of any talent, certain to be carried off to more important duties;
> (4) that it was desirable that a little more attention should be paid to the *personnel* of the boys, and it was also thought that lay-brothers were hardly adequate to the charge of little boys just come from home.[34]

In a separate seven-point memorandum Bellasis listed the principal features of the promoters' plan: a first-rate classical school where the religious element would be secured by the Oratorian connection: a school for lay boys only, 'somewhat more select as to the class of boys' than some of the colleges; acceptance of boys aged seven to twelve years old, providing them with proper female care and attention; special attention to habits of dress and cleanliness; the best possible masters, whether lay or clerical; everything to be 'superintended' by Newman; fees of about £70 per annum.[35]

The evidence shows that the promoters' uppermost objective

---

[34] Bellasis, *Memorials*, pp. 193–94.
[35] Bellasis, 'Memorandum respecting the proposed School at Edgbaston', n.d., BOA.

was to secure an education that would prepare boys to compete on an equal footing with their Protestant counterparts; it was to be achieved by imitation of the English public school, whatever its shortcomings. This wider goal of furthering the cause of Catholic emancipation explains the involvement of those who did not stand to gain directly: priests, such as Rock and Macmullen; and those unmarried or without sons, such as Acton and Hope-Scott. There is no evidence for McClelland's claim that the two main aims were to 'exclude episcopal oversight' and gain a socially exclusive education.[36] To the extent that either aspect was present, it was in consequence of the central idea: gaining full access to English life through a public school education. Inevitably the setting up of a lay school entailed a diminution of ecclesiastical involvement, but at no time was deliberate evasion of due ecclesiastical jurisdiction contemplated: the point in question was the exercise of the parents' legitimate right to secure a suitable education for their offspring.

Reference to the sons of the gentry and professional classes acquiring 'provincialisms' and 'vulgarities' implied that, to achieve social equality in later life, the boys needed to acquire modes of behaviour that would not disqualify them from social and professional circles. The wish for 'a certain degree of selectiveness',[37] as Bellasis put it, was in keeping with the times; it matches the conclusions of historians of education such as John Roach, who has described the second half of the nineteenth century as a period of growing stratification in the public school system, when schools became increasingly aligned to social class.[38] At Rugby, Dr Arnold had fostered the school community by consolidation in ability, age and social class, and he discouraged sons of the aristocracy from applying because the majority of his boys were, in his own words, 'sons of gentlemen of moderate fortune'.[39] In criticising the school promoters for fostering class snobbery, McClelland has overlooked the

[36.] V.A. McClelland, 'School or cloister? An English educational dilemma, 1794–1889', *Paedagogica Historica* 20, 1980, p. 116.
[37.] Bellasis to Newman, 15 June 1859, BOA.
[38.] J. Roach, *A History of Secondary Education in England 1800–1870* (London: Longmans, 1986), p. 160.
[39.] Honey, *Tom Brown's Universe*, p. 16.

social pressures of the times and the tensions this gave rise to even within the Catholic colleges. At Oscott, a serious incident of discrimination occurred in 1853 on account of antipathy to church students of humble origins, who were nicknamed 'bunkers'; it was at a time when the president favoured lay boys and, as Newman observed, 'ever acted *against* the Church boys'.[40] In 1866 an Irish judge took the President of Oscott to court after his son was expelled for fostering anti-bunker prejudice. According to the Taunton Report, there was also some ill-feeling at Stonyhurst on account of the mixture of classes, though apart from church boys the lowest class admitted there were sons of wealthy tradesmen.[41]

Gathering support

With the decision to solicit backing from a wider circle, the scheme moved into the public domain. No doubt the project was discussed at length in educated Catholic circles, for a radically different type of school was being proposed, prompting Catholics to reconsider their assumptions. In the process of gathering support, the promoters also sparked off a debate on the perceived strengths and shortcomings of the colleges; furthermore, the responses of those they approached identified and explored the weaknesses of the proposed new school, in the process hammering out important educational principles. For the promoters, the exercise served the purpose of a survey; for us, it sheds light on how parents and others viewed schooling at the time.

The response from converts was predictably favourable. Lord Charles Campden gave his cordial approval, though on the express understanding that he was not committing himself further. The future Lord Rudolph Feilding was more wholehearted, declaring that the planned school had 'long been a great desideratum, as the existing ones leave much to be desired'.[42] W.G. Ward expressed himself in typically pugna-

---

[40] Newman, memorandum, 4 May 1865, *L&D* XXI, p. 457n.
[41] Taunton Report V, p. 330.
[42] Feilding to Dodsworth, 18 February 1858, BOA.

cious fashion by declaring that there was not one 'of our present English colleges or schools to which I could dream of sending my son'. He thought 'every one of them as bad as bad can be; and that the religious education is almost as low as the intellectual; though such a feat might seem almost impossible'. His main reservation about the plan was whether Newman 'would give sufficient prominence to definite religious *teaching, instruction*, in fact *theology*, as distinct from *training*'. This attitude reflected both his high-minded aspirations and his misgivings 'as to the effect of any really high intellectual education, unless the truths of revelation are also imparted in a most distinctly intellectual shape'.[43]

Simeon needed little prompting to lend his support for 'a higher, more complete, more rigorous, more intellectual and more extended education' than he believed existed in the colleges. He told Bellasis he had 'often mourned over the educational advantages forfeited by converts'; but he confessed he was pessimistic, fearing there was

> not much chance of such a general movement as will secure the advantage of a large public school. Old Catholics from old associations, from the habit of being satisfied with the education forced on them by circumstances, and from their long acceptance of a cheap and short and therefore necessarily imperfect education will see no necessity for a change.

He predicted that some of the converts would take the same view; most of the clergy would too, having been educated at the colleges. The bishops, faced with the financial necessity of maintaining the colleges, which would become unviable 'if a really good school on a large scale were established, [. . .] will be in their hearts opposed to the plan, whatever they may say'. He anticipated that the experiment would begin with as few as a dozen sons of those 'giving a security for gentlemanlike habits and ideas'.[44]

One of these gentlemen was the wealthy convert Charles

[43.] W.G. Ward to Dodsworth, 15 February 1858, BOA.
[44.] Simeon to Bellasis, 15 February 1858, BOA.

Scott-Murray, who was so dissatisfied with Catholic educational provision that his sons (aged ten and eleven) were being educated at home, though the disadvantages were becoming more apparent to him with time. He told Bellasis he had 'long felt the want of the sort of school you speak of', and hoped that Newman might be 'induced to inaugurate' one.[45] He promised his sons for the new school, with the proviso that it was situated in the country, though he supposed this was unlikely to happen. (This strong preference for a rural setting was to resurface later.) Scott-Murray offered to gain the support of others, including his father-in-law Lord Lovat and Sir Piers Mostyn – both old Catholics.

Not every convert the promoters contacted was convinced of the plan, as can be seen from the reaction of Robert Monteith, the only son of a rich Glasgow cotton merchant. He told Bellasis he would support it despite some uncertainty as to how the school would provide formation in human virtue, particularly 'the point of honour'; for its acquisition, he suggested 'the performance of a sort of informal vow of Perfection in certain branches of conduct in which Perfection is by no means difficult'. It was generally accepted that a gentleman abhorred 'small lies – any thing approaching to grossness of eating – dirtiness of person – dirty talk (I do not mean impure – *that*, of course)'; yet Catholics seemed confident 'that considerable imperfection in these things is a topic about which Religion has no voice with which to speak to them'. More generally, Monteith wondered if Newman could do something to bring religion to bear on such points 'and thus sanctify the instinct that is in man [...] yet without exaggerating?' Still, he doubted 'whether mischief can be kept out of a school without some amount of espionage on the part of the masters'. Unless he felt sure the new school showed the same 'alertness and sleepless care' as Stonyhurst, he would not send a son.[46] To obtain this security, he was prepared to tolerate all the imperfections of the colleges.

In a second letter Monteith returned to the 'troublesome' subject which Bellasis had avoided in his reply, '*viz*, the imita-

[45.] Scott-Murray to Bellasis, 20 February 1858, BOA.
[46.] Monteith to Bellasis, 22 April 1858, BOA.

tion of the Jesuits, so far as possible, in all the devices suggested to them by experience for the guarding of morals'. Surely it was 'impossible for wise men commencing such an enterprise not carefully to investigate these devices, and not to copy, except where a positive objection can be alleged. I am for "espionage", except in the sense of any *unworthy* employment of boys as spies on each other.' He declared he would wait for the marked success of the venture before deciding on a school for his sons, but promised £100 on condition that the promoters 'enter into this matter – learn what is done (e.g. at Stonyhurst) – and only decline to imitate on well considered grounds'.[47] While not allowing himself to be drawn, Bellasis was certainly alive to the issue, for on the document listing his 'Four reasons' for a new school he jotted down two additional phrases: 'whether flogging' and 'whether surveillance in bed rooms'.[48] Two reasons why he might have held back from discussing the matter with Monteith are a reluctance to pronounce on behalf of the promoters as a body, and, more importantly, his conviction that it was Newman's prerogative to decide.

The most negative response from the convert quarter came from the ecclesiastical historian William Maskell, who thought the plan had little chance of working. He argued that the educational need for youths aged sixteen to nineteen was greater, though he doubted whether the masters or pupils could be found for this either. Maskell was unconvinced about a school under the Oratorians, and declared he would rather send a son to Oscott or Ushaw; and he added that he thought Newman's 'experiment in Ireland' had been a failure.[49] Maskell's cold reply was a salutary warning to the promoters that they could not take support from converts for granted.

Herbert of Llanarth was one of several old Catholics who welcomed the plan, and he promised his three boys when they were old enough. Recollections of 'an infinitesimal dose of *learning* drilled into me at Prior Park' convinced him that there was a real need for a school to which there was 'no admission

[47.] Monteith to Bellasis, 30 June 1858, BOA.
[48.] Bellasis, memorandum, 12 February 1858, BOA.
[49.] Maskell to Dodsworth, 28 February 1858, BOA.

on cheap terms for boys who imagine they have a *vocation* or whose parents have a wish to get education for nothing. If all the boys paid alike the teachers could then have sufficient remuneration which is not the case at most Catholic schools.'[50] Other leading old Catholics, such as Sir Robert Throckmorton and Robert Berkeley, are known to have expressed their support, but written evidence of their views has not survived.

Highly influential among the old Catholic families, and hence crucial for the backing of the school, were the names of Fitzalan-Howard, Petre and Weld. Henry Fitzalan-Howard, MP for Arundel, had returned to the Catholic Church and become a pious and generous layman; his support as Duke of Norfolk was regarded as critical, among other reasons because 'it would smooth our way with the Cardinal'.[51] The £50 he offered the venture may have seemed a routine gesture, but Hope-Scott considered it 'sufficient evidence of support' to include his name on the list of supporters.[52] Lord Petre's reaction was different; he asked Bellasis for a copy of the correspondence between the promoters and Newman in order to understand the promoters' plan more fully. On reading through it, he judged that the school's only chance of permanent success lay 'in immediate and intimate' connection with the Oratory. The school would undoubtedly be all that was wished for so long as Newman was at its head, but thereafter Petre feared that it might lose that 'thoroughly religious spirit' which all wished to maintain in Catholic educational establishments.[53] As even a partial connection with the Oratory seemed uncertain, he had doubts about the success of the plan.

Thomas Weld Blundell, a leading old Catholic with strong Stonyhurst connections, provided the most convincing case for preserving the college system. He was open in acknowledging the three educational principles he held to: that 'A boy is, generally speaking, better at home under the eyes of his Parents than at a Public school, until he is 11 or 12 years old'; that however much knowledge a boy acquired by the age of fifteen, 'the system by which his intellectual and moral facul-

---

[50.] Herbert to Bellasis, 14 February 1858, BOA.
[51.] Bellasis to Hope-Scott, 11 February 1858, BOA.
[52.] Hope-Scott to Bellasis, 3 March 1858, BOA.
[53.] Petre to Bellasis, 27 February 1858, BOA.

ties are trained and developed is of far greater importance'; and that this system is best carried out in a school with at least one hundred students (what *he* called a 'public school'). Weld Blundell spoke for many when he claimed that the ecclesiastical element in the colleges was of the highest importance in 'tending to the moral and religious benefits of the scholars'.[54] The lay boy would suffer considerably from any separation, as the young ecclesiastic students, usually older and more mature, invariably provided him with 'an example of assiduity, earnestness of purpose and religious feeling, which cannot fail to exert an advantageous influence on his mind and character'; and friendships begun at the colleges led later on to 'the return of many to the paths of virtue'.[55] The atmosphere Weld Blundell referred to was, of course, diametrically opposed to that at the public schools, 'where the principal controlling force was a rough public opinion, the product of boyish minds'.[56]

Weld Blundell was similarly forthright in his opinion of Newman: he considered him 'a man singularly qualified to create a new establishment for Catholic Education' but at the same time, despite Newman's involvement and that of others he admired, he declined to offer active support, for he had many reservations about 'Dr Newman's way' and preferred to wait and see. 'The difficulty that he will have to contend with, in selecting and marshalling a staff of teachers and managers, would I should think daunt a man of the strongest resolution' – although he conceded that Newman probably knew suitable people, particularly among 'the learned and pious converts who have been left without any means of subsistence'. Weld Blundell challenged the promoters' view that the college teachers were below par; in his opinion the teaching at Stonyhurst was very good. However, this was of secondary importance: the primary aim of a public school was how best to train the moral and intellectual faculties, 'how they can be best developed and fitted for what is to be demanded of them hereafter'. As far as the system of teaching at Stonyhurst was concerned, it had

[54.] Weld Blundell to Bellasis, 17 March 1858, BOA.
[55.] Weld Blundell to Bellasis, 24 March 1858, BOA.
[56.] Chichester, *Schools*, p. 35.

been 'founded principally on a foreign model and I believe it to be very effective and useful'.[57]

It was instructive for the promoters to receive replies such as Weld's, since it gave them an insight into the diversity of views among Catholics about their own educational system. It was natural that, with the prospect of significant restructuring, some should react by dwelling on its defects and weaknesses, while others should express alarm at the risk of forfeiting its recognised advantages. The correspondence confirms that there was considerable dissatisfaction with the general condition of Catholic education, not only among converts, but also among hereditary Catholics; however, there was uncertainty over how best to maintain proper discipline and guarantee moral and religious education, as they attempted to anticipate the outcome of establishing a new type of Catholic school. Somewhat depressingly, the one factor which all were agreed upon was that the undertaking would be immensely difficult to carry out.

The difficulty with assessing observations about the strengths and weaknesses of the public schools and colleges is that most were based on an intimate knowledge of just one tradition. The dilemma over the wisdom of shared (i.e. lay–clerical) education is conveyed by the change of view of a convert priest, John Morris, over a thirty-year period. After reading the documents sent him in 1858, Morris pronounced that the promoters would be making 'a most excellent bargain' if they accepted Newman's offer. Just as 'the Church never intended her future Priests to be at such schools as Eton and Harrow [...] it is equally clear that she never intended future lawyers, or diplomats, or Members of Parliament to be trained in her seminaries'. Besides, it was clear 'that your sons injure our seminaries, and that our seminaries do not suit your sons. [...] If the Oratory school promotes this entire and most necessary separation, it has my hearty prayers for its success.'[58] When Morris re-read these comments in 1887, as a Jesuit at Stonyhurst (after having been vice-rector of the English College in Rome and secretary of first Wiseman and then Manning), he was taken aback by their dogmatic tone. While he

---

[57.] Weld Blundell to Bellasis, 24 March 1858, BOA.
[58.] Morris to Bellasis, 17 May 1858, Bellasis, *Contribution*, pp. 10–11, BOA.

assumed everyone wished to see lay and church boys separated by the time of university studies, he *now* reckoned that all would wish them to begin together, as it was difficult to tell them apart 'before they know their own minds'. And whereas he used to consider that boys were best separated at the age of eleven or twelve, he would *now* draw the line through the middle of public school life.[59]

It is evident that, in the eyes of the converts, the colleges succumbed to the defect of being un-English because they derived from a foreign tradition. An education that was perceived to be inferior merely because it was different was liable to prove a handicap to Catholics in later life. A public school classical education was considered to make the gentleman; whether it did so or not, the bond of a shared culture united the upper classes into one caste. The promoters and those they contacted, even Bellasis with his scientific bent, were all convinced of the merits of a classical education. The matter of discipline, however, divided opinion sharply. Many converts disliked the system of surveillance used at the colleges; it bore similarities to private schools and was the antithesis of the public school constitution which relied so heavily on a system of self-governance. On the other hand, old Catholics could not conceive how discipline would be enforced and morals safeguarded without adequate oversight. The promoters were confident that Newman had the ability to solve the problem, but old Catholics were unconvinced and their wariness was reinforced by tales of Newman's reputation at the Catholic University. Another huge imponderable for old Catholics was the impact of removing church boys. It was all very well to speak of 'Eton, minus its wickedness', but what guarantees were there for ensuring high moral standards? The public schools were considered by most Catholics to inculcate only 'worldly' virtues. It should therefore come as no surprise that Cardinal Wiseman regarded Acton's presence among the promoters as 'his only security' in the foundation.[60]

[59.] Morris to Bellasis, 5 November 1887, BOA.
[60.] Acton to Simpson, n.d. [March 1858], *The Correspondence of Lord Acton and Richard Simpson* I, ed. J.L. Altholz and D. McElrath (Cambridge: CUP, 1971), p. 17.

Before the promoters' next meeting Bellasis was in a position to show Wiseman that the scheme was backed by thirty-two prominent Catholics, all but one of whom were, according to Bellasis, 'decidedly friendly'. Three-quarters of the signatories were converts. Of the twenty-one names on the promoters' original list, seven were missing, all but one of them old Catholics; and nine new names were added – four old Catholics and five converts. Although the list looked impressive, Bellasis knew that few of those on it would be willing to help financially as those most anxious about the plan were the least able to aid it.

The cardinal's questionnaire

Acton and Bellasis heeded Newman's advice, and informed Wiseman of the school plan before starting to gather support. (Newman was reluctant to write himself because he felt he was owed an important reply from Wiseman: the previous year he had been officially invited to undertake a new translation of the Bible into English, had started preparations for the project, but then had heard no more about it – and never did!) Wiseman was non-committal at first, but afterwards sent them a questionnaire containing forty-one questions. After eight years at Ushaw, another twenty-two at the English College Rome (twelve as rector) and seven as president of Oscott, Wiseman declared he was in an unrivalled position for proposing 'the necessary questions to be seriously considered in founding any Institution for education'.[61] He suggested that those the promoters were unable to answer would be useful in helping them decide what was necessary for the plan to be complete and invite confidence. Bellasis sent him a brief reply outlining the plan.

The questionnaire enquired into all aspects of the proposed school: about the head (whether he would be a layman or priest, who would nominate him and how, and for what reasons he could be dismissed); the teaching staff (whether they would all be laymen or some be clerics); religious instruc-

[61] Wiseman to Bellasis, 5 March 1858, BOA.

tion (the 'permanent arrangement', given that the Oratorians would only undertake the spiritual care for a limited time); spiritual directors (the relation between them and the head, whether they would be able to carry out their duties without interference, who would appoint them, and who could remove them); the age of admission and whether there would be any guarantee for a boy's morality; general management (the ownership of the property, the power of the trustees, and provisions for the disposal of assets in the event of the plan failing). The questions clearly assumed the structure of a college, not a school, for they also referred to the discipline of rising, prayers and common duties of masters as well as boys, the regulation of the boys' spiritual reading, and the scheme for covering the philosophy course.[62]

The task of drafting a response to the questionnaire was begun by Newman, who answered on behalf of the Oratory. The headmaster would be a secular priest, he began, not a layman, 'because in the public schools of England, his being a clergyman is in many ways a gain; and that, for office as such';[63] only he would be required to live in. Either laymen or ecclesiastics would fill the other posts. The two offices of teaching and maintaining discipline would be considered distinct (as at the colleges), though in practice they could be 'accidentally united' (as at the public schools). College disciplinary procedures were to be followed, 'except with those changes which are implied in the idea of school': the replies to several questions were in a similar vein, indicating that he envisaged a different regime 'inasmuch as a school is different from that of a College'. The school would operate the form-system (in which individual boys moved up, when ready, to the next level – 'form' – each of which had its own master) rather than the class-system (in which a cohort of boys progressed together

[62] Wiseman, Questions on the subject of the proposed lay-school at or near Birmingham, *L&D* XVIII, pp. 284–87.
[63] public school headmasters continued to be clergymen until the twentieth century. The first laymen to be appointed were at schools predominantly for day-boys, such as St Paul's in 1877. The turning point for boarding schools came with the first lay head at Marlborough in 1903; among the last to change were Harrow (1926), Eton (1933), Winchester (1935) and Westminster (1937).

through the school, often with the same master); classics was to be the main subject taught.[64]

Newman's draft replies were passed to Hope-Scott who expanded and amended them on behalf of the promoters. He clarified that the headmaster would be appointed by the Oratorians and be 'removable by them, and, of course, also by any other authority having jurisdiction over secular Priests'; he would have no salary except, say, £50 for incidental purposes. The criteria for the appointment of staff would not be lay or clerical status but 'the capacity and power of teaching', the aim being to attract the best available talent. Newman's assertion that masters would enforce discipline over the boys during school hours was extended to include the eventuality of boys lodging in masters' houses. As for internal discipline, the school would not differ substantially from the colleges; in some respects it would be more strict, and in other respects less so. Either way, it would be preserved 'in the usual manner, by the birch'. As regards the curriculum, the extent of modern language teaching would partly depend 'on the wish of the Parents'. Newman's proposal that boys be admitted at any age was tightened up: the earlier a boy came, the better, 'as less guarantee would be required as to his morality or antecedents' – the only guarantee for morality Hope-Scott suggested was that of 'vigilant caution'.[65] (It was customary at the time for the colleges to request references from parish priests about the moral standing of the boys applying to them.)

At their meeting on 8 March the promoters concurred that Newman's view of the school, as revealed in his draft answers, matched their own. They were now all agreed that matters would be simplified if the school began 'as an Oratorian school, leaving the future to take care of itself'; if it proved burdensome the Oratory could sever its links, but there seemed no need to refer to this possibility at the outset. They intended to inform Wiseman that, although Newman had spoken of a 'mere temporary supervision', it was 'not *now* necessary to

[64.] Newman, Answers to the cardinal's questions, *L&D* XVIII, pp. 284–87.
[65.] Hope-Scott, 'Proposed answers to the Interrogatories of his Eminence Card. Wiseman', March 1858, BOA.

provide for its continuance by means of masters or otherwise', as in the event of a separation the necessary arrangements could be made when the time came.[66] The promoters sought clarification from Newman on two points: whether the Oratorians were secular priests; and why Newman continually spoke of the connection of the school with the Oratory as 'temporary'. Newman explained, via Bellasis, that the Oratorians were indeed secular priests, living in community. As for the 'temporary' connection, one reason for not pledging the Oratorians to the school for good was 'that it might be hard on our successors'; the most Newman had ever spoken of was twenty years, and this was longer than he preferred to say. However, he saw no objection to calling it 'our school absolutely', although 'properly speaking, the school would be mine and Darnell's, not the Oratory's'.[67]

Bellasis's first, brief reply to Wiseman had been accompanied by a copy of the important communications between Newman and the promoters. After reading through these papers Wiseman felt that the questionnaire was in fact out of place, as the 'whole plan is essentially to have a lay school under not only Oratorian management, but under the same roof as the Oratory'.[68] It is not surprising that Wiseman should have had second thoughts, since the plan represented a departure from the collegiate system; he recognised the complexity of the issue and took the opportunity to distance himself from it by arguing that it was not a matter necessarily under his jurisdiction. Ever sensitive to ecclesiastical authority, Acton thought Wiseman had overstepped the mark by sending such a detailed questionnaire in the first place; the promoters would commit a similar mistake by answering it fully – 'The details I take to be entirely Newman's affair'.[69] Nevertheless it is clear that Wiseman was perfectly justified in asking, among other things, what the power of the bishop would be as to visitation, correction, the removal of the chaplain, and spiritual supervision.

[66.] Bellasis to Newman, 8 March 1858, BOA.
[67.] Newman to Bellasis, 12 March 1858, *L&D* XVIII, pp. 292–93.
[68.] Wiseman to Bellasis, 8 March 1858, BOA.
[69.] Acton to Bellasis, 7 March 1858, BOA.

Between the idea and the reality

On Newman's advice, Acton and Bellasis went to see Ullathorne about the movement for the new school. Newman prepared him for their visit by describing the Oratory's position: that it was not yet committed to the plan; that they had been asked to 'nurse' the school, while it was in its infancy; and that only Darnell had the qualifications or taste necessary for the work. At the meeting Ullathorne told the promoters that he approved the principle of a lay school, but expressed misgivings over whether the means proposed would enable it to match the discipline and general management at the colleges. It is likely that his concern stemmed from the anticipated absence of cradle Catholics – and, perhaps, because of the likely predominance of lay teachers who, at the time, were looked upon by many as a necessary evil; in old Catholic circles, even private tuition was almost exclusively in the hands of the clergy. Acton interpreted Ullathorne's remarks as a declaration of war, reflecting the hostility to the plan of Ullathorne's household and his fellow bishops. Nevertheless, Ullathorne convinced them to postpone the plans for building at the Oratory and instead to rent a house nearby. It seems that Ullathorne had been frightened by Wiseman, who had told him that he would have entire responsibility for the scheme; in turn, Wiseman had been influenced against it by others. By now the promoters were aware that, to protect the collegiate system, and Oscott in particular, various bishops intended to oppose the plan.

For his next move Bellasis heeded Newman's warning that 'it will never do to have it said (*which will otherwise be said*) that we, you and ourselves, began against the expressed wish of the Bishop of the diocese'.[70] He wrote to Ullathorne to explain that he and Acton, the spokesmen for others, had 'no notion of committing your Lordship to an approval of it [the school] or of putting you in the position of being in any way responsible for it';[71] they had merely considered it a duty to inform him of the plan as it was in his diocese, and Bellasis now asked for

---

[70.] Newman to Bellasis, 1 April 1858, *L&D* XVIII, p. 310.
[71.] Bellasis to Ullathorne, 2 April 1858, BOA.

confirmation that he did not intend to veto the scheme. Ullathorne obliged, putting in writing that he was 'in no wise disposed to offer any opposition or discouragement to the contemplated experiment at Edgbaston'.[72] Ullathorne's lack of enthusiasm is understandable; although, in Newman's opinion, he was the *only* bishop who was not against the scheme, and 'if left to himself would be for us'.[73]

All along Newman had bargained for a measure of resistance, but now he was taken aback by a remark made by Ullathorne that he, the Oratorians and other converts considered the discipline at the colleges to be too strict. Ullathorne's attitude, Newman thought, was influenced by the reputation he had acquired for lax discipline and liberal attitudes at the Catholic University, where he had allowed the young men in his hall of residence to go to dances and keep hunting horses. Newman explained to Bellasis that, while 'I have it as little in me to be a good schoolmaster [. . .] as to be a good rider [. . .], this does not hinder my feeling the *need* of strict discipline for boys – for many a man approves what he cannot practise'. He emphasised that 'The only point of *principle* on which we should differ from the Colleges, is that we should aim at doing every thing above board', forbidding spying, listening at doors and the like. He was uncertain whether or not they ought to open the boys' letters, as was customary at the colleges; in any case he desired 'such honesty and openness in our conduct to the boys, that they would have no temptation to *distrust* us'. Only time and experience would remove doubts about his ability to keep order and the various other reasons for the lack of trust in 'our school plan'.[74]

On 11 April the Oratorians began a novena of prayer prior to deciding on whether to sanction the school plan. Bellasis, finding out about it when it was already under way, asked what prayers were being said so that he could participate himself and encourage others to do likewise: Newman apologised for not informing him. On 21 April it was decreed unanimously

[72.] Ullathorne to Bellasis, 4 April 1858, BOA.
[73.] Newman to Hope-Scott, 18 October 1858, *L&D* XVIII, p. 490.
[74.] Newman to Bellasis, 6 April 1858, *L&D* XVIII, pp. 314–15.

that the Congregation gives its sanction to Fr Nicholas
Darnell's being Fr Superior's representative in undertaking, at the instance of friends in London, the
establishment and formation of a school for lay boys of
the upper classes, of the nature of such public schools as
Winchester and Eton, his relation to it being not materially different from that which a Father of the Oratory
would bear towards a Ragged School, a Reformatory or
Workhouse, and the other Fathers of the Congregation
being in no way connected with the boys except as having
their direction in spiritual matters and in ecclesiastical
functions and devotions.[75]

At once Newman set about informing the heads of the
Catholic colleges of the decision, just as he had in 1850 when
about to begin the St Wilfrid's scheme. He explained that the
promoters 'wish lay boys to be kept distinct from ecclesiastical –
and our Bishop is as strong for ecclesiastical being kept apart
from lay'; and he argued that the new school was unlikely to
interfere with the colleges, since they were beginning with boys
under eleven and with much higher fees. Sharing his bishop's
anxiety as to 'whether a lay portion can be kept religious
without the element of ecclesiastical', he explained that the
beginning would be small enough to result in little harm if the
experiment failed.[76] While the president of Oscott assured
Newman there was no fear of collision – they would be like
different trees growing together in the same soil, 'each searching out and drawing up its own peculiar juices' without
interfering with the other – he only agreed in theory to the
separation of lay and ecclesiastical elements; and argued that
the colleges were far from being able to survive on their own
resources and maintain expensive buildings without 'large
subsidiary aid'.[77] The prior of Downside took a longer-term
view: he agreed that 'the great and important work of Catholic
Education must be promoted by such a step'.[78]

[75.] The decree is transcribed in Newman to Bittleston, 22 April 1858,
    L&D XVIII, p. 328.
[76.] Newman to Newsham, 13 April 1858, *L&D* XVIII, p. 321.
[77.] Weedall to Newman, 3 May 1858, BOA.
[78.] Sweeney to F.R. Ward, 5 April 1959, BOA.

Informing Bellasis of the Oratory's decision to sanction the undertaking, Newman waxed eloquent on the responsibilities of the parents and other promoters. They needed to secure about thirty boys, and promises for more, for the sake both of financial support and of appearances, and build up a number of backers and patrons who would speak on behalf of the school among Catholics so as to counter the inevitable 'prejudice, opposition, criticism, adverse whispering, and ready belief of tales told to our disadvantage'. The problem of securing initial help, and 'the *continuance* of such interest and support' during the difficult early years, would be solved along with the pressing financial problem 'by making them [the promoters] responsible for the first expenditure and risk of expenditure which will be incurred'.[79] Newman analysed the finances and translated this parental commitment into figures: an initial down-payment of £600 for fittings and alterations; a loan of £1000 for works on the church; and a guarantee of the deficit if numbers fell short. He pointed out that this was just a first sketch, and that he awaited the promoters' views. In the interests of working in tandem with them, he suggested liaising with Bellasis, Hope-Scott and possibly one other, 'whom we might privately and confidentially consult on the details of our plan of proceeding'.[80] But Bellasis was not able to do more than acknowledge the news of the Oratory's decision and the accompanying proposals, since he was extremely busy with the Shrewsbury Peerage case,[81] as was Hope-Scott; Acton and others were abroad. After a hectic three-month period, all communication ceased until Newman took the initiative in October, six months later.

The change in tempo was dramatic. The promoters' commitment to the enterprise had induced Newman and the Oratory

[79]. Newman to Bellasis, 23 April 1858, *L&D* XVIII, p. 331.
[80]. Newman to Bellasis, 6 April 1858, *L&D* XVIII, p. 315.
[81]. Bellasis and Hope-Scott had been advisers to the Earl of Shrewsbury, and managed his landed estates until his death in 1856. The Shrewsbury Peerage case began in 1857 and dragged on for a decade. The contention for the title and possession of the property lay between the heir, Earl Talbot, and the Duke of Norfolk, to whose son it had been devised by the recently deceased Earl. During these ten years Bellasis and Hope-Scott had the entire control of the estate.

to combine with them; having deliberately held back previously, Newman now intended to throw himself wholeheartedly into the scheme. No sooner had he done so, than he seemed to be left in the lurch. During these months of waiting he had to resist the temptation to step in and engage in the 'temporalities' that he had insisted were the promoters' responsibility – no easy course for one who had recently masterminded the establishment of a university. His unwillingness to force the issue by softening his demands for parental backing makes it abundantly clear that Newman considered such involvement a *sine qua non* for the plan.

There was, however, one practical matter Newman could involve himself in: finding a school agent. It was impossible to proceed with the school, he felt, 'unless the Gentlemen who are interested in it appoint some one to act for them in gaining promises of support, in raising funds, in securing pupils, etc and in transacting business with the Oratory Fathers'. This was the promoters' business, of course; Newman's aim was not just to set the Oratory free from the chance of loss, but 'to interest the Gentlemen [...] in the project in some especial way, by making its success an object of personal concern to them'.[82] Newman spoke from his experience in Dublin, where he had learned that '*you cannot have a University, till the gentlemen take it up*'.[83] First Francis Ward, and then Pollen was invited to act as school agent with a salary of £100 per annum, but both declined. Newman's letter to Pollen is significant, as it gives yet another indication of his sensitivity to the joint nature of the enterprise: fearful lest he trespass on the domain of the promoters, Newman's invitation included the caveat that the job 'depends on yourself on the one hand, on Bellasis & Co on the other – not on me'.[84]

What Newman dreaded was 'beginning and creeping on with a few', for besides incurring debt, low numbers meant falling short of 'the idea of a school'.[85] In May, Darnell travelled to London to see why school matters flagged. The problem was money: Newman's friends were unable to raise funds for an

[82.] Newman, memorandum, 19 May 1858, *L&D* XVIII, p. 332.
[83.] Newman to Capes, 1 February 1857, *L&D* XVII, p. 514.
[84.] Newman to Pollen, 20 August 1858, *L&D* XVIII, p. 444.
[85.] Newman to Scott-Murray, 7 July 1858 *L&D* XVIII, p. 402.

uncertain venture. The news drew Newman to the bleak conclusion that 'the whole plan is at an end'. Reconciling himself to the outcome, he reflected that there was no point in bemoaning the lost opportunity: 'We have many ways of serving God and St Philip.' The remarks of his fellow-Oratorian Ambrose St John provide a more objective view of developments: Newman was overworked and worn out, while Bellasis was preoccupied with the Shrewsbury job, but St John was certain that the promoters 'will never let the school drop'.[86]

With no-one willing to undertake the role of school agent, and despite being 'wholly unable to dedicate any time to our educational scheme', Bellasis somehow managed to keep the momentum going.[87] His approach is illustrated in a begging letter to Monteith, which describes the undertaking and emphasises how it met a pressing need. Here was a window of opportunity, Bellasis urged: Newman was ready to begin but needed backing before he could announce his intention; he was not expecting any profit from it, but he needed £2000 to cover the cost of outlay and to provide a guarantee; only three contributions of £100 had been received. 'As having an equal interest with ourselves in the improvement of Catholic education', could Bellasis count on his help?[88] Monteith's reply reveals that the attraction of the plan was not only Newman's involvement: 'the working interest which you and H[ope-]S[cott] take in it is no small guarantee that it will be thoroughly made'.[89] The winning of the convert Thomas Gaisford to the school cause also owed a good deal to Bellasis's persuasive powers. Gaisford had already spoken of the plan with Simeon and Sir Robert Gerard, an old Catholic, but still favoured Downside. A week later, after meeting Bellasis, he had undergone a profound change: he decided to contribute £50, to guarantee the scheme with a further £50, and to write to three others about it.

A major impediment to the plan was that many of the influential Catholics contacted were already committed to other

86. Newman to Bittleston, 21 May 1858 (containing comments of St John), *L&D* XVIII, pp. 352–53.
87. Bellasis to F.R. Ward (draft), n.d., BOA.
88. Bellasis to Monteith, 27 June 1858, BOA.
89. Monteith to Bellasis, 30 June 1858, BOA.

undertakings. Robert Biddulph Phillips was candid about his situation: he said he would be truly grieved if the plan collapsed for lack of support, but confessed he was unable to promote it with boys or money, 'for the calls on one's surplus funds are more and more numerous and seem to increase every year, whilst one's income cannot be accused of any such tendency'.[90] He offered to help on a lower level, by mentioning the plan to others. By late June, Bellasis had exhausted all avenues, and matters had come almost to a standstill. By now he realised the predicament in which the plan found itself: if Newman were to announce his intention to begin, he was sure to have enough pupils offered, but he would not do this without parental backing; however, the parents were holding back because there was no full commitment to the plan. The argument went full circle and explained the stalemate reached. Bellasis suspected that even a large benefaction would have been insufficient to attract many boys and break the deadlock, as there were parents like Monteith and Gerard who were willing to provide financial support but intended to hold back from sending their sons until the school had started and showed signs of success.

The dilemma was neatly conveyed by Gerard, who thought the scheme was 'extremely good – but not perfect'. Certainly, it would answer a need in providing more pastoral care for small boys than was currently available, but 'what guarantee does a school not yet formed offer for this desirable end?' Having a few subscribers and Newman as 'nominal Head – and living anywhere' guaranteed nothing: the real head might be another Oratorian and less suitable. Until the real headmaster and regulations had been announced, he thought, few would be willing to subscribe. So far none of the old Catholics had 'joined the movement'.[91] In fact, only a handful of converts were willing to risk all and give their full backing: money *and* sons.

For Newman the suspense and uncertainty were punctuated by occasional indications of progress. One promising new recruit was Mrs Barbara Charlton, an old Catholic and a friend

[90] Biddulph Phillips to Bellasis, 6 May 1858 BOA.
[91] Gerard to Bellasis, 27 July 1858, BOA.

of Mrs Bellasis, who requested books so that she could prepare her sons for the school. Since the colleges and convents were 'so undeniably behind the times, in all things relating to education', she declared, rather patronisingly, that it would distress her to entrust her sons to 'well meaning, but, untutored "ecclesiastical" ploughboys'![92] It was to the aid of converts that they, the old Catholics, looked for the prosperity of the old Faith. Three months later she reacted with disbelief to a rumour that the plan had collapsed. How could the bishops be 'so insane as to break down an undertaking which could not fail eventually to be of the greatest advantage to the Catholic gentry – the eyes of the most bigoted, must be open to the cruelty and disadvantage of sending sons to our underbred Colleges'? It was sad for parents like herself to feel the 'everlasting dragchain *"bigotry"* ever is keeping us, from all social improvement'.[93]

Despite her wholehearted support Mrs Chalton, like Gerard, was not intending to send her eldest son until he was ten. For others, like Ward, the problem was the reverse: his two sons, aged ten and twelve, were too old, as the plan was to start with small boys and to accept older ones three years later. Early hopes of a solution receded by the end of 1858, as Downside became the likely destination for the Ward boys. Another difficulty concerned the school's future. Like Gerard, Mrs Charlton asked what was to become of the boys once they were twelve. Surely Newman intended to 'superadd and carry out his plans more extensively – otherwise, it will be mere cruelty, placing boys in a "gentlemanly school" with the certainty, they must undergo afterwards the painful feeling of receding in civilisation, as no old Catholic establishment can come under the denomination of a *"gentlemanly* College" '.[94]

Newman waited until October to put his gloomy case to Hope-Scott. He would not have attempted the school, he explained, but for the need itself, together with Darnell's 'wish and capacity to undertake it'. The idea had been for a small, discreet beginning, letting 'the fact of its existence grow on people's minds'; but, due to his friends' interest, it had become

[92]. Mrs Charlton to Mrs Bellasis, 13 July 1858, BOA.
[93]. Mrs Charlton to Mrs Bellasis, 8 November 1858, BOA.
[94]. Mrs Charlton to Bellasis, 11 February 1859, BOA.

'a formal intention, and a sort of recognised, public undertaking'. Of late it had 'subsided again into something like its original state'; however, because of the public airing it had received earlier, it would now 'be measured, not by what it is, but by those greater ideas which were to come after, and which have been divulged'. Furthermore, whereas before he was answering a call from a number of respectable names and was personally protected, he was now alone, a priest in a diocese, challenging Oscott, Stonyhurst and Ushaw with a great plan. He was also feeling the inquisitory gaze of church dignitaries: 'It may be represented at Rome, that I am setting up a convert school and perpetuating a convert spirit and party' – a claim he dreaded having to refute. 'Now, as my friend, what would you advise me to do?'[95]

The parliamentary lawyer set to work on Newman's doubts. The difficulties, Hope-Scott explained, were of two kinds: those that would arise whatever the plan, and those arising on account of the delay. The latter presented no problem because of the crying necessity for the school 'among a definite number of people who know and trust you'; they would send their sons to it, certain they would get what 'they *know* they cannot find elsewhere'. As for the first set of difficulties, the public airing had in fact diminished them, because it had 'exhausted the feelings of hostility', and because so much had been said 'of the *want*' that 'attempt at supply [...] will now appear the smallest part of the mischief'. His advice was: 'go on by all means'.[96]

The way forward

On 25 November, after his final visit to Dublin and resignation of the rectorship, Newman broke the deadlock. He sent Bellasis a draft manifesto, requesting his opinion 'on the *whole* – and again in *detail*', and suggesting that a number be printed and sent to friends.[97] Bellasis and Hope-Scott were delighted. Taken at face value, Newman's decision had all the appear-

[95]· Newman to Hope-Scott, 18 October 1858, *L&D* XVIII, pp. 489–90.
[96]· Hope-Scott to Newman, 21 October 1858, BOA.
[97]· Newman to Bellasis, 25 November 1858, *L&D* XVIII, p. 518.

ances of a U-turn, for it seemed that he now intended to abandon his demand for full backing and, instead, to strike on without it. Had he reneged on his original conception of partnership after striving so long to preserve it? The question is clarified in a diary entry, written two years later, which reveals Newman's analysis of the situation and explains his apparent change of mind. The Oratory had indeed taken the initiative with the establishment of a school for the Catholic upper classes, Newman recorded, but 'it must never be forgotten that, as that very object implies, the duty and the interest rest with that upper class, and not with the Oratory'. That duty and interest had been made explicit earlier with the request for an advance of £2000, but the money had not been forthcoming as parents were not convinced that 'we were the men to do the work. The project in consequence was in a lock: the Oratory waiting for the money, and the parents for a trial of the Oratory.' Newman resolved that the Oratory should begin, using its own resources, in order to 'furnish [...] that trial of our capacity, which it was natural for parents to demand'.[98]

The two lawyers set to work on the draft manifesto and excised the greater part of it, reducing it to the bare minimum: the originator – Newman, 'at the urgent instance of friends'; the name – Edgbaston Catholic School; the starting date – 1 May 1859; the pupils – boys under twelve 'not destined for the ecclesiastical state'; the bishop's approbation; its location – by the Birmingham Oratory; female care for the boys; and the headmaster – Darnell.[99] To avoid provoking arguments, Hope-Scott considered it enough that people should know '1. That it is a lay school. 2. That parents want it. 3. That the Bishop approves.'[100] Three sections of the manifesto were removed in their entirety: the first, about the need for the foundation, because it 'affords a point of attack'; the second, Newman's hope that it would support the Catholic University, because it 'will allow people to say that the school is a mere feeder to the Dublin University'; the last, the claim that the colleges would not be damaged, on the grounds that *qui s'excuse, s'accuse.*[101]

[98]. Newman, memorandum, 5 February 1861, *L&D* XIX, p. 463.
[99]. Newman, draft manifesto, n.d., BOA.
[100]. Hope-Scott to Newman, n.d., BOA.
[101]. Bellasis to Newman, 29 November 1858, BOA.

Besides these alterations, other smaller ones were made. Newman's original phrasing that the house was to be 'managed by ladies residing in it' was altered, as the term 'ladies' was sometimes used at the time to mean nuns. The relevant section of the revised draft then read: 'The boys will be under the care of an experienced matron and female assistants who will have the management of the house; and the School-room and its masters will be under the rule and superintendence of Father Darnell.' After meeting again, the promoters suggested another minor change. They thought 'rule' should be omitted from the text, if there was to be a distinguished classics master, such as Thomas Arnold, the younger son of Dr Arnold; Newman agreed.[102] Besides the inducement of a salary, it was suggested that a classics master could be offered extra payment for each boy over a certain number; and failing Arnold, they wondered if someone else could be found at the Catholic University. Newman again heeded their advice.

The heavy editing of Newman's draft document shows how sensitive Bellasis and Hope-Scott were to the prospect of opposition. While amused at their 'lawyer-like caution, in cutting off every unnecessary word', Newman told them of his growing awareness of the cause of their tact, the 'hard and wrong things' said of him. He used the occasion to issue them with a forthright warning that the criticism levelled at him might 'tend seriously to involve the prospects of the school', and that he intended to ignore it, even if his friends urged him to answer the accusations for the sake of the school; he would continue to refrain from speaking even when the school had grown from a personal project into an established public one. 'Therefore, I think all those who are earnest in the plan of a school, should carefully think over these contingencies first, and see their way clearly as regards them.'[103]

Though Newman's decision to push ahead marked a new stage in the foundational process, there was no suggestion that the promoters were to be absolved from securing funds and pupils; and suggestions concerning masters, fees and other matters continued to pour in via Bellasis, as the promoters sought to secure the best possible arrangements. While it was

---

[102.] Bellasis to Newman, 14 December 1858, BOA.
[103.] Newman to Bellasis, 4 December 1858, *L&D* XVIII, pp. 527–28.

their wish that Newman should be unhampered in his work of setting up the school, Newman used his freedom of movement precisely to work with them. Mounting doubts about the plan's financial viability led him to abandon his search for an assistant master, and he compiled a leaner budget based on lower numbers. The danger of incurring a deficit was considerable, for by Christmas 1858 contributions amounted to just £500. Newman asked Bellasis, 'can we move without a guarantee, in some shape or other, against losses, or without a larger sum to begin with?'[104] And he wondered whether the 'opposition against us reduces our probability of success so low that it is unwise in you to risk any sum', asking Bellasis and Hope-Scott to consider whether the £500 fund was not 'a middle measure, too little to succeed with, and too much to throw away'.[105]

Newman surmised that some of the promoters supporting their scheme might, quite understandably, be wishing to cover themselves with a backup scheme near London under the patronage of the provost of the London Oratory, Frederick Faber. But Hope-Scott and Bellasis dismissed all such thoughts. Hope-Scott, like many, regarded London as unsuitable for a school; Bellasis, although he thought a location in the south of England more attractive in itself, and was alive to the possibility of 'active opposition' from Faber 'in the form of a rival school near London', felt that 'the attraction to me of the proposed Birmingham school consists in the founders'.[106] (It

---

104. Newman to Bellasis, 21 December 1858 (first letter), *L&D* XVIII, p. 553.
105. Newman to Bellasis, 21 December 1858 (second letter), *L&D* XVIII, pp. 553–54.
106. Bellasis to Newman, 18 December 1858, BOA. Relations between the two Oratories, and indeed between their provosts, were strained from the beginning, in 1847, when Wiseman asked Newman to accept as Oratorians a group of seventeen converts led by Faber. Their addition to the six original Oratorians drastically altered the chemistry of the Oratory and placed together two leaders with contrasting, if not incompatible, characters. More significantly, Faber's idea of an Oratory was markedly different from Newman's. The solution was to allow Faber to begin an Oratory in London, where it soon acquired a marked 'Roman' and Ultramontane reputation. Among other points of difference, the two Oratories diverged in their approach to educational work, particularly as Newman's emphasis on it was held by Faber to be a departure from the intentions of the founder.

was in keeping with his self-effacing nature that Bellasis should not have entertained the idea that he was himself a co-founder.) Acton managed to ascertain that the London Oratory objected to the school plan because it was judged to be inconsistent with the Oratorian Rule, and doomed to failure on account of Newman's supposed incompetence. Faber had, however, previously mentioned to Acton that he would not only tolerate but assist the school, and Acton was prepared to make this statement public if the need arose.

In view of the threat of a rival school, opposition from Faber, and what Bellasis described as 'a certain amount of hostility from the convert side', Bellasis and Hope-Scott decided to guarantee the school a further £500 from their own funds.[107] On receipt of this welcome news, Newman considered it decided that they should begin. (There was one day remaining of the second novena for the school, about which Newman again failed to tell Bellasis in time. Newman had asked the Oratorians to meditate on the intention: 'O, St Philip, give us no new mortification – but either prevent the school, or prosper it'; and he told them that their 'great difficulty lies in a quarter where we might have expected neutrality, if not sympathy.'[108]) With the likelihood that the school would begin small, the anticipated fees had risen to £100: now, at Newman's initiative, the three decided to lower them to £80. The debate about fees was not merely a budgetary matter; it was linked to the idea of a first-class school. Scott-Murray had insisted that the fees should not be lower than £70, which he considered with his 'protestant idea *very* low indeed';[109] Darnell wanted them raised to £100; Gaisford was concerned that the school would not be sufficiently select. The decision not to capitulate to this pressure for a narrower upper-class clientele reflected Hope-Scott's contention that there were balances to be struck: between affording the salaries for good masters and making the school really public; and between catering for the upper classes and being able to hold a mixture of classes safely. After the school opened, Bellasis took up the matter with Newman,

[107.] Bellasis to Newman, 25 December 1858, BOA.
[108.] Chapter address, 20 December 1858, *Newman the Oratorian*, pp. 380, 383.
[109.] Scott-Murray to Newman, 5 July 1858, BOA.

as Gaisford and William Monsell (the future Lord Emly) kept pressing; both had guaranteed the school £50, but neither had boys ready for it.

During the four months preceding the opening of the school, Newman kept Bellasis abreast of developments, such as his efforts to secure a second master and Darnell's visits to London, but otherwise the school barely featured in his correspondence. This reflected not only Newman's preoccupation with other matters, but also the extent to which Darnell was masterminding preparations. Meanwhile there were indications that opposition was widespread and on the increase: Acton noticed how people were 'most prepared to criticise' the plan and prejudice mothers with tales of Newman's lax discipline.[110] The months leading up to May 1859 were anxious ones. In January, three boys were enlisted, two Scott-Murrays and a Bellasis; in February, the son of Charles Stokes was added; in April, the Wards changed their minds about Downside and added their two eldest boys; the son of Frederick Capes brought the total to seven. It is significant that all seven were offspring of converts: not one of the old Catholic families was willing to risk a son at the outset.

May 1859

Newman's diary entry for Sunday 1 May reads simply: 'New School began'. But what exactly was begun? Comparisons of Edgbaston Catholic School with other foundations at the time are problematic as the school bestrode two distinct systems, each with its own variety of types, each defying a systematic description. Besides, it was open-ended: it began as a preparatory school but with the prospect that it might develop into a public school. As such it was an early example of that class of school whose characteristics were to become fully developed by the end of the century. The new school satisfied three of the four criteria proposed by the school historian Donald Leinster-Mackay for designation as a preparatory school: separation (a physical and moral separation from a public school); rustica-

---

[110.] Acton to Darnell, 3 February 1859, BOA.

tion (being located away from a city or large town); and preparation (as a feeder for the public schools or the Navy).[111] The fourth characteristic – the profit motive – was absent. In the light of its development into a public school on the same site and the intention to feed this one school, thereby forfeiting the characteristic of separation, it might be more appropriate to categorise it as a junior school or preparatory department, and as such it could claim to be one of the first. (Of course, the usual order of starting a public school and adding on a junior school later was, in this case, reversed.) Alternatively it could be viewed as a public school from the outset. This interpretation is eminently plausible as Eton, the school it sought to imitate more than any other, admitted boys as young as eight; indeed the *average* age of entry for Eton was only ten years and three months, significantly lower than the corresponding ages for schools such as Harrow and Winchester.

The list of thirty-two names backing the scheme reveals neither the true identity of the founding group nor its composition. Acton argued against the list becoming public knowledge, as 'the few native Catholics [on it] would be alarmed at the smallness of their numbers';[112] in fact the list, if anything, disguises how feeble the support was from old Catholics. Further confirmation of the dominance of the convert input comes from the list of subscriptions and guarantees, which shows that a total of £100 came from two old Catholics and £800 from nine converts. At the same time, apart from Scott-Murray, convert peers and gentry were not among the leading promoters: Campden would only give the plan his simple approval; Feilding was supportive but his money was fully occupied; Simeon was convinced of the need, but expressly wished not to be one of the first promoters of the undertaking. It was from the professional classes predominantly that the chief executors of the plan and its true supporters hailed. Bellasis and Hope-Scott were barristers; Capes and Ward solicitors; Charles Stokes was a private banker and his brother Scott Stokes (who paid his nephew's fees)

111. D.P. Leinster-Mackay, *The Rise of the English Prep School* (London: Falmer, 1984), pp. 12–18.
112. Acton to Bellasis, March 1858, BOA.

worked in education, as did Allies; Gaisford served in the army; Wilberforce was a journalist; Dodsworth a writer; Monsell a politician; Pollen an artist and architect. The only nobleman, Acton, was a dedicated historian. These men were the driving force; they were the ones quick to respond to Newman's idea; they made it their own and backed it with time and money. Above all they were willing to take the ultimate risk and entrust to it their sons. Effectively the foundational group was comprised entirely of Newman's friends and admirers: they wished to begin a school under someone in whom they had complete confidence. Likewise, trust was a *sine qua non* for Newman to agree to undertake the task on their behalf.

Newman recognised the difficulty of parents at the outset in 'our not yet having boys enough to make a real school or offer its advantages – it is the difficulty which comes first and is greatest in our attempt'.[113] On this score, it is surely those who sent sons at the start, who planned the enterprise and gathered support for it, that deserve to be called the school's founders. On account of their vital contributions, the *chief* founders can be identified as Newman, Bellasis and Hope-Scott: Newman for his central role; Bellasis as the leading promoter and man of action; and Hope-Scott as advisor to both. Hope-Scott's contribution might appear relatively lightweight, but he suffered two family tragedies in 1858: his first wife took ill in the spring and died in October; and two of his three young children died in December. Acton does not quite qualify, though *he* thought he had contributed more than anyone to the foundation.[114] However, he could be included in the wider sense, for Newman later referred to the fund-raisers as 'the real authors of the undertaking'.[115]

The promoters decided to entrust the establishment and formation of their school to 'the mature deliberation of some one mind' rather than to a committee. But it would be an oversimplification to say that they devised the outline of a plan which they asked Newman to complete, because the plan was

---

[113.] Newman to Mrs F.R. Ward, 30 March 1859, *L&D* XIX, p. 95.
[114.] Acton to Döllinger, 28 January 1862, J.J.I. Döllinger, *Lord Acton Briefwechsel, 1820–90* II, ed. V. Conzemius (Munich: Beck, 1963), p. 247.
[115.] Memorandum, 19 December 1864, BOA, A.26.5.

negotiated. In fact, a harmonious balance can be discerned between the roles of the two parties involved, the promoters and Newman. The task of raising funds and finding pupils was carried out, not by the usual means of public advertisements, but by a diffusion of ideas through personal contacts; undoubtedly this discreet approach was considered the most effective in the circumstances. It was Newman's intuition regarding duties and responsibilities that guided the arrangements; and it was an intuition that reflected his understanding of the role of parents in the educational process.

Bellasis and Hope-Scott were heavily involved in Newman's 'mature deliberation'. Bellasis's pivotal role was that of a channel of communication between Newman and the promoters: he kept Newman informed of parental hopes and demands, and, when asked, sounded out others on Newman's behalf. Hope-Scott provided mature advice that was all the more objective for his being removed from the centre of activity. It was these three who were chiefly responsible for determining the school's characteristics. Evidently a partnership was at work. It was achieved through the efforts of Newman, who laboured to encourage the promoters' initiative, a characteristic that informed the enterprise and made it truly a joint venture. That the details concerning the practical running of the school were left to Newman in no way contradicts this assertion; it simply marks out the limits to the competences of parental involvement.

The foundational story makes clear Newman's explicit motives for involving himself and the Oratory: Darnell's enthusiasm and capacity for schoolmastering; the great need of Newman's close friends; his desire to be of service; and the search for suitable activities for the Oratory. Newman's prolonged reluctance to commit himself to the scheme provides a further rebuttal to McClelland's claim that he was determined to see it through at all costs. For McClelland, Newman was bent on forging links with the Catholic aristocracy and saw the school as a means of doing so, despite teaching not being part of the Oratorian vocation and despite deep-rooted opposition from within the Birmingham Oratory to the foundation of a boarding school.[116] But events do not

---

[116.] McClelland, 'A Catholic Eton', pp. 6–12.

bear this interpretation out; indeed, Newman was criticised for not striking when the iron was hot, in January 1858.

The foundational period reveals the tactics Newman adopted. There were no public lectures outlining theory before engaging in practice, as at Dublin; instead he worked tentatively, trying to find common ground with those willing to share his vision. To those closest to him, he divulged his thinking, but only gradually. He waited for the agreement and commitment of others before advancing; if the response was less than satisfactory, he called a halt to proceedings. This was Newman at his most cautious. What explains Newman's stance? Besides reasons of expediency (that he would be more effective acting with others, than alone) and lessons taught by recent experience at Dublin, another explanation suggests itself. Newman saw himself as helping his married friends solve the problem – *their* problem – of how to educate their children; thus he held back from whatever displaced an involvement more proper to them. By design, his collaboration enabled them to put into effect their rights and duties as the first educators of their children. Many years earlier, in a sermon he preached on the purpose of education, he had urged that 'parents should consider that from the earliest infancy of their children they are their natural guardians and instructors; that sending to school is merely an accidental circumstance, and but a part of education'; and had questioned the action of those who think 'they have done all that can be required of good and wise parents' when they have sent their children to school at the proper age.[117] This abiding conception of the educational task evidently guided Newman in the setting up of Edgbaston Catholic School.

[117.] 'On popular mistakes as to the object of education', sermon no.128 (preached in 1826), BOA.

Chapter 3

Darnell's School

The seven young boys who arrived at the beginning of May 1859 would have found no physical reality they could have called 'school'. They boarded with Mrs Wootten and a young convert Edward Ransford at 97 Hagley Road, ten minutes' walk away from the Oratory. The large three-storied red-brick Georgian house contained a makeshift chapel on the top floor, where one of the Oratorians said Mass daily, and on the ground floor a schoolroom furnished with heavy oak desks. The house had a long strip of garden, which served as a playground, and what they called a 'racquet court'; for larger games a nearby public field was used. This and no more was what Edgbaston Catholic School amounted to when it opened. For the greater part of the school day the boys were under the supervision of Ransford, who acted as Darnell's assistant; of Newman they probably saw little, because they only went to the Oratory for Mass on Sundays.

The Edgbaston dame

The basic structure of the school, as devised by Newman the previous year, relied on three key roles. The headmaster was to be the president's 'representative in undertaking [...] the establishment and formation' of the school;[1] the boys were to

[1.] Congregation decree, 21 April 1858, BOA.

live near by in a house 'committed to the management of an experienced lady', called a matron or dame;[2] and the president was to retain overall control. For each of these key roles the foundation was blessed with gifted individuals. The headmaster, Nicholas Darnell, had been a scholar at Winchester, prefect of Hall (head boy) and captain of Lords (cricket). He went up to Exeter College Oxford, then became a Fellow of New College, but resigned in 1847 on becoming a Catholic, and a year later joined the Oratorians. In 1859 he was an active, capable and self-confident man in his early forties with a taste for schoolmastering. The dame, Mrs Frances Wootten, was the widow of the Oxford doctor who had been popular among the Tractarians. She converted to Catholicism in 1850 and became one of Newman's most loyal friends, moving to Birmingham in order to assist him at the Oratory, and there she had struck up a close friendship with Darnell. By 1859 she had become the Oratory's main benefactress, having put over £6000 into Darnell's hands for Oratorian purposes. Newman regarded Mrs Wootten and Darnell as 'the two pillars of my undertaking';[3] and he expressed their two-fold contribution succinctly when he reduced the promoters' reasons for the new school to just two desiderata:

1. that boys should have their private needs, as boys, attended to [...] the care of their persons, their cleanliness, health, and the superintendence of their childish weaknesses and troubles, and
2. secondly that they should be well grounded in their books and have a really liberal education.

Mrs Wootten was to supply one and Darnell the other, while 'their intimate friendship was an additional reason for their undertaking those offices'.[4]

Although Newman had envisaged a role for Mrs Wootten at the outset, added impetus had come from the promoters –

[2.] School manifesto, 21 February 1859, BOA.
[3.] Newman, Paper proposing a compromise, 24 December 1861, *L&D* XX, p. 86.
[4.] Newman, Second paper with proposals for a compromise, 28 December 1861, *L&D* XX, p. 90.

many of whom were Eton men[5] and urged Newman to imitate the 'Eton dame' arrangement.[6] Even though the dames' houses were being gradually phased out at Eton, Newman was enthusiastic about the arrangement since it met one of the promoters' key demands; besides, he had experienced something similar as a boy at Ealing School, where the boarding houses were also under the jurisdiction of dames. The Ealing dames ensured that boys were properly dressed and cared for them when sick, and they also ran the tuck shops. As a sensitive boy Newman seems to have appreciated this arrangement, and the happy memories he cherished from his Ealing schooldays no doubt influenced his decision to accede to the promoters' wishes and establish a dame system at Edgbaston. Unlike Newman, Darnell had only second-hand knowledge of the dame system because at Winchester there were no dames in the Eton sense; and in any case Darnell had been a scholar and had lived in college, while the 'commoners' lived in one single large establishment, not in houses, and mixed little with the 'collegers'. His idea of a dame was that of the 'Winchester matron', a subordinate to the headmaster.

The dame's role at Edgbaston was shaped by the powerful personality of Mrs Wootten. She took her duties seriously, and

[5.] One quarter of the thirty-two prominent Catholics who had been willing to back the school publicly were Etonians, and four of them were among the leading promoters: Allies, Hope-Scott, Pollen and Scott-Murray. Of the 425 public school converts identified in *Converts to Rome*, approximately a quarter were Etonians.

[6.] The dual system of houses under masters and dames had developed more by accident than design at Eton in course of its history, as it had elsewhere, though the dames' houses at Eton were more fully integrated into the fabric of the school: they were nominally under the control of a classics tutor, but the dame was the ruling power. In the 1760s ten of Eton's thirteen houses for the fee-paying pupils were under dames. A century later only a quarter of the boys were living in dames' houses: by then, most other public schools had followed the example of Dr Arnold, who had raised the entry age at Rugby to twelve, abolished the dames' houses and promoted the housemaster system. In part, the pressure for change had come from masters who were eager to boost their earnings with the substantial profits a boarding house could provide. At Eton, however, the dames' houses were allowed to die out naturally, ceasing in 1905.

was able to send for a boy without fuss or difficulty; equally, boys had easy access to her for their various needs, as described in her own words:

> an extra pocket handkerchief, a collar, *a dry pair* of stockings and so forth [...] Also *boys may* want to give me messages from their Parents about their health, or clothing, or shoes, or about an advance of money, or to exchange stamps for money, or to have letters read or written for them, or corrected for them without publicity. Or they may want their sore feet, hands and so forth attended to without a doctor or any special notice.[7]

She had the discretionary power of putting boys into such dormitories and beds as she thought best for them, taking into account the masters' suggestions. Naturally, she had the entire care and management of the sick, and communicated directly with doctors and parents in these matters. Mothers entrusted her with special requests for their dear ones: one boy required a glass of wine and a biscuit every night, while the Wilberforce boys were supplied with compresses for stomach aches – both of which required discreet application. She also kept accounts of each boy's personal expenses and sent them to parents on a termly basis. In fact, her duties were similar to those of the present-day Eton dame, while her overall responsibilities matched those of the nineteenth-century dame.[8] But her duties went beyond these and her remit included helping her charges grow in virtue and good habits; if she noticed anything faulty in a boy's dealings with his friends, or in other small matters, she would try to help him out of it. Newman, in fact, thought the dames had a huge contribution to make: 'By throwing the boys into houses, we shall secure, as far as that is possible, superintendence and care both of their souls and of their bodies.'[9] Far from merely tending to the boys' material needs, the dames had a role that in some respects put them on a par with the Oratorians, for Newman was of the opinion that the

---

7. Mrs Wootten to Newman, 7 December 1861, BOA.
8. See N. Byron, *Eton: a Dame's Chronicle* (London: W. Kimber, 1965), pp. 19–31.
9. Newman to Lewis, 26 August 1860, *L&D* XIX, p. 398.

school would slip into 'subordinating religion to secular interests and principles [...] but for the presence of Matrons of a high class, and of spiritual directors'.[10]

One episode that occurred a couple of years after the school had begun highlights the dame's elevated role: Bellasis thought his eight-year-old son showed signs of a vocation to the priesthood, and wondered whether Edgbaston Catholic School was appropriate, given that it was for those not intended for the priesthood. Although Bishop Grant had encouraged him to send the boy to one of the Catholic colleges, Bellasis sought Newman's advice. In his reply Newman set out his thinking – untypical for the time – on early vocations, which helps explain his attraction to the idea of a lay school, even for those called to the priesthood or religious life. True vocations, he maintained, were not destroyed by contact with the world. Many boys showed signs of a vocation early on, which often faded away, not because it was lost, but because it had been present only in appearance: avoiding such deception could only be a positive good. The more likely danger for the Church was not

> losing priests whom she ought to have had, but gaining priests she never should have been burdened with. The thought is awful, that boys should have had no trial of their hearts, till at the end of some 14 years, they go out into the world with the most solemn vows upon them, and then perhaps for the first time learn that the world is not a seminary.[11]

Moreover, early separation from the world tended to foster a 'spirit of formalism, affectation, and preciseness'; by contrast, many saints had received a vocation when young and cherished it and matured it in the course of a secular training. In his opinion it was '*more* common in this age for false vocations to be made by an early dedication to the religious or ecclesiastical state, than for true vocations to be lost by early secular education'. As it happened, before receiving Newman's reply,

[10.] Newman, Second paper, 28 December 1861, *L&D* XX, p. 91.
[11.] Newman to Bellasis, 5 August 1861, *L&D* XX, p. 21.

Bellasis had decided that the boy should join his elder brother at the school. The boy went on to become a lawyer – while the elder one, who had shown no signs of a vocation, became an Oratorian.

There are two incidental aspects of the episode which bring out the dame's role. Firstly, Newman had delayed his response to Bellasis, partly, as he said, because he wished to talk first to Mrs Wootten – no reference was made to consulting Darnell or any of the other Oratorians. Secondly, it contained a surprising suggestion: 'I found Mrs Wootten take the same view, as far as she spoke upon it. She spoke from such experience as she had – I wish you would write to her.'[12] Evidently she so identified with the spiritual dimension of the school that Newman could rely on her in this way. On another occasion Newman thanked her for using 'her influence among the boys to excite devotion to St Philip [Neri] and an affectionate loyalty towards his Birmingham House'.[13] (This may explain why, when the boys were confirmed in May 1860, no fewer than twenty-five took the Confirmation name of Philip!) Mrs Wootten was, as Newman once commented, 'more like a Saint than most people';[14] though his description of her as *mulier fortis et sapiens* suggests she also had other, more down-to-earth qualities. For the boys, she represented a strong maternal figure; for the masters, a force to be reckoned with. Newman relied on her virtually to run the school when Darnell was away during vacations; and she even received applications from parents. In this way Newman confirmed his intention that the school be run as a partnership between her and Darnell, under his presidency.

That Mrs Wootten was a lady of independent means reinforced the notion of her dedication above and beyond the call of duty. Newman was later to boast that, 'If we have one point, which we lay stress on, more than other schools, it is in the quality of our matrons. They are ladies, who do not make a livelihood by their places, but have means of their own – and they take peculiar care of the boys.'[15] It is likely that Newman

---

[12.] Newman to Bellasis, 5 August 1861, *L&D* XX, p. 22.

[13.] Newman to Mrs Wootten, 5 December 1861, *L&D* XX, p. 77.

[14.] Newman to Mrs F.R. Ward, 8 August 1859, *L&D* XIX, p. 188.

[15.] Newman to Miss Holmes, 22 November 1861, *L&D* XX, p. 68.

wished to emphasise their financial independence, because a major reason for the abandonment of dames' houses in the first half of the nineteenth century was the abuse of the system by exploitative dames. At the outset, Darnell seems to have submitted to Newman's system of dual control, with the headmaster supreme in the school and the dame supreme in her house, though he may not have appreciated the full implications of the arrangement or how different it was to be from the system at Winchester. Alternatively, it is possible that he *did* appreciate the difference but dismissed it on the assumption it would prove unworkable or, more likely, merely temporary, since in a few years the majority of boys would be considerably older.

Early developments

Darnell had effectively assumed control as headmaster around Christmas 1858, for Newman had granted him a free rein in accordance with his claim that 'My rule has ever been to give a generous liberty to those I put in trust with any work'. Assertive, dominant and impatient as Darnell was to see the school develop rapidly, it was not long before Newman realised that, 'having put power out of my hands, there was no way of getting it back'.[16] At the same time, it must be said that Darnell showed initiative and flair. In February 1859 he offered the post of second master to Robert Moody at £150 per annum, with free places for all his sons and the prospect of taking in boarders. A recent convert who had been educated at Eton and Christ Church Oxford, Moody already had some teaching experience, and so Darnell sought his advice on the timetable and a system of studies. Despite Darnell being a Wykhamist they agreed that, as Moody noted in his diary, 'we are to work the School pretty much on the Eton system, and ground them well in classics'.[17] Nevertheless Darnell chose the Winchester Latin grammar for the school and asked all fathers to buy a copy before their sons arrived.

[16.] Newman to Wilberforce, 26 January 1862, *L&D* XX, pp. 138–39.
[17.] Moody's diary, 2 March 1858, BOA.

Moody's diary provides an inside story of the school's early development, coloured by his strong preferences and eye for detail. His eldest son joined the school in mid-May 1859 but only in July, at the very end of the first term, did Moody move his family to Edgbaston and take up his duties. His first impression of the Oratorians was of men in awe of their leader and constrained in his presence, which in turn made Newman awkward in their company and deprived him of conversation; although affable, Newman looked frail and ill, and wore an expression of sadness and disappointment. In the school Moody found a complete lack of order; Ransford, who acted as tutor and usher, was warmly religious and dutiful, but a liability as a schoolmaster, being without tact, management or refinement, and he frequently over-reacted to the boys' provocations. Outside lessons Ransford had charge of the boys, though Darnell and Moody joined him for cricket and weekend walks. Moody soon formed a negative impression of the neighbourhood as a place for a school: land was hard to come by and expensive, the air was smokey, and, besides, there was no Catholic society for him. However, he felt able to fall back on Darnell's assurance that once the school was strong enough to exist by itself, it was at liberty to establish itself elsewhere.

By all accounts Darnell was a natural schoolmaster, though his style was autocratic, which meant that he was unable to appreciate the more complex role of headmaster intended by Newman, with its modification of conventional power. Newman had hoped to excise his role as president with a light touch, but Darnell's obstructive attitude became apparent as early as the first term, when Newman's request to sit in on examinations was refused. At first Newman took a generous view and assumed Darnell simply wanted the boys better prepared, but he soon realised that his advice and recommendations were being ignored. Nevertheless it is clear that Newman's energies were devoted elsewhere, because his *Letters and Diaries* contain just one reference to the school during the first three terms, apart from noting the arrival and departure of boys. Newman even admitted to one parent that 'I have no time nor strength to give to the school personally'.[18]

[18.] Newman to Wilberforce, 13 January 1861, *L&D* XIX, p. 452.

In fact Newman's time was largely taken up with his duties as superior of the Oratory. After leaving the Catholic University he had intended to devote himself more fully to the small community of Oratorians which cared for the large and growing parish based in Edgbaston, characterised by its urban poverty. From the parish the Oratory looked after orphanages, poor schools and a workhouse: they had even tried to start a hospital for the poor, but it had failed to get off the ground. The running of the Oratory itself involved many domestic tasks: those of librarian, sacristan, music master, novice master and treasurer (this last complicated because each Father retained his own property). Two of the Fathers were in the process of leaving the Oratory; of the remaining seven, two had contracted pleurisy and a third tuberculosis. Although they gradually recovered, Newman had to shoulder much of the weight, particularly in the summer of 1859, at the very time the school had just started, when he found himself virtually alone. Newman cared for the invalids in the parish, oversaw the enlargements to the church, and later, in January 1861, took over the school accounts from Darnell; he also spent up to four hours a day in the confessional.

One of Newman's major preoccupations at the time was the escalating confrontation between *The Rambler* and the Catholic hierarchy – a dispute that came to have a notable effect on the school on account of the favourable attitude shown towards it by the journal's proprietors and contributors. These wider developments reveal the tensions existing within the English Catholic body as a whole. *The Rambler* had clashed with the episcopate over education twice before, in 1848–50 and 1856–57, and the dispute was reignited in January 1859 when Scott Stokes, uncle of one of the first seven boys and a government inspector of Catholic schools, criticised the bishops' handling of the question of state support for Catholic schools. In striving for unanimity, the bishops claimed the sole right to discuss and decide the educational issue; rather than officially censure the journal, they asked Newman to intervene as the only *persona grata* to both sides. Just as Edgbaston Catholic School was about to open in 1859 Newman undertook the editorship, but his attempt to exculpate Stokes landed him in serious trouble. His article 'On consulting the faithful in matters of doctrine' in the July issue irritated Ultramontane sensitivities by pointing out that during the Arian controversy in the fourth century the majority of the bishops were unorthodox, while the laity remained faithful. It was delated to Rome for heresy by Bishop Brown of Newport, who pointed out to the authorities that both Oratories were filled with converts rather than 'original Catholics' and complained that they possessed Protestant notions and instincts instead of Catholic ones. Then a vital letter from Newman to Cardinal Barnabò (Prefect of Propaganda Fide and in charge of English Catholic affairs), in the resolution of the matter, was misplaced due to an administrative error. Barnabò came to believe that Newman had refused to explain himself, whereas Newman, having heard no more, presumed the matter was settled: it was not, and for years afterwards Newman remained under a cloud at Rome. Although Newman lasted only two issues in charge of *The Rambler* – May and July 1859 – before relinquishing his duties to Acton, his association with the journal led many to regard him as the leader and guide of a 'Catholic opposition'; even when he made his resignation public – dismaying Acton and leading to a forty per cent drop in the readership – it was commonly assumed that he was still the *eminence grise* behind the journal.

The school had been in existence for only two months when Newman observed that Darnell was 'ambitious perhaps to have a tip-top school',[19] though he was pleased to note that when it reopened for the Michaelmas term numbers had grown to fourteen, and that among the newcomers were sons of old Catholics. Newman managed to conduct a two-day examination of the boys in November and another in December, and was satisfied – but no more – with progress. Although Darnell laid great stress on the academic side, he ensured that work was balanced with play, and after being tested by Newman on their Caesar and Euclid, the boys had apple-bobbing to lift their spirits. Like any youngsters they enjoyed the half or whole holidays, such as Michaelmas (29 September) and St Edward the Confessor (13 October), which were marked by special games of football. Oratorians as well as masters joined in – and both alike were knocked to

[19.] Newman to Mrs F.R. Ward, 8 August 1859, *L&D* XIX, p. 189.

ground by Darnell, whose strength and skill were in a class of their own. Staff participation was in keeping with the times, for the masters joined boys in games of football at Eton and Harrow, as did ecclesiastical staff at Stonyhurst. Besides the grammar book, another Winchester import Darnell oversaw was the singing of *Dulce Domum* after the concert to mark the end of the Christmas term; the song supposedly originated from a boy at Winchester who had been kept back during the holidays as a punishment, and who died of grief, but not without first giving musical expression to his feelings.

Moody turns sour

Just before the end of the Christmas term, fire broke out one night in Mrs Wootten's house and disaster was narrowly averted; had she not raised the alarm in time, the house, full to capacity with twenty young boys asleep inside, would have burnt down. When the Lent term began in 1860, Moody was allowed to start taking in boarders at his house, 112 Hagley Road; he had expected to do so earlier but Darnell had told him that the policy was to fill Mrs Wootten's house first. Moody was eager to see greater financial rewards, and his ambition was fuelled by his beautiful wife (known to her friends as 'Lady Apricot') and the needs of a growing family that eventually numbered nine children.

Another change that term was the appointment of the part-time French teacher, Henri La Serre, whose duties included leading French conversation with the boys at meal times. Unfamiliar with the public school system, he was baffled by various aspects of school life. In his 'Memoirs' he recounted how he had once intervened in what appeared to be a riot in the boys' dormitories, where he found Darnell in their midst being pelted with pillows and bolsters. Though the boys turned on La Serre and forced his retreat, Darnell seems to have been (more or less) in control of what amounted to a customary end-of-term pillow fight.[20] Moody had already noticed that Darnell

[20.] H. La Serre, 'Memoirs on the late Cardinal Newman and the Oratory School', n.d., pp. 31–32, Arundel Castle archive, MD.2119.

was a lax disciplinarian who was over-familiar with the boys during school hours and prone to remitting punishments set by masters, and his exasperation with Darnell's easy-going ways led him to urge Darnell to introduce 'flogging for the incorrigibles'.[21]

The spring of 1860 turned out to be a crucial moment in the school's early life because it was during this period that, in the course of discussing its future development, two groups began to form, each with its own agenda. The immediate matter to be dealt with concerned priorities: whether a larger playing field was the most pressing need, as Moody and many parents thought, or whether the moment had arrived to construct the main school building, as Newman proposed. There was also the question of how to accommodate new pupils: Oscott's instability – after two changes of president within five months – raised the prospect of a rush of pupils, and Darnell wanted to prepare for the eventuality by opening a second dame's house.

Although Darnell must have spoken at length with Newman about the school, it is probable that practical considerations dominated their discussions and that they skirted over problems associated with its future development: otherwise their differing long-term aspirations would have become apparent. That they could have been working to separate agendas is all the more curious since the Oratorian Rule required them to report and submit to the whole Congregation their plans for the joint undertaking. Given the school's financial dependence on the Oratory, as well as its use of the church and other amenities, it was natural that the Congregation should play a part in its governance, and their minute book indicates that school-related business dominated many of their meetings. After discussing the question of accommodation on 9 April, the Oratorians met again a fortnight later. By then Darnell had found a house in Monument Road with a large field, which he suggested they rent. But he also read out to the Fathers a separate proposal from Bellasis which objected to the system of tutors' and dames' houses, since they would be independent of the Oratory; for Bellasis the aim was to have the boys under the eye of the Oratorians, and he anticipated that difficulties would arise in

---

[21.] Moody's diary, 17 February 1860, BOA.

the tutor's houses if boys lived with families where there were daughters growing up and governesses around. Although not stated, his concern over the dames' houses was on account of complaints that the boys were left alone at night – presumably neglected by the live-in tutor, Ransford.

Within a month of this meeting several major changes had taken place. The lease on the property in Monument Road was acquired so that the building could be used as the girls' orphanage and its eight acres of meadowland as playing fields for the school. By leasing another nearby property, 6 Vicarage Road, the school was able to provide further accommodation under a second dame and to take the pressure off Mrs Wootten. The new dame was Miss Elinor Ffrench, a former governess, one of the 'nunnish ladies' who helped at the Oratory and whom Newman had once hoped would run a girls' boarding school. On 2 May, the school's first anniversary, Newman celebrated High Mass for the boys and the staff in St Philip's Chapel. That day the school's centre of gravity moved definitively to the Oratory: the chapel, which was then connected to the church, was where the boys now attended daily Mass; a large room on the ground floor of the Oratory House came into operation as the main schoolroom; and the playground at the Oratory (supplemented by an adjoining field) began to function as the main play area. From this time onwards, the boys were escorted to the Oratory early in the morning and only returned to their houses in the evening.

With the prospect of increasing numbers and Ambrose St John inheriting £4400, Newman considered (in his first major memorandum about the school) that they were presented with an ideal opportunity to further 'the material (and so moral) establishment of the school'. He thought they should take advantage of their good fortune and lack of troubles, and place themselves boldly before the world, putting the school 'on a more formal and firmer basis, and in a more visible position. [...] what the school needs absolutely, and also to give it character and make it imposing, is School-rooms – and the only thing which it will ever want, if the plan of Dames Houses is continued'.[22] His proposal was to build these central school buildings

22. Newman, memorandum, 30 May 1860, *L&D* XIX, pp. 348–49.

between the Oratory and the newly-acquired houses adjacent, 67 and 68 Hagley Road, as his intention was to cease using the outlying houses and gradually close in round the Oratory. This strategic change reflected a general feature of the Victorian era, the slow but progressive divorce of the public school from its surroundings: instead of boys eating and sleeping in town, in boarding or dames' houses, they came to be lodged in central buildings or boarding houses contiguous to them. The change had two crucial advantages: it brought boys under the power of the masters, and it ensured that boarding profits remained within the school. For Edgbaston Catholic School, there was the additional benefit that it placed the boys in closer contact with the Oratory: for this reason Bellasis was delighted with the proposed development.

In part Moody must have been very pleased with the scheme too, as he had grumbled at the school's poor facilities, which made it look like a small private school, and had called for improvements to convince parents about the imitation of the Eton system. However, he was dismayed when he realised that the occupation of the two houses threatened to throw overboard his cherished boarding-house. The plan was also at odds with the aspirations of two influential Etonian parents. Scott-Murray had understood that the school was virtually independent of the Oratory and that Darnell could act as independently from it as Newman had in setting up the Catholic University; and he had presumed Darnell intended to leave the Oratory once the school was flourishing and move it into the country. He expressed his strong disapproval of any plan which involved the school establishing itself properly in Birmingham, and recommended Henley instead. Another Etonian, Lord Thynne, visited the Oratory in mid-April, hoping to use the opportunity of accompanying his son on his first day to talk over the school's future with Newman; in Newman's absence he spoke with Darnell and Moody. Like Scott-Murray, Thynne thought the school ought to move to a country location if it was to become a public school, and he promised to lobby for a new site near Reading so that boys could remain at school as they grew older. It was ideas such as these, coming from a handful of parents and his main ally Moody, that encouraged Darnell to develop his own agenda

for the school, and misled him into assuming that it reflected
the thinking of the whole parental body; effectively they pressurised him by laying more and more stress on adopting the
public school system.

Isolated from this current of thought, Newman was unaware
of the pressure to re-locate. His own preoccupations were very
different: the one theme that comes up constantly in his dealings with parents is that of the school acting *in loco parentis*.
Expressions like an 'awful responsibility', 'a tremendous
anxiety' and a 'great mark of confidence' appear in his correspondence and reflect a keen sympathy with those parents who
were entrusting their dearest ones to the experimental undertaking; it was 'a most serious charge to have the care of so
many boys, on whom the well being of English Catholicism in
the next generation, humanly speaking, materially depends.
[...] The greater the act of confidence on your part, the keener
is our anxiety.'[23] The transmission of responsibility was manifested in symbolic fashion by the handing over of boys at the
start of each term, above all at the start of a boy's school career.
On his return to the Oratory, Newman apologised to Thynne
that his absence meant he was unable to

> have had Charlie put into my hands by yourself, as you so
> kindly intended. I feel deeply both the confidence shown
> me, and the responsibility incurred by me, in such a
> charge – and assure you that neither myself, nor any of
> us, should ever view the new School in any other light,
> primarily, than that of a public institution for the advan-
> tage of the Catholic gentlemen of England. We should
> consider ourselves happy, if we are made the instruments,
> in the Hands of Providence, of supplying what is on all
> sides felt to be a great desideratum.[24]

Newman added: 'As to the ultimate destination of the
School, in years to come, we must wait for the actual coming of
those years, and the advice we get from friends like yourself, to

---

[23.] Newman to the Duchess of Norfolk, 7 March 1861, *L&D* XIX, p.
476.
[24.] Newman to Thynne, 25 April 1860, *L&D* XIX, p. 328.

determine us what is best.'[25] However, Newman played little part in the school's working arrangements. He was scarcely to be seen about the place, and communicated little with the masters; and neither they nor the majority of parents were involved in discussions about the school's development, but only Bellasis and Hope-Scott. Newman's lack of direct involvement in school affairs – perhaps due to his underestimating how much he would have to be involved to form the school along his own lines – allowed a gap of understanding to open up.

At the start of the school's fourth, term numbers were up to twenty-four and there were promising indications of further additions: several boys had switched from Downside, and there were some notable gains from Oscott, while several boys from Ireland (owing no doubt to Newman's influence there) opted for Edgbaston instead of Stonyhurst. An architect was consulted about the various schemes for expansion, including Hope-Scott's plan for a large dormitory in the Oratory House, and on account of the complexity of the matter the Congregation decreed 'that Newman, Darnell and [William] Neville be appointed a Committee to arrange definitively and without appeal the question of providing new Rooms for the Oratory School'.[26]

By this time Moody had set himself against the changes and begun to turn sour. Newman tried to placate him by doubling his salary to £300 per annum, as compensation for losing his boarders, but it had little effect. Moody was a sound schoolmaster and popular with the boys, but he now began to introduce a subversive element into the school as his opinions hardened. Soon he was arguing to Darnell that the school ought to be independent of the Oratory, that the headmaster should be the only authority, and that the Congregation should exercise no more control over it than the provost of Eton did over his school. Together with his wife, he began spreading rumours

[25] Newman to Thynne, 25 April 1860, *L&D* XIX, p. 328.
[26] Congregation decree, 28 May 1860, BOA. The first and only time Newman is known to have used the expression 'the Oratory School' before the Darnell crisis is in this decree and in the title of a memorandum of the same date, both of which were intended for Oratorian eyes only.

that Newman was nearing a state of physical and mental collapse. Their actions soon began to have an effect. The Oratory choir master and organist at the time was Sebastian Okeley, a talented Etonian convert who had been a Cambridge wrangler (first-class mathematician). In May he had begun helping in the school by taking a mathematics class, but in August he decided to leave on account of the Moodys.

In September the Moodys' gossip reached Mrs F.R. Ward, and she asked Darnell to put a stop to it. By chance Newman came across her letter and decided to take the matter up himself, seeking the advice of Thynne, who had once had Moody as his curate. Thynne described him as an honest man, but bad-tempered, conceited and forceful, and his wife as having little regard for the truth. He confirmed they had both spoken against both the Oratory and the school and all connected with it, including the boys. Thynne was reluctant to say more about Moody, as his life after conversion had been a great struggle against poverty, bad health and loss of friends; he realised how harmful it was for the school 'to have those about it who do not cordially support it', but he believed that, in a way, Moody *did* wish for the school to succeed, though 'it must be under *his* management and under *his* direction'.[27] Primed with this intelligence Newman drew up a list of charges, called the Moodys for an interview, and confronted them with the main points; but they denied everything and demanded to know who their accusers were. Mrs Ward's husband, a solicitor, advised Newman to let the matter drop: a warning had been delivered, and they were likely to do more damage if Moody was dismissed. If Newman really thought that the question at stake was too serious to let it pass, he added they should try to gather written statements. After weighing up the alternatives Newman sent a tactful reply to reassure the Moodys of his goodwill and explain that he did not want to pursue the matter further. This did not satisfy Moody, who complained that he and his wife would now feel the restraint imposed on them by knowing that they had 'enemies' about the place. And so the matter was left, with its uncertain outcome.

27. Thynne to Newman, 19 September 1860, BOA.

Out of touch

The Michaelmas term of 1860 began with thirty-six boys and an extra master, the abbé Rougemont, a French priest who spoke English fluently and taught mathematics. But not long after appointing him, Darnell began to have second thoughts about Rougemont's ability to keep discipline. Meanwhile, Ransford was regularly having run-ins with the boys; on one occasion he set half the school a heavy imposition for throwing stones, after which Darnell decided to remove him from responsibility for the younger boys. Moody attributed the general disorder to Darnell trying to do too much at once. However, Darnell seems to have taken a firmer line that term, since at the end of it he thanked the boys for their improved behaviour, though he went on to lecture them about conduct in the dormitories and the behaviour of those given permission to go into town. He spelt out to them the *Prefect's Dormitory Rules* that Newman had composed after hearing complaints about the lack of dormitory supervision. The rules stated:

1. Silence.
2. No going into each other's rooms.
3. Each boy to dress and undress and say his prayers behind his own curtain.
4. All lights out by half past nine.[28]

It was the responsibility of the tutors, who slept in rooms next to the dormitories, to ensure – as the prospectus declared – that 'the rule of silence is strictly enforced'. But Newman knew only half the story; there was also gambling and smoking among the boys which Darnell was aware of but did little to eliminate.

Besides catechising the boys every Sunday, examining them once a term and giving out prizes, Newman was intent on exercising the wider dimension of his role as president. To understand how he intended to oversee the school it is useful to look at the scheme he had worked out in December 1860 for its administration, and which the Congregation adopted provi-

[28.] Arundel Castle archive, C.581.

sionally, on a majority vote, for a year. In what was the closest he came to drafting a school constitution, Newman defined the school's personnel as the 'Father Prefect' (headmaster), the assistant masters, the secretary, the confessors, the dames and the servants. The establishment was to consist of dames' houses for boarding and lodging the boys, and a central building. The appointment of all masters, dames and servants was to lie with the headmaster, but required confirmation from Newman; the confessors were to be appointed by Newman himself, independently from the headmaster.[29] The headmaster was to deal with the routine finances while Newman, as the representative of the Oratorians and with their consent, was to deal with all financial arrangements concerning school properties, including alterations and furnishing. He was also to fix the salaries of the masters and the 'pensions' (boarding fees). Each house was to have its own dame (though the same dame could, with Newman's permission, have more than one house); she was to receive from the headmaster, in advance and on a monthly basis, the pensions corresponding to her boys.[30]

Darnell was probably unhappy with this scheme and the prominence it gave Mrs Wootten, particularly since he had fallen out with her of late after she had taken to lecturing him for not complying with Newman's wishes. Aware of the discrepancy emerging between Newman's vision and the line Darnell was beginning to adopt, she tried to compensate for it; because of her long friendship with Darnell, she did not inform Newman, but resorted instead to a policy of non-cooperation, telling Darnell she would not fulfil her duty to him so long as he did not fulfil his to Newman. Darnell found her policy immensely irritating, but, though he vented his frustrations in a letter to Newman in January 1861, he could not bring himself to send it; and so Newman was kept in the dark about the rift that was developing within the school. On 14 February next, nearly all the Oratorians, including Newman, received

---

[29.] This arrangement was similar to that at the Woodard schools where the chaplains were appointed by the provost and Fellows, not the headmaster. This was because Woodard wanted his chaplains to provide individual spiritual attention to boys and to have nothing to do with teaching or discipline.

[30.] Congregation minute book, 4 December 1860, BOA.

unpleasant Valentine cards, and there was strong evidence the Moodys were responsible; more alarming was that most of the Fathers thought Darnell was involved too.

Although out of touch with school affairs, Newman was occasionally drawn in, as when he became involved in resolving a clash between Ransford and a son of his friend Henry Wilberforce. Newman tried to ease matters by urging the Wilberforces to have trust in the school but admitted that, while 'Boys are not ruined in a day', he was 'provoked and troubled at his [Ransford's] hacking and hewing the delicate natures submitted to him'. To sort out the matter, the Wilberforces not only wrote to Darnell but travelled to the Oratory where they spoke at length with St John – a most unusual measure for the times. For this, Newman was very grateful: 'It is the part of a true friend. We cannot get on, unless we know just how things are going.'[31] Parents, he told them, should be 'perfectly sure that I hold the welfare of the boys committed to me above the existence of the school itself – and would rather they all went, than that they should get harm instead of good by remaining'.[32] (By contrast, Wilberforce had received very different treatment when a son of his died at Radley. Instead of apologising or commiserating with his loss, the founder Sewell blamed Wilberforce for sending the weak boy to his boarding school and, as a consequence, injuring Radley's reputation.[33])

In February 1861 Newman composed a second major memorandum about the school. It explained why both sides had held back in November 1858, the Oratory waiting for the Catholic laymen to supply the finance and pupils, and the majority of parents wanting proof that the Oratory could run a school; Newman had eventually decided to break the deadlock and 'furnish to Catholic gentlemen that trial of our capacity'. But by February 1861 the school and the Oratory had been 'on trial' for almost two years, and Newman judged that the Oratory should revert to its former position and demand from the parents the means for the 'adequate establishment' of the

[31]. Newman to Wilberforce, 13 January 1861, *L&D* XIX, p. 452.
[32]. Newman to Mrs Wilberforce, 15 January 1861, *L&D* XIX, p. 454.
[33]. T. Mozley, *Reminiscences: Chiefly of Oriel College and the Oxford Movement* (London: Longman, Green & Co., 1882) II, pp. 27–28.

school. In founding a school for upper-class Catholics, it was not to be forgotten that, 'as that very object implies, the duty and the interest of the undertaking rest with that upper class, and not with the Oratory'. So far, parents had provided just £550 for capital expenditure, while the Oratory had put in over £7000, of which £4000 had been spent on enlarging and decorating the church for the school's needs. While the immediate benefit accrued to parents, Newman admitted that the Oratory had a considerable interest in the school prospering. There was no more direct way of fulfilling their mission from the Pope than that of 'keeping school'; it provided work that suited some Oratorians, and for Newman it 'falls under those objects, to which I have especially given my time and thought'. In general, however, he felt that other works would have been more suitable for an Oratory. Viewed as a commercial speculation, the school was bringing in an adequate interest on the capital, but for the need to plough it back in for buildings and additional staff. And there was another drawback:

> The parents of the boys, not only have the direct interest in the school, but also a real power over it. Our dependence upon them is as great, as if they were a committee of management; for they have only to withdraw their children and the school falls to the ground. Of course there is a date in the history of most undertakings, when they are established beyond the power of individuals, however many or influential, to affect them prejudicially; such are not our circumstances at present. A run might suddenly take place against the school; as there is at present a run in its favor.[34]

Clearly, the reputation and prospects of the Oratory, as well as their capital, were tied to the school. And there was another risk arising from their pledge to 'keep school', for the Oratorians supplied the headmaster, and if he became ill another Oratorian would have to 'throw up his existing engagements, buckle on his Latin and Greek, and rub up his knowledge of boys'. A similar argument applied to Mrs Wootten; so that 'it might happen we could supply neither

[34.] Newman, memorandum, 5 February 1861, *L&D* XIX, pp. 463–64.

Head Master, nor Head Dame to the satisfaction of the parents', in which case the school would collapse. Another scenario Newman envisaged (and which eventually took place some sixty years later) was that 'The school might outgrow the place. Or parents might begin to find that we were perfection, had we but a better situation, amid pleasant meadows and upon an available river. After discussion the school goes away from us into the country, with our benediction indeed' – but with a loss to the Oratory.

Although Newman thought it unbecoming for the Oratory to engage in financial speculation, its funds had been committed to overcome an otherwise insurmountable obstacle. The school required further investment of £3000–£4000 to give it a fair chance.

> Under these circumstances, we wish to know of our friends, whether they will give, advance, or lend us a sufficient sum for us to proceed with the plans which we have begun with such good promise – and, if so, on what terms.
>
> Such a sufficient grant of money on their part, will not only trim the balance of expense, in the prospect of a further outlay, but will also serve as our safeguard against, and our compensation under the contingency of the school going out of our hands into some other locality, or being superseded by some newer institution elsewhere.[35]

The practical proposal Newman put to Hope-Scott was that parents and friends of the school should pay for the purchase of the field adjoining the playground, namely £1750.

Because the Congregation had devised as many as five plans for further expansion, a professional accountant was brought in to analyse the financial implications. His up-beat report was read to the Congregation, and shortly afterwards Bellasis and Hope-Scott visited the Oratory to discuss the building plans with Newman. Although he had boarded at an Eton dame's house, Hope-Scott fully approved of Newman's proposal to turn the vacant rooms in the top storey of the Oratory House

[35.] Newman, memorandum, 5 February 1861, *L&D* XIX, pp. 464–65.

into boys' dormitories, with a capacity of up to forty. A record of Newman's conversation with Hope-Scott was read out to the Congregation, and after deliberation it gave his plan the go-ahead, with one proviso: that the alterations to the House be made without expense to the Congregation or sacrifice of its privacy. Newman's grand plan entailed two further steps: converting the two houses adjacent to the Oratory (belonging to St John) into dames' houses, and constructing a central school building along the road-front joining the two sites. The provisional time-scale for development was drastically reduced when news arrived that the dowager Duchess of Norfolk was to send her eldest son to the school and donate £500 for improvements in anticipation of his arrival.

In April the Congregation sanctioned a seven-year lease on St John's houses for school usage, and in May the school committee was empowered to proceed with the rest of the plan, to the extent of £3000. The intention was to use the Duchess' gift as a down payment and to take out a loan for the amount outstanding, which was to be serviced by the increased income generated by raising school fees from £80 to 80 guineas. With these measures in place, and after protracted negotiations with the architect, works were begun in July. The upper storey of the Oratory building and the two houses were ready by September, but it was not until February 1862 that the purpose-built schoolroom and playroom were. The main edifice, which survives to this day, was the only major school structure erected in Newman's time. Measuring 78 by 27 feet, it housed winter and wet-weather playrooms and a gymnasium on the ground floor and a typically cavernous Victorian schoolroom above.

Forcing the pace

Undoubtedly the school's most significant entrant was the young Duke of Norfolk, who arrived for the Trinity term of 1861, the year after his father's death. This remarkable success was due to the influence of Hope-Scott; he happened to be the Duke's trustee and guardian and had managed to persuade the Duchess of the merits of the dame system, and of the merits of Mrs

School of the Oratory, Edgbaston

His Grace the Duke of Norfolk

1863. _____ Michaelmas _____ TERM. Sept. 10–Dec. 20.

        £ . s . d   £ . s . d

EXPENSES OF THIS TERM—

   1 Scholastic—   July 20. 1863   Principia Latina &c sent back   3 6

     Books   — — —   as by bill   1 13 6

     Stationery -   for the Term   5 6

     Printed Music -

     Hire of Piano

     Drawing Materials

                                           2 3 0

   2 Personal—

     Clothes—Tailor   - Repairs

       Shoemaker -   - Do.   11 0

       Linen Draper -   Cap 3/6 Tie 3/

       Hair Dresser   1 6

       Pocket money—Allowance   at 6 per week   7 0

         Additional -   Dec. 1st & Dec. 10th   6 0

         For Journeys - Railway Sept. 25/   ditto 9/6 Fly & Cab   2 16 10

                Dec. 19. 28/

     Letters, Stamps, &c.

     Carriage of Parcels   1

     Seat in Church -   for the Term .   7 0

     Medical Attendance, &c. -

       Amusements :- Repair of violet, 4/9 Broadway Apparatus   1 6 3

          Engine 4/ Leather 1/6 and Cab 4/

          Biscuits . . . .

          Port wine . . .   2 7 2

          Entrance to asking of links .   1 0   11 14 9

PENSION IN ADVANCE FOR NEXT TERM - - - - -   13 17 9

The Lent Term commences on Monday Jan 25.   —   28 0 0

                                      £ 41 17 9

                      TOTAL...

Termly expenses of the Duke of Norfolk,
Michaelmas Term 1863.

Wootten, into whose care the young Duke was placed. By now the Edgbaston version of the dame system had become fully formed, with the dame acting as surrogate mother to the young boys and 'mistress of the house'. Entrusted with the pastoral care of the boys in her house or houses, she was to correspond directly with the parents – usually the mothers – about the general welfare and health of their sons. This conformed to the Victorian pattern whereby mothers of the middle and upper classes regarded early schooling as their responsibility, while their husbands had more to say about public school arrangements. A measure of the confidence Newman had in Mrs Wootten was the way he could depend on her to take charge of the young Duke, and she exchanged letters with the Duchess in much the same way as with other mothers. Though none from the dowager Duchess survive, twenty letters from Mrs Wootten do: nine about the Duke, and eleven about his younger brother, Lord Edmund Howard. The absence of formality in them is striking. Their matter-of-fact content ranges over standard boarding-school matters: moods (especially homesickness), foibles and the development of good habits; patterns of sleep, matters of diet and dressing habits; bruises, blisters and other minor ailments arising from schoolboy knocks and falls; toothache, colds and sicknesses requiring medical attention; the acquisition of social virtues, friendships and choice of dormitory comrades; pleasures (cricket, outings, gardening and pets); and dislikes – usually school work. On one occasion she told the Duchess she wished anxious mothers would communicate with her more readily, though she found it difficult both 'to write enough and avoid giving an undue importance to trifles'.[36]

Just one of Darnell's letters to the young Duke survives; in it he specifies the Duke's daily dose of vacation Latin, encouraging him to 'get this dreadful bore [. . .] over as soon as possible after Mass and breakfast', then to practise music and French with his sisters, and to prepare the first canto of the 'Lady of the Lake' with a view to competing for a school prize.[37] The

36. Mrs Wootten to the Duchess of Norfolk, n.d. [1861], Arundel Castle archive, C.581.
37. Darnell to the Duke of Norfolk, 21 July 1861, Arundel Castle archive, C.581.

School of the Oratory, Edgbaston.

Lord Edmund Howard

187*2*   *Lent*   TERM. *Jan. 20 - Ap. 20*

			£	s.	d.	£	s.	d.

EXPENSES OF THIS TERM—

1 Scholastic—

			£	s.	d.	£	s.	d.
Books	*German 4/ . Lardner Philosophy 4/3 Chem's 10/*		1	7	3			
Stationery				5	6			
Printed Music								
Hire of Piano								
Drawing Materials						1	12	9

2 Personal—

			£	s.	d.	£	s.	d.
Clothes—Tailor				3	9			
Shoemaker				8	9			
Linen Draper	*1/2 - 17/6*			18	8			
Hair Dresser				3	0			
Pocket Money—Allowance				5	0			
Additional	*. Watch mended*			5	6			
For Journeys	*Cabs &c*			3	6	9		
Letters, Stamps, &c.					2			
Carriage of Parcels				10	2			
Seat in Church				7	0			
Medical Attendance, &c.								
	Meat at Breakfast 23/4 Pale Ale at Dinner 15/		1	18	4			
	Double washing of Linen		1	1	0	11	0	10

PENSION IN ADVANCE FOR NEXT TERM   33   6   8

Trinity Term commenced on *Ap. 20*ᵗ.

£44 7 6

BANKERS FOR THE ORATORY SCHOOL :—BIRMINGHAM & MIDLAND BANK, BIRMINGHAM. LONDON CORRESPONDENTS :—UNION BANK OF LONDON.

Termly expenses of Lord Edmund Howard, Lent Term 1872.

letter may be indicative of Darnell's drive to force the pace of the school in order to achieve his goal of establishing an academic public school. Certainly there were several indications of an impatience for quick gains: at one time the younger boys were forced on in their mathematics and made to do algebra early, but this had to be abandoned.

It seems that Darnell, exasperated at the boys' behaviour, was capable of resorting to extreme measures once matters had escalated. La Serre has left his vivid (if tongue-in-cheek) impressions of one of Darnell's 'most impressive executions':

> When lo! Darnell burst in, whose index-hand
> Holds forth the virtue of the dreaded wand:
> His wrinkled brow a birchen garland wears,
> Dropping with infants' blood and mothers' tears.
> Over every boy a shuddering horror runs;
> Th'Oratory School shake through all her sons.
> All flesh is humbled. Edgbaston's bold race
> Shrink and confess the genius of the place:
> Each pale young offender yet tingling stands,
> And holds his breeches close with both his hands.[38]

Parents were not long in complaining about his use of corporal punishment, which sometimes involved a boy receiving up to two dozen strokes. Gaisford thought this too severe; and he also objected to floggings before the whole school for small offences, citing the practice at Eton and Rugby, where such floggings were reserved for 'a disgraceful or heinous offence'.[39]

By all accounts Darnell was a very competent schoolmaster. Nevertheless, Newman (like Moody) attributed the disorder in school affairs to 'Darnell letting no one do any thing but himself, and he having no time to spare'.[40] Moreover, as Newman observed, Darnell excluded the other Oratorians 'from any knowledge whatever of school matters and made the School simply his'.[41] Newman had intended that the Fathers

[38.] La Serre, 'Memoirs', p. 6, Arundel Castle archive, MD.2119.
[39.] Gaisford to Newman, 11 January 1862, BOA.
[40.] Newman to Allies, 26 January 1862, *L&D* XX, p. 135.
[41.] Newman to Monsell, 5 January 1862, *L&D* XX, p. 110.

should care for the boys, 'having their direction in spiritual matters and in ecclesiastical functions and devotions',[42] but Darnell's possessive manner stifled this vital contribution; he even fixed the times for First Communion and Confirmation without consulting the other Oratorians, though the prospectus stated that 'The Confessors, with consent of the Father and the Head Master, prepare and send boys to the Sacraments.'[43] It was the old Catholics, being more in tune with expectations at a Catholic establishment, who noticed the lack of spiritual care and instruction under Darnell. They thought that the confessors ought to have a more exclusive and fuller jurisdiction in spiritual matters, and were dismayed to find there were no extra religious activities for boys to attend on a voluntary basis. The teaching of religion was also unsatisfactory: boys did not learn their catechism properly and were unable to say even ordinary prayers. The prospectus stipulated daily attendance at Mass, saying the Rosary before dinner, and a visit to the Blessed Sacrament after evening lessons, but this was far from being the reality.

Naturally, Darnell's outlook was reinforced by the staff he selected, since all appointments lay with him – 'not nominally, but really', as Newman deemed 'it simply necessary that he should be uncontrolled in the matter'.[44] However, when Darnell appointed Henry Oxenham in August 1861, Newman reacted vigorously and complained that he had not been consulted: the constitution required his confirmation of the appointment, but this arrangement, like others, had never been enforced. Oxenham had been educated at Harrow, and had won a classical scholarship to Balliol; after becoming a Catholic in 1857, he had tried his vocation first at the London Oratory and then at St Edmund's, where he gained a reputation as an agitator against authority. Acton later described him as 'a most pungent and persistent fault-finder'.[45] Not surprisingly, Newman was very reluctant to accept Oxenham,

[42]. Congregation decree, 21 April 1858, BOA.
[43]. School prospectus, n.d. [1861], BOA.
[44]. Newman to W. Wilberforce, 3 June 1861, *L&D* XIX, p. 501.
[45]. Acton to Gladstone, 19 February 1875, *Selections from the Correspondence of the First Lord Acton*, ed. J.H. Figgis and R.V. Laurence (London: Longmans, 1917), p. 267.

although Manning had twice sent him to Newman so that he could be given work at the school. Although at the time Newman did not welcome his arrival, he came to regard it as providential, 'for, tho' with us only three months, he brought to a head what otherwise would have lurked in the system, felt but not ascertainable'.[46]

An additional cause of Newman's concern stemmed from the controversy that had blown up in July 1860 as a result of an anonymous letter from Oxenham to *The Rambler*, which amounted to a denunciation of the seminary system. His letter objected to the separate training of clergy from boyhood; the extensive restrictions imposed on reading, which depressed imagination and stunted intellectual development; and the deficient general education. Above all, it deplored the effects of the 'vigorous system of police inspection': 'the Spartan principle, that there is no disgrace in dishonesty, but much disgrace in being caught', a slavish and material obedience, the tendency to make sneaks by the score, the crushing of the affections, and the lack of character formation by personal influence and discriminating sympathy.[47] As Oxenham buttressed his arguments by using Newman's Dublin lectures and mentioning the counter-example of Edgbaston Catholic School, Newman felt obliged to respond. His letter to *The Rambler* objected to the discussion of clerical education in a lay magazine, implying that, 'if the laymen of the *Rambler* wanted the bishops to keep their hands off lay education, they in turn should abstain from criticising that of ecclesiastics'.[48] By chance, Newman chose to sign himself 'H.O.', probably for 'Henry of the Oratory', but also Oxenham's initials. Annoyed that his cover had been blown (or so he thought), Oxenham objected strongly that H.O. had misunderstood Newman; when he realised his blunder – that H.O. *was* Newman – he immediately withdrew from the controversy.

In the debate Oxenham's letter inspired, Simpson sang the praises of the Protestant public school system over the un-English collegiate one, while W.G. Ward vigorously defended

46. Newman to Hope-Scott, 12 January 1862 (not sent), *L&D* XX, p. 122.
47. X.Y.Z. [Oxenham], 'Catholic education', *The Rambler*, July 1860, p. 251.
48. C.S. Dessain, *L&D* XIX, p. xv.

the principles of the collegiate system.[49] The question of whether a Catholic public school was conceivable continued to be debated fiercely over the next two decades, without either side relenting, and since there was no clear verdict the vast majority of old Catholics remained unconvinced and sided with caution. The staff of Edgbaston Catholic School were all too aware that many old Catholics regarded the school as an unwelcome intruder and harboured deep suspicions about it. It is against this background that the public school aspirations paraded in the school's 1861 prospectus need to considered:

> Its object is to afford to Catholic youth the benefit of a system of education similar to that of our great English Public Schools, as far as circumstances will admit. It embraces the same classes of pupils, with the same variety of destinations in life, as are met with and provided for at Eton, Winchester and Harrow.
>
> The Masters and Tutors are chiefly persons educated at those Schools or the English Universities, or at both. [. . .] The School-Hours, Order, Discipline, and Books, are those of an English Public School, so far as they are consistent with Catholic habits and requirements.[50]

[49.] One of the questions discussed was whether it was the Catholic colleges or the public schools that were the true inheritors of pre-Reformation education. In *The Rambler* (September 1861, pp. 346–60) the statutes of Eton and Winchester were analysed to illustrate the extent to which the structures were permeated by religion, and to argue that they could not be equated to current public school practice plus the sacraments. But in a reply (*The Rambler*, November 1861, pp. 119–24) several counter-arguments were presented: that no provision for espionage had been made in the Winchester statutes; that the Eton statutes only applied to the foundationers there, not the great mass of oppidans (just as, at Oxford colleges, rules for the foundationers were aimed at preparation for the priesthood, not as an educational ideal for the majority); that Dr Arnold *developed* a ready-made prefect system at Rugby – he did not *begin* one; and that the *onus probandi* regarding continuity lay with his opponent, as the present-day Catholic system was largely based on the post-Reformation Jesuit model.

[50.] School prospectus, n.d., BOA.

Only six of the school personnel were named: Newman as president, Darnell as headmaster, Moody as second master, Rougemont as third master, and Bittleston and Flanagan as confessors. The prospectus added that the masters were assisted by two tutors (Oxenham and Marshall) and by French, music, drawing and drill-masters. James Marshall, who replaced Ransford, was a bachelor who was popular with the boys, and a good singer and sportsman. Worthy of note is that the three public schools mentioned were precisely those attended by Moody, Darnell and Oxenham respectively. No less striking is the fact that, other than Rougemont, all the academic staff were convert clergymen who had been educated at Oxford, and that the two dames were also converts. Among the Birmingham Oratorians, the only cradle Catholic was John Stanislas Flanagan, who had left the social life and hunting fields of Ireland to study for the priesthood; the other confessor, Henry Bittleston, was another Oxford-educated convert clergyman.

A crisis looms

On medical advice, Newman had left the Oratory in July in order to rest and recover from the stress and insomnia induced in part by his powerlessness to remedy what was patently wrong in the school. The powerful drugs he was taking to combat the psychological strain had brought about a state of complete exhaustion; and his recent fits of absent-mindedness and look of depression suggested he was near to a nervous breakdown – a condition the Moodys had tried to exploit with their gossip. Convinced that he had been elbowed out of his school, Newman made one final attempt to put matters right. At the end of August he wrote to Darnell, warning that the forthcoming six months would be critical as there had been 'indications some time past that a trial may be at hand', and he listed his concerns. There was so much talking in the dormitories at night that the rule of silence no longer held, and other rules had also fallen into neglect; they either needed reinforcing or amending, for 'if one rule is transgressed, others are also; and general idleness is sure to follow on impunity'.

Parents had spoken to him of idleness and lack of progress, and this had been reflected by the poor Easter exams. What system of weekly and monthly 'repetitions' was in place?, he asked. The end-of-term exams needed to be conducted with more solemnity. Discipline was suspect, and he doubted whether Rougemont was up to it. The sudden influx of older boys from schools with different regimes had contributed to a general slackness. Religious education had been neglected; in particular, the confessors did not have adequate access to the boys – and this after Newman had ceded to Darnell's request not to have retreats or confraternities.[51] In short, he hoped Darnell was ready for his 'arduous campaign at home'.[52]

Another cause of unrest that summer was the construction work taking place at the Oratory. The two new houses (67 and 68 Hagley Road) were being converted for school use; a covered stone staircase was erected up the side of the Oratory House to provide direct access to the new dormitories at the top of the Oratory House; and work on the main school building was begun. The sight of expensive and handsome buildings being erected, instead of temporary ones, disappointed parents like Scott-Murray as well as the masters, for it meant that the school was now physically connected to the Oratory and permanently established in Edgbaston. When Scott-Murray visited the Oratory in October he told Newman plainly that he considered absence from a town part of the very essence of a good Catholic school: location by a large conurbation would not allow the boys the freedom of a public school, and he foresaw difficulties if the older boys remained there. Newman's attempted explanation only made matters worse. He agreed with Scott-Murray about the problem, but suggested there was no remedy, on account of the Oratorian Rule; though he went on to talk about whether a reformed Oscott could provide the solution, 'whether it could be *worked* [by the president] *into* a public school – the Seminary and the Bishop giving it up'.[53] Several parents already regarded Edgbaston Catholic School as

---

[51.] Confraternities were devotional associations, whose members were supposed to be earnest in their desire to lead a good Catholic life and eager to uphold the moral tone of the college or school.

[52.] Newman to Darnell, 29 August 1861, *L&D* XX, p. 39.

[53.] Newman, memorandum, 16 February 1862, *L&D* XX, p. 98n.

a feeder for Oscott, but what Newman had in mind for his pupils was rather a reformed college; back in 1846 he had tried to convince Wiseman to remove the 'divines' from Oscott and turn it into a boys' school. Being on friendly terms with the current president of Oscott, Newman obviously had good reason to think this was still a distinct possibility fifteen years later, but the indications that presaged such a radical change have not survived; in fact, the reverse happened, and Oscott ceased taking lay boys in 1889.

After Scott-Murray's departure, Newman realised he had probably misled him with his remarks, which he attributed to being 'in a state of great despondency from having no control over the school, yet seeing many things wrong with it – with a conviction that Fr Nicholas [Darnell] was not up to these wrong things or their removal'.[54] He had not intended to exclude a move to the Oratory's retreat house at Rednal, eight miles away and in the country – a scheme that was revisited a decade later. The episode highlighted the problem of not fully involving all those interested in the project: if a loyal friend like Scott-Murray could be misled so easily, it is not therefore surprising that others should have become confused about the direction of the school's development. The close contact and confidence between Newman and his friends eased some problems, but it is not clear that Newman ever managed to make provision for those parents who were not among his circle of friends. As the parental body grew and the proportion who knew him personally began to drop, other means of communication were called for. Newman only coped by relying heavily on Bellasis, who kept him informed of rumours circulating; sounded out parents about changes, such as fee increases; and made enquiries, obtained character references, and even conducted the interviews when parents who were unknown to Newman applied to the school.

In the autumn of 1861, under the influence of Moody, Scott-Murray and Thynne (all Etonians), Darnell began investigating alternative sites for the school. The attraction of a rural setting and greater independence from the Oratory had become irresistible as the first step towards the attainment of their goal, a

---

[54.] Newman, memorandum, 16 February 1862, *L&D* XX, p. 98n.

true public school. It is difficult to ascertain how developed Darnell's plans were when the affair finally erupted, and who else was involved in them. Moody was undoubtedly a prime mover, as he had always opposed the Edgbaston site, and some of the Oratorians were at least aware of Darnell's investigations – but both Newman and the majority of parents had been kept entirely in the dark. Effectively two distinct groups had formed within the school, each with its own aspirations and schemes; but the whip hand was with Darnell, as he was privy to most of Newman's plans.

Since Darnell's part in the conspiracy was pivotal, it requires some explanation. He had long been granted broad scope to develop the school and had put his heart into it – so much so that his loyalty to the school had displaced his loyalty to the Oratory. Out of touch with the main parental body, and influenced by a small côterie who had a one-sided appreciation of Newman's scheme, he nurtured plans of his own and deluded himself into thinking that he had the backing of Newman for what he did. The plan to move the school into the country, for instance, while always part of Newman's long-term strategy, was not on Newman's immediate horizon. It would seem that Darnell was wilfully deaf and unable to bring himself to face the fact he was no longer working to Newman's plan. Whatever the reason, once the building works had commenced in the summer of 1861 and Newman had begun to question the running of the school, he resorted to a drastic solution.

Darnell made no reply to Newman's letter questioning school policy, either by word of mouth or in writing, a fact which should not have surprised Newman, knowing as he did how sensitive Darnell was to criticism and how hard he took correction. The atmosphere in the school began to show signs of strain as Darnell and Mrs Wootten attempted to consolidate their positions. Darnell made inroads into her domain by depriving her of one of her rooms and interfering with her servants; for her part, she refused to undertake responsibility for the infirmary, which entailed caring for boys with infectious illnesses or requiring night-nursing. The battle, which had been going on for about a year, intensified when Mrs Wootten moved into her new houses next to the Oratory in the summer of 1861.[55] By then a rift had opened up between her and all the masters, leading them to disregard not only Mrs Wootten but Newman himself, and to reduce their part in the school to a minimum. She was held up to ridicule and called names, especially by Marshall, the tutor assigned to her house. Darnell's colourful description, although expressed to Newman in the heat of the moment, once the affair had blown up, indicated the extent of the division:

> she has utterly lost my confidence, has thrown contempt and defiance at all my Masters and Tutors, who have ventured within her circle (reaping in return from each enduring dislike and disgust) has treated with scorn such of my intentions in regard to the external working of the School as I have ventured to mention to her, has thwarted them to the utmost by encountering them with embarrassing propositions of her own, has endeavoured to tamper with the loyalty of my boys, as also with the fidelity of my servants – has made house arrangements without reference to me, has scor[n]ed dormitory rules with her remarks on their non observance and *in fine* has generally acted as 'plenâ potestate Praefecta', in expressed assurance of indemnity and absolution from Fr Ambrose [St John] and yourself.

And he accused her of being 'a german Princess regnant with a back way to the Emperors of Russia and Austria when she falls out with Prussia'.[56] Though the charge of being a tale-bearer was quite false, her behaviour may have been erratic as she was in delicate health; that autumn, unbeknown to Darnell or Newman, she had been spitting blood and was convinced she was about to die.

With Darnell and his masters on the lookout for an opportunity to diminish Mrs Wootten's power, it did not take much to trigger the crisis. The trivial incident which did so occurred in

---

55. When Michaelmas term began, there were twenty-five boys at 67–68 Hagley Road and six at 6 Vicarage Road, all under Mrs Wootten, and another twenty under Miss Ffrench at 97 Hagley Road.

56. Darnell to Newman, 10 December 1861, BOA.

early December when a boy confined to bed was spotted out of
school with Mrs Wootten's permission on two successive days,
first at a local bazaar and then at the Birmingham Dog Show:
the treats had been intended to lift the boy's spirits and placate
his anxious mother, not as an act of defiance. In response,
Darnell ordered the boy back into school and sent Mrs
Wootten a copy of the school notice he had issued, which
declared: 'The Head Master will allow no boy who is not on the
sick list, to enter a Dame's room on any pretext whatever
without leave from his Tutor. No boy on the sick list, can leave
his own house and premises without the Head Master's express
permission.'[57] Mrs Wootten's immediate response was to ask
Newman how she was to proceed under the circumstances; she
offered to resign, or else to stay 'as Matron to the Boys, or
Housekeeper over the servants',[58] for the new instructions
meant she would be unable to fulfil her duties – though, she
added, if *Parents release me from these duties to which I have pledged
myself*, I can be the sort of dame the new rule calls for'.[59] To
continue in her former role, she demanded that certain conditions be met: boys should have access to her in their playtime,
those entrusted to her needed to be lodged in her houses, and
she should have the command of her houses and servants.
There had been occasions when Mrs Wootten proved tiresome
and had driven Newman to distraction with her dithering – but
these demands were serious. Newman was alert to the immediate implications of the dispute: if Darnell gave up his post 'it
would ruin us with the world – if Mrs W does it will ruin us
with the mothers, and rob us of the *only* real advantage that we
have over other schools'. St John's first reaction was similar: he
wondered how Darnell intended to answer the inevitable
furious parents. But Newman was unsure how to proceed
because Darnell regarded him as having sided with Mrs
Wootten, and therefore as an unsuitable arbitrator.

Newman decided to urge Darnell to accept Mrs Wootten's
conditions, suggesting that rules could be drawn up to allow
both of them to act in their respective spheres without collision;

[57.] *L&D* XX, p. 76n.
[58.] Mrs Wootten to St John, 4 December 1861, BOA.
[59.] Mrs Wootten to Newman, 7 December 1861, BOA.

where their provinces overlapped she should give way. Darnell thought otherwise. He felt that Newman, by focusing on Mrs Wootten's grievances, was avoiding the issue: the 'practicability of a renewal, of the entente cordiale' between Mrs Wootten and the rest of the school staff. He regarded it as absurd that he, Darnell, should concede her establishment as an independent authority; and he declared he was not prepared 'to sacrifice the School and my own independent action there as its Head Master (involving of course that of all who are cooperating with me in it) to the hypothetical interests' of two or three boys requiring Mrs Wootten's special care – though he conceded that a *few* boys could be assigned to her. To achieve a reconciliation and a working relationship, Darnell argued, new guidelines for the dames were required. He added that his remarks about Mrs Wootten were made strictly in his capacity as headmaster; otherwise he regarded her 'as my most unselfish benefactress, my most willing servant, and most tender nurse and second mother'[60] – a remark which vividly illustrates the extremes of mood to which he was prone.

Newman's reflex action at the first sign of trouble had been to contact Bellasis, to ask for his advice and that of Hope-Scott and anyone else they considered it worth consulting; he confided that he found himself taking sides with Mrs Wootten. Meanwhile, he reminded Darnell that without his (Newman's) name the school would not exist, and that the majority of parents had made him responsible for it; Darnell's dismissal of the right of appeal, on the part of subordinates in the school, to Newman as president was unacceptable. Only now, it seems, did Darnell finally grasp that Newman 'intended to inflict Mrs Wootten on the School and me for the future [...] a coordinate jurisdiction – Mrs Wootten supreme in the house – myself in the School'.[61] This is surprising to say the least, because Newman's intentions had been spelt out clearly not only in the school manifesto (issued in February 1859) but also in his scheme for the administration of the school (approved by the Oratorians in December 1860).

In his outright rejection of the dame's right of appeal to the

[60.] Darnell to Newman, 10 December 1861, BOA.
[61.] Darnell to Newman, 19 December 1861, BOA.

president, Darnell effectively rejected Newman's whole scheme. For Darnell, Mrs Wootten was his subordinate, not Newman's, and so her appeal to the president must pass through him. He now invoked public school practice in support of his case: at Eton or Harrow it was unheard-of that dames should appeal directly to the provost or the governors, respectively; nor did any such right exist at Winchester – there, as elsewhere, it was doubtful whether even the masters (except for the second master) could appeal against the headmaster. 'Here, as there, the only remedy is for the insubordinate Dame to return to her duty to her proper Superior – or to go.'[62] Darnell declared that concession to Mrs Wootten's demands would be tantamount to a vote of non-confidence in him as headmaster; and he told Mrs Wootten that he would regard her stay beyond Christmas as the signal that his services in the school were superfluous. Undoubtedly he was egged on by Moody and Oxenham, who meanwhile had pressurised Marshall and Rougemont into signing a letter which declared that they would all resign if Darnell did. The presumption was that they were in a strong enough position to be able to dictate terms, as Newman would be unable to accept a general resignation.

Before receiving Darnell's ultimatum, Newman had already had a long conversation with Bellasis, after which he decided to insist on three points 'without which, as first conditions, the school had better not be'. In the first place, Newman was the 'immediate Superior of the school', so communication between him and the staff did *not* have to pass through the headmaster; a right of appeal to Newman existed, as the counterpart to his right of supervision over all of them. Secondly, all property belonged to the Congregation, whereas Darnell had 'kept back certain engagements or leases' – these anomalies had to be removed. Finally, confessors had to be 'allowed their free influence upon the boys, and not be dealt with in any peremptory manner'.[63] But however vital these clarifications were, once he had received the ultimatum Newman realised it was now too

---

[62.] Darnell to Newman, 19 December 1861, BOA.
[63.] Newman to Darnell, 17 December 1861 (draft; not sent), *L&D* XX, pp. 82–83.

late to insist on them, so instead he put Darnell under obedience not to proceed further until they met, and requested Mrs Wootten to do likewise.

For much of autumn 1861 Newman was away in London convalescing, returning to the Oratory for Sundays, and so most of his dealings with Darnell and Mrs Wootten were by letter; at this moment he was nearing the end of a four-week stay at the Bowdens, convert friends who had a son at the school. Anxious to glean what he could about the dispute before the likely showdown in Birmingham, he broached the topic with Mrs Bowden. She turned out to be remarkably well-informed and was able to name fourteen boys who had shown exceptional loyalty to Mrs Wootten, after Darnell's notice forbidding them to see her. Both the Bowdens urged Newman to submit to 'almost any inconvenience to retain her', so much did they value her 'care and tender management'.[64] When Bellasis first heard that Mrs Wootten might retire, he immediately relayed the news to Darnell. He explained that he had of course contradicted the rumour; and he pointed out what seemed obvious to him, that her retirement would be a fatal mistake because, although the school was prospering, it was unable to do without her. Unaware of the political situation at the school, he reported that some boys spoke disparagingly about her and suggested Darnell remove the master encouraging them.

A practical solution to the whole problem was proposed by one of the original promoters, Richard Macmullen, who suggested that, since sooner or later the school would have to be divided into upper and lower parts, now was a propitious moment to enact this division, with Darnell assuming full control of the upper school, leaving the younger boys under Mrs Wootten's care. Bellasis agreed with the strategy and, after sounding out a few parents, he informed Newman that their reaction was favourable. Primed with this (limited) information Newman entered the final phase of the crisis he was later to describe as the most acute, though the briefest, he ever had to face.

[64.] Bowden to Newman, 25 December 1861, BOA.

The Oratorians meet

Since the dispute involved two Oratorians, himself and Darnell, Newman decided that it should be resolved as an internal matter of the Oratory. On Christmas Eve the Oratorians met and Newman presented his view of the situation. Quoting from the school manifesto and the decree sanctioning the plan, he asserted that the school was his insofar as it could be separated from the Congregation, and insofar as the 'origination and administration can be separated from money matters'; the point at issue was whether Mrs Wootten was Darnell's 'servant'. Newman then unveiled the compromise solution of splitting the school into two. Darnell would become headmaster of the upper school, with Moody and Oxenham as under-masters and 'no Dames in my sense of the word', only servants, appointed by Darnell and with no right of appeal; Newman would become headmaster of the lower school, assisted by dames like Mrs Wootten. As president of the school as a whole, Newman would determine the precise moment the transfer of boys from lower to upper school would take place; it would be at about thirteen, but taking into account 'the particular case, the wishes of parents, and the opinion of the Masters'. Dining arrangements would continue as they were, the older boys eating at Miss Ffrench's and the younger ones at Mrs Wootten's. Besides providing a way round the impasse, the plan had 'in its rudiments been in the idea of various persons from the first' and would, Newman believed, meet with the approval of masters and parents.[65] The meeting was then adjourned for three days to allow Darnell to consult friends; it also gave Newman the opportunity to consult his.

To judge from their insights and suggestions, Bellasis and Hope-Scott appear to have been more alive to the deeper issues than Newman. Bellasis told Newman he thought the underlying issue was one of control: was Darnell the 'real sole acting head', with Newman and the Oratory as *nominal* superiors in authority, or was he in real terms Newman's subordinate? Everyone Bellasis had spoken to thought that the link between the school and the Oratory was essential. Hope-

[65.] Newman, Paper proposing a compromise, *L&D* XX, pp. 86–87.

Scott had told him that Darnell's view was wholly inadmissible: it was Newman's name and, to a degree, Mrs Wootten's that had 'brought the school together' – not Darnell's. There had to be no doubt who was in charge. The 'Wootten case', as Hope-Scott dubbed the crisis, was a mere incident: there was no point in patching it up, because the underlying problem of Darnell's independent action was bound to resurface. Hope-Scott recommended that the Oratorians go beyond the immediate issue, and address 'the question of the continued authority and action upon the school of yourself and the Fathers'; Darnell had to submit or go. It was better to have a clean break than to delay and allow gossip to spread. Sensing that the independent action extended beyond Darnell, Hope-Scott recommended that Newman's authority be explicitly acknowledged by all the masters, for there was 'probably a crisis in the school, upon which its future welfare may depend'.[66] He advised against any further airing of the issue with parents and friends of the school, and urged Newman to act decisively.

But some damage had already been done. Darnell accused Bellasis of interfering, by influencing a parent against him, and warned him that 'I am a public school man, and that I have public school men on and by my side; and that with their assistance, I at least believe myself to be going straight towards our great desideratum in the present day – a public school'. He accused Bellasis of taking sides, and challenged him to reveal whether he had broached the idea of partitioning the school with 'parents or friends of any [of our] boys who are public school men', as he had with old Catholics; and he ended with a demand for 'the most ample and unqualified apology'.[67] To his discomfiture Bellasis replied that, of the six people he had approached, three were public school men; and so it was Darnell who had to apologise.

When the Oratorians reconvened, two days after Christmas, Darnell declared that he was resolutely against Newman's proposal and would resign immediately unless Mrs Wootten left at once, and raised the stakes by hinting that all the masters would do likewise. He dismissed the proposed division of the

[66.] Bellasis to Newman, 24 December 1861, *L&D* XX, p. 88.
[67.] Darnell to Bellasis, 26 December 1861, BOA.

school as unworkable, since buildings would be shared and boys divided arbitrarily. Despite lengthy and repeated protestations from Newman, he adamantly refused to accept any compromise, even the possibility of remaining until Easter so as to avoid scandal. Faced with these stark alternatives, the meeting was adjourned once again. To add to Newman's worries, he received a note the same evening from Ignatius Ryder, the youngest Oratorian, who warned that the Congregation was likely to back Darnell. What had begun apparently as a dispute within the school now revealed serious divisions within the Oratory: three of the other seven Oratorians were siding against Newman.

Addressing the meeting the following morning, Newman summed up Darnell's case: unwilling to compromise, he wished, by his 'strong act of supremacy', to prove that he had 'supreme power over the school' to the exclusion of everyone else. Newman's case was that the school was his, just as the boys' orphanage was Flanagan's; it could be taken away from him or even closed, but until that time it was under his control. 'I believe the parents have entrusted their children to *me*', he said, and added, 'I believe in my heart that Mrs Wootten has been the real cause of its growth'. The parents had asked for personal care for the young boys and a liberal education, and these two desiderata were to be supplied by Mrs Wootten and Darnell. From the nature of the case, the second object could not be fulfilled so quickly as the first:

> I believe the fruit of Fr Nicholas's exertions are to come, and those of Mrs Wootten have been immediate. The great care taken of the persons of the boys, of soul and body, has, in my judgement, been the cause of the success of the school. And [...] in giving up Mrs Wootten, I give up the chief cause of the school's prosperity.[68]

It was for the Oratorians to decide whether the school was Newman's, as direct originator of the undertaking, or Darnell's, under the supremacy of the Congregation over them both. This, he ventured, was the very question that had been

---

[68.] Newman, Second paper, 28 December 1861, *L&D* XX, p. 90.

contested between the Moodys and Mrs Wootten all along. He had found it hard to convince himself that Darnell's view of the school differed from his own, but having realised that this was indeed the case, he warned that 'if things were as he [Darnell] would have them', there was trouble ahead, because 'the mode of conducting the great schools of Eton, Winchester etc, necessarily end[s] in subordinating religion to secular interests and principles; and that this consequence would ensue in ours, but for the presence of Matrons of a high class and of spiritual directors'.[69] He proposed that he and Darnell take their leave and let the remaining Oratorians decide who the head of the school was, though, from what he had heard, it seemed likely they would rule against him.

Once the provost had spoken, the other Oratorians were given the opportunity to state their views. St John argued that they should ascertain the real cause of the 'direct formal unyielding opposition' between Newman and Darnell, as Mrs Wootten was clearly not the cause but only the occasion of the dispute. No one doubted she would resign if asked, but greater principles were involved, and if these could not be resolved, he felt that the school should be closed. Flanagan then spoke, protesting that Newman's claim – that the school was Newman's – was quite new to him, and probably to others too; he had assumed that Newman was 'president of the school in virtue of being superior of the Congregation to whom the school belonged', and that when it sanctioned Darnell as Newman's representative, Darnell became the representative of the Congregation too. He conceded that the documents quoted supported Newman's case, but asked if it was possible to ignore the 'real practical position': the Oratory was pledged to the school, it had invested heavily in it, and in the eyes of the world it was identified with it. In a matter of such vital importance, he thought, the Congregation deserved a voice; for him, the question to be decided was whether the loss of Darnell or Mrs Wootten would be the greater blow to the school, and therefore to the Congregation; as a compromise, he suggested that Darnell remain until Easter, on condition that Mrs Wootten took leave until then.[70]

[69.] Newman, Second paper, 28 December 1861, *L&D* XX, p. 91.
[70.] St John's and Flanagan's papers, BOA.

Newman requested time to think matters over and consult friends, but Darnell and Flanagan demanded an instant reply. Newman refused, and eventually they gave way and the meeting was adjourned for a third time. And so matters would have rested, but for discussion on how best to secure silence; Newman, naturally enough, presumed that news of Darnell's threatened resignation was not in the public domain – whereupon Darnell dropped his bombshell and revealed that he had made his resignation public in writing to friends in London the previous night. He must have realised how startling this revelation was, because he immediately declared that he was, in fact, unwilling to remain, even if the Congregation decided in his favour; he then produced the resignation letter signed by all the masters. The news that Darnell's resignation was already public meant that a compromise was pointless, and the meeting finished abruptly; without further ado, Newman took the opportunity to remove Moody by accepting his resignation. Darnell assumed his fate was also sealed, and he asked to be released from his obligations to the Oratory, though protracted attempts were made to persuade him to change his mind on both counts.[71] Miss Ffrench, a great friend and supporter of Darnell, resigned too. Thus the combined effect of Darnell's gamble was that Newman was left with just one dame. Newman alerted Hope-Scott: 'I come to Town to get some Masters etc at once. I must go into the School myself for a while'.[72]

Four years after these events, Darnell admitted that 'my conduct was insufferably violent, headstrong and conceited generally to the Congregation, and still more insufferably insolent, ungrateful and ungracious to the Father [Newman]'.[73] His admission confirms that although personality and mood played an important role in the crisis, the reasons for it need to be looked for elsewhere. Much the same could be said about Moody's animosity towards Newman, which was a contributory factor but not a cause of the crisis. When Edgbaston Catholic School opened in May 1859, the future looked rosy; and the early developments appeared to give substance to the initial

---

[71.] Newman, memorandum, 4 January 1862, *L&D* XX, pp. 91–93.
[72.] Newman to Hope-Scott, 28 December 1861, *L&D* XX, p. 94.
[73.] Darnell to Caswall, 15 October 1865, *L&D* XXII, p. 75n.

optimism. It began, too, with a promising team – Newman, Darnell and Mrs Wootten – which looked ideal for the task in hand. Why, then, did the staff mutiny take place? Historians have come up with a variety of explanations, attributing the crisis variously to a clash of personalities, faulty organisational structures, disagreement about the rate of achieving independence from the Oratory, and the battle for overall control of the school. As we have seen, there is an element of truth in each. Fortunately, the surviving letters and other documents relating to the school's early life and the crisis itself – over three hundred of them – virtually eliminates the need for guesswork. From the evidence it is plain that Darnell was set on matching the best public schools, but at the expense of vital aspects of the foundation; he 'concentrated on making it only too like a public school, without the Catholic and indeed human and gentle counterweights, that Newman considered necessary'.[74] Newman was later to remark that, but for the crisis, 'the school would have become essentially a Protestant one, if we had gone on, as it was going'.[75]

In agreeing to undertake the project of establishing the first Catholic public school, Newman had counted on those undertaking the key roles to identify themselves with his vision. This was particularly important because of the inbuilt bias, due to the preponderance of converts involved in the school plan, leading to the risk that the Catholic dimension would be neglected in striving after the more familiar goal of a public school. As events showed, only Mrs Wootten among all the staff held out for the coherent whole envisaged by Newman. The affair was, at root, a battle for control of the school and the right to determine its destiny; yet it can also be viewed more broadly as another example of the tensions that characterised the Catholic body at the time. Newman found himself between two camps, both of which suspected him of belonging to the other. From outside the school and the Oratory those with Ultramontane tendencies suspected him of holding dangerously secular ideas about education; many old Catholics

---

[74.] Dessain, *L&D* XX, p. xiii.
[75.] Newman to Hope-Scott, 12 January 1862 (not sent), *L&D* XX, p. 122.

thought that the converts were unable to pass on the Church's teaching adequately, and their suspicions can only have been reinforced by reports they heard of the neglect of religious education. By contrast, those with Liberal Catholic tendencies suspected Newman of favouring a narrow Catholic education: this small but influential lobby happened to be well represented among the masters, parents and friends of the school. Thus Ker is entirely accurate in his analysis of the crisis, that Newman 'occupied the middle ground [...] between conventional Catholic educators and those like Darnell who wanted the Oratory School to be as like an English public school as possible'.[76] The staff's failure to grasp the importance of Mrs Wootten's role was indicative of a more general failure to appreciate the personal and spiritual side of the school, precisely the aspect that Newman was particularly keen to emphasise. Darnell's assertive and inflexible attitude was a secondary cause of the crisis because, by blocking Newman's involvement, he prevented a remedy being applied. Undoubtedly the dispute was allowed to fester because of Newman's lack of involvement in school affairs; but it is hard to judge to what extent this stemmed from the pressing nature of Newman's other commitments, to what extent from his underestimation of the attention the new foundation would require. In the day-to-day functioning of the school there were countless decisions to be made, many of which would ultimately determine its nature as a lay Catholic school, and the process required the judgement and long-term vision of a Newman.

In founding the Catholic University in Dublin, Newman had thought long and hard about how to supply the absence of a tradition. Given that his friends were expecting him to adopt a similarly painstaking approach with the school, it is surprising that the crucial task of shaping and forming it should have been delegated. At the same time, Newman thought (reasonably enough) that it was easy for people to say, 'Oh, Dr Newman has neglected to look after the school', and 'rather cool' to ask someone over sixty to do more than 'confide the school to a trustworthy person. Such I thought Fr Darnell to

[76]. I.T. Ker, *John Henry Newman: a Biography* (Oxford: Clarendon Press, 1988), p. 505.

be, and they thought so too, independent of me.'[77] It was a mistake he would not make again.

Newman's line of action during the crisis is also worthy of note. He had been effectively cut off from school affairs and, despite a late rally and vigorous liaison with parents, had had to form judgements deprived of much relevant information. In defending his vision of the school, he had represented the parents. The sheer pace of events had given him no alternative other than to take decisions without the consultation he would have preferred, and it is noteworthy that on the few occasions he could, he sued for time in order to confer with those he represented. By contrast, he did not consult the Oratorians, for he was acting not on their behalf but on the parents'. In remaining loyal to Mrs Wootten, Newman remained loyal to the school founders – the parents and promoters who desired a public school that was fully Catholic.

78. Newman to Bellasis, 20 April 1862, *L&D* XX, p. 190.

Chapter 4

Rescue Operation

Crisis management

On 28 December 1861 Newman suddenly found himself in charge of a school with fifty-six boys, one dame and no masters, and which was due to begin term within a month. The rescue operation undertaken during this four-week period was masterminded by Bellasis, Hope-Scott and Newman. Together they functioned as a caretaker management committee, engaging new staff at short notice, communicating with parents, limiting the damage the rebel masters could cause, and deliberating over changes. To accomplish their mission the three-man committee kept in close contact with each other; over fifty letters survive from a hectic three-week spell during which they passed on information, exchanged opinions, and circulated important draft replies or notices. To the first emergency meeting in London, on 30 December, Bellasis brought a strongly-worded letter from Scott-Murray which expressed his disappointment in the school, and it provoked discussion on several important questions: how many parents felt like Scott-Murray; would they able to have a school for older boys; and should the Oratory apply to Rome for permission for a large school? They drew up a list of possible masters, and also discussed whether any of the former ones could be taken back. Hope-Scott argued against re-engaging them, as they had effectively taken part in a conspiracy, and he urged Newman to involve himself fully in school business.

Newman decided to act on the recommendations of Thomas Allies for prospective candidates for the posts of first and second masters, Robert Campbell and Richard Pope respectively. (Both were married converts, with families.) Pope telegraphed from Gibraltar, where he was vice-principal of St Bernard's School, to accept the post of second master; he turned out to be a superb appointment and remained at the school for thirty-eight years. Campbell, however, had just been appointed master of the newly-opened grammar school in Dublin and did not feel he could accept. St John was dispatched to Dublin with a 'shopping list' from Newman comprised of lecturers at the Catholic University, topped by the name of Thomas Arnold, the younger son of the famous headmaster of Rugby. He had been educated at Rugby, Winchester and University College Oxford, and had become a Catholic during his stay in Tasmania, where he worked as a school inspector. Arnold had declined Newman's original offer of a mastership in May 1858 because he was enthusiastic about the prospects of the Catholic University, where he was professor of English literature; besides, he saw 'no *future*, no likelihood of promotion' at the school.[1] At the insistence of several promoters, Newman had been on the point of asking him again later that year, despite the risk of appearing to poach him from the university, but had withheld his revised offer on account of the financial uncertainty of the school plan. Now Arnold accepted the offer made him, and St John proceeded to negotiate his loan until Easter, Arnold being unwilling to commit himself for longer unless offered the head-mastership.

Though two of the rebel masters were quick to repent and asked to be reinstated, the committee had doubts about doing so, foreseeing the problems this would give the new headmaster; yet they also realised the importance of breaking up the coalition, as this would both reduce the impact of the rebellion and provide the school with much-needed continuity. The abbé Rougemont apologised first, attributing his actions to the pressure exerted on him and pleading ignorance of the character of English schools; and, after writing what Newman considered a 'very proper' letter, he was received back.

[1.] Arnold to Newman, 1 May 1858, BOA.

Newman was against receiving any such overtures from Marshall, though Bellasis was inclined to think otherwise – except that his antipathy for Mrs Wootten remained. Marshall's third letter to Newman seems to have tipped the balance and the committee agreed to take him back, though Marshall still felt honour bound to see Darnell before accepting. Consequently, within a fortnight, a full complement of masters was found. (La Serre, the French priest who had arrived from St Omer the previous year, continued as a tutor and part-time French teacher; being on the periphery of school affairs, he had not been involved in the staff mutiny.) The replacement for Miss Ffrench was Miss Sophia Mitchell, former governess of a friend of Newman's. Before she applied, Mrs Ward had explained what her duties would involve. At her interview Newman emphasised the responsibility her job entailed: she would be independent, with her own servants at her command and a salary, and under no-one but one of the Oratorians. Though she was forty-four, Newman thought she looked too young for the job, but she felt confident the boys would not be 'uppish with her'.[2]

One of the most complex matters the committee had to address was the business of communicating with parents, deciding what to tell them, when and how. As the situation kept changing, the committee's cautious approach paid dividends. No sooner had he resigned than Darnell began visiting parents and friends, speaking freely about taking boys to set up a rival school.[3] Besides being a means of saving face by telling his version of events, his visits were an attempt to apply leverage so that the rebel masters could be reinstated. The five of them met on 2 January and debated whether they should communicate jointly with the parents. Rougemont and Marshall objected; Darnell was unhappy too, and distanced himself by staying away from the next meeting two days later. Moody and Oxenham decided to press ahead with a manifesto, which they circulated to a few friends, but without Darnell's

[2.] Newman to St John, 15 January 1862, *L&D* XX, p. 128.
[3.] In the context of the mid-nineteenth century this would have been the normal course of action for a man in his position, except that he was a subject of the Oratorian Congregation.

signature it lacked credibility; over the following weeks they tried to persuade him to sign, but in vain.

While it was obvious to the caretaker committee that neither Moody nor Oxenham could return, Darnell's case posed a problem: he was a priest of the Oratory and Newman was his superior. Darnell had asked to be released from the Oratory, but three days later suspended his request: his behaviour continued to be unpredictable. He had been staying with the Pollens, who tried their utmost to convince him to return to the Oratory; they were in close communication with Newman and Bellasis, and asked the committee to try to keep him nominally in office by giving him six months' leave of absence and reorganising the school in his absence. Indications that Darnell was undergoing a change of heart led Hope-Scott to advise against issuing any list of staff until the new term was under way. At this juncture, Newman envisaged Darnell 'returning to his post [after six months], *if he would* – or else, attempting something in the way of an incipient upper school under him to be placed near Rednall'.[4]

Despite the positive indications, hopes for Darnell's return receded as other friends managed to undo the efforts of the Pollens – at which point Bellasis diagnosed the problem: 'he is so weak that the last speaker has him'.[5] Pollen was able to send the uplifting news that not one of Darnell's London friends was backing him in the dispute. Nevertheless Newman was wary that Darnell might continue to see parents and attempt to siphon off boys for a school of his own, and so the threat of a rival school lingered on. In fact, Moody continued agitating with Oxenham even though Oscott had taken him on. Meanwhile, Darnell was granted six months' leave from the Oratory, which he accepted. Despite Hope-Scott's earlier advice, Newman had a list of staff printed for circulation to the parents; he was keen to use the opportunity of advertising 'so great a gun as the son of Dr Arnold',[6] and thought that if the list accompanied the bills for the coming term, it would dissuade wavering parents from withdrawing their sons at

[4]· Newman to Hope-Scott, 5 January 1962, *L&D* XX, p. 109.
[5]· Bellasis to Newman, 8 January 1862, BOA.
[6]· Newman to Hope-Scott, 8 January 1862, *L&D* XX, p. 114.

Easter. He considered adding a few lines restating the aims, 'the object of the School being to unite the system of the English Public Schools with the careful personal religious training which is a first necessity with Catholics',[7] as he was concerned that they might be forced to make a public statement if Darnell and his supporters appealed to parents.

With the start of the new term approaching, the question arose of whether the school would be ready in time. Gaisford and Hope-Scott recommended delaying a week, but Newman was adamant that a delay would gain them nothing. So, on 18 January parents were sent the new list of staff and a circular letter, together with their bills. The letter explained that several parents had requested clearer arrangements for the start of term, as the existing confusion made some unwilling to send them to a partially filled school; in future the day of return was to be 'imperative', but in view of the short notice being given Newman declared that Monday 27 January would be the *last* day of return.[8] Parents were quick to welcome the new arrangements. On 24 January all the masters were in place ready to receive the boys, and by night-prayers on 27 January the schoolroom was full: with the exception of boys who were ill, only one was missing, and notice of his withdrawal (on account of excessive punishments meted out by Darnell) had been given the previous term. Not only had the parents given Newman their full support, but they had gone to some trouble to cooperate with the new arrangements. There were several new boys, too.

Hope-Scott's advice

Once term began the caretaker committee was *de facto* dissolved, since their immediate goal, the rescue of the school,

---

[7.] Newman to Hope-Scott, 12 January 1862 (not sent), *L&D* XX, p. 122.

[8.] Newman's insistence on a crisp, coordinated start to an academic session had been in evidence at Oxford; as a tutor at Oriel, he had proposed that undergraduates be admitted once a year, all together, whereas previously new college members were admitted three times a year, or more often.

had been achieved, and in a manner beyond their expectations. Yet the committee did much more than patch up; they addressed the deeper issues at play and effectively set the school in a new direction. For this reason, their deliberations in the run-up to 27 January need to be looked at in some detail. Newman regarded the Darnell affair as one of those early difficulties that were to be expected – 'such catastrophes take place in all nascent and inchoate institutions',[9] he remarked. More remote from the catastrophe than Newman, Hope-Scott was alert to its purgative effects. He sensed that 'this disturbance, painful in all ways, may be the appointed means of determining the future character of the School';[10] it was 'an opportunity for bringing into play, for the benefit of the School, all the lessons which experience has taught: and probably alone could teach'.[11] Many of the insights that led to a re-formation and reorganisation of the school issued from his mind, and during these critical weeks Newman constantly sought his counsel.[12]

To enable Bellasis and Hope-Scott to help him resolve the 'Darnell affair', Newman decided to provide a clear picture of its origins, and to this end he compiled a selection of the important documents relating to it (fourteen in all) together with some connecting narrative of his own. Hope-Scott was the first to inspect this, and on the evidence gave his verdict that Mrs Wootten had acted reasonably. It was plain that Darnell and some of the masters had been 'gradually framing a new constitution for the school, different from that announced in the

[9] Newman to Ornsby, 31 January 1862, *L&D* XX, p. 143.
[10] Hope-Scott to Newman, 4 January 1862, BOA.
[11] Hope-Scott to Newman, 5 January 1862, BOA.
[12] Besides their close friendship, Newman sought Hope-Scott's advice because he was an expert in educational matters. As a Fellow, he was asked to compile a report for reforming Merton College Oxford along the lines of its medieval statutes, and soon afterwards embarked on an extensive *History of the Colleges* with his friend Roundell Palmer, the future Lord Chancellor. In 1840 he began collaborating with William Gladstone to found 'an Eton, on very moderate terms' (Ornsby, *Memoirs II*, p. 209) to provide the Episcopal Church with a much-needed collegiate institution for the education of its ministers. Gladstone's growing political commitments meant that the organisational burden of establishing Trinity College Glenalmond fell on Hope-Scott.

prospectus, and having a distinct tendency to withdraw it, at no distant period, from all real connection with the Oratory'; a crisis would shortly have occurred in any case, with or without Mrs Wootten. To avoid confusion about the relationship between the school and the Oratory, one principle was clear from the affair: 'If the Oratory is to lend its name and incur responsibility, the Congregation must be supreme; and so far as individual Oratorians take part in its management, they must do so with the constant sense that they are merely officers of that body.'[13] This would eliminate a perception of the school which led to Marshall speaking of '*our* Headmaster' and, more seriously, Darnell's reference to '*my* Masters'. (In a similar vein, Acton had begun to refer to the school as 'Darnell's school'.) When suggesting modifications to Newman's draft letters to returning masters, Hope-Scott urged him not to miss the opportunity of replying more fully on the question of authority 'so as to lay the foundation of a better system hereafter'.[14]

Hope-Scott's analysis effectively ratified the change in the school's name. In the first prospectus it had appeared as 'Edgbaston Catholic School', but in 1861 it was called 'School of the Oratory, Edgbaston'.[15] The change of name reflected a change of control, from the school as an undertaking of individuals – Newman and Darnell – to one of a body, the Oratory. This progression from individual enterprise to corporate undertaking was an inevitable part of growing up, though the rite of passage had come earlier than expected. Hope-Scott certainly approved: before the school had even opened he had advised Bellasis that, if Newman were to take the lead, it should be an Oratorian school, since in his view education best thrived under a religious body. In putting safety first and yielding to an arrangement that was tried and tested, Newman retreated from grappling with a new solution such as Scott-Murray's – the idea that the school could be 'independent of the Oratory as a body, and even possibly in lay hands'.[16]

13. Hope-Scott to Newman, 4 January 1862, BOA.
14. Hope-Scott to Bellasis, 5 January 1862, BOA.
15. In the three decades after 1861, two names were used on the prospectuses and other school documents: 'The School of the Oratory, Edgbaston' and 'The Oratory School, Edgbaston'.
16. Scott-Murray to Bellasis, 22 December 1861, *L&D* XX, p. 98.

Analysing the affair, Hope-Scott opined that Newman's proper consideration of the dispute had been rendered impossible by the precipitate action of Darnell and the masters, and that *they* were therefore the cause of the scandal and disorder. Newman's authority had been undermined. The school had been founded by him, with the assent of the Congregation, on the principle that it depended on the Oratory and was under him as its chief; he had allotted the house to Mrs Wootten and the schoolroom to Darnell as 'coordinates' under himself. Darnell's claim that Mrs Wootten and the whole school were under him alone was a departure from this idea. The results of Darnell's attitude had been painfully illustrated in his attempt to dictate terms to Newman and the Congregation. The question of defining the limits of jurisdiction lay ultimately with the Congregation: in trying to win the dispute by force, Darnell's action was subversive not only of the primary idea of the school but of the discipline of a religious body. The question of Mrs Wootten's position was subordinate to the question of authority. In Hope-Scott's view, Darnell could not complain if others should interpret his claims and acts as a deliberate intent to withdraw the school, 'morally if not locally', from its dependence on the Oratory.[17]

Hope-Scott's analysis of the affair was masterly, and Newman relied on it for numerous explanatory letters; he also heeded his practical suggestions. Hope-Scott favoured the proposal to send Darnell away for six months, to enable Newman to form the school on his own lines, and then allow Darnell to return to run it; he advised against adopting Scott-Murray's plan – Mrs Wootten asking for six months' leave for reasons of health – as it was likely to prolong the uncertainty and provide fresh disruptions. In his opinion, Newman was master of the situation and ought not to surrender his position. The separate question of an upper school, favoured but not founded by the Oratory and at some distance from it, was best postponed. Hope-Scott thought the Oratory 'should supply the whole *authority*', and do so by providing a president and vice-president (or 'Prefect of studies'); the senior and junior masters should come under them.[18] This

---

[17.] Hope-Scott, memorandum, 5 January 1862, BOA.
[18.] Hope-Scott to Bellasis, 31 December 1861, BOA.

view was endorsed, and the new staff list gave the names and titles of four Oratorians before those of Arnold, Pope and Rougemont. On it Newman was described as 'Prefect of studies and discipline', William Neville (who had been educated at Winchester and Trinity College Oxford) as 'Prefect of dormitories and playground', and Flanagan and Bittleston as spiritual directors. Thus it seems that masters and tutors were replaced by Oratorians in supervising the dormitories and playground (though the next prospectus altered Neville's title to 'Prefect of houses'). In terminology and structure, the changes brought about a closer resemblance to the Catholic colleges.[19] The staff list did not indicate who the real headmaster was. Hope-Scott thought it did not matter if it was Newman or not: the important point was for the Oratory to '*go at it*'.[20] He later added a strong proviso: 'It is most desirable that for the future, however little *you* may actually do in the School itself, *you* should know, day by day, and in detail, what is being done.'[21] His suggestion that St John be appointed headmaster was implemented only at the very start of term, and in the next prospectus he was described as 'Vice-Prefect (*ad interim*)'.

Hope-Scott advised Newman to investigate the comments he had heard from old Catholics that attributed to Darnell the 'want of due spiritual care and instruction' and the excessive use of corporal punishment. He also recommended that, in reorganising the school, Newman should define very carefully Mrs Wootten's future position; the strong outcry against her suggested an error of judgement and temper on her part, and he suggested enquiries be made. (In La Serre's 'Memoirs', her strong personality comes across in her adeptness at talking masters out of the punishments they had given boys from her house, typically with the excuse: 'He is such a delicate boy.'[22]) Hope-Scott had heard from people outside the school that her

---

[19] In fact, from the outset Newman had employed terminology which was not used at the public schools: 'Prefects of the playground' and 'Prefects of the dormitories' in his manifesto (21 February 1859, BOA); and the term 'usher' in his correspondence. They were names (and roles) associated with the Catholic colleges.

[20] Newman to St John, 30 December 1861, *L&D* XX, p. 99.

[21] Hope-Scott to Newman, 7 January 1862, BOA.

[22] La Serre, 'Memoirs', p. 28.

influence was too great, particularly as the school was 'assuming a new character – too old and too extensive for anything like a female preponderance in the management'.[23] Newman replied that he was 'alive to the necessity of keeping her under great restraint',[24] and set about altering the school prospectus. The previous version had stated: 'The houses are superintended as at Eton, etc., by Tutors and by Dames. The latter are Ladies of experience in the care of boys.' In the new prospectus it read: 'Especial attention is paid to the diet, health, and comfort of the boys; who are committed to the care of Ladies experienced in such duties, and are lodged either in the Oratory Building, or in houses in its immediate neighbourhood.'[25] Reference to the Eton dame system had been dropped, but otherwise there was no change, as Newman continued to use the term 'dame' interchangeably with 'matron'.

Hope-Scott may have had a hand in another significant change: the old prospectus referred to three public schools – Eton, Winchester and Harrow – while the new version mentioned Rugby in place of Harrow. Two equally likely explanations can be given: the arrival of Arnold, a Rugbeian, and the departure of Oxenham, a Harrovian; and Hope-Scott's opinion that Rugby had a healthy mix of classes, unlike Harrow, which was solidly aristocratic. More significantly, while still claiming to offer 'the advantages of the great Public Schools of England', the revised prospectus balanced this claim by alluding to 'the evils which are incidental to the system therein pursued'.[26] By openly acknowledging the dangers of public school life, Newman must have hoped he could dispel the fears of at least some old Catholics.

The caretaker committee suspected that Darnell must have viewed the school as a private venture managed by himself, not as a public institution attached to a body, the Oratory. Confirmation came when Bellasis asked Scott-Murray to try to prevent Darnell and the masters from writing to parents. Scott-Murray refused, declaring that he had always considered the

23. Hope-Scott to Newman, 7 January 1862, BOA.
24. Newman to Hope-Scott, 8 January 1862, *L&D* XX, p. 115.
25. School prospectuses, n.d. [1861, 1862], BOA.
26. School prospectus, n.d. [1862], BOA.

school to be independent from the Oratory, and Darnell's position with respect to the school to be the same as Newman's had been with regard to the Catholic University.[27] From this premise Scott-Murray argued that, as the boys were entrusted to the headmaster, *he* was the one responsible to parents, and therefore no other master should communicate with the parents except the headmaster: he considered Bellasis's letter about upper and lower schools to be an act of interference. Since Scott-Murray admitted he had regularly discussed his views with Darnell, it was obvious to the committee that 'those views have been the origin of the whole difficulty, Darnell imagining that other parents partook of them'.[28]

To resolve the long-standing canonical dispute among the Oratorians over the Birmingham Oratory having a school, Newman again consulted Hope-Scott, sending him the relevant sections of their *Brief of Institution* and decrees, along with explanations of his own. Opposition to the school from within the Birmingham Oratory (as well as the London one) rested on the contention that teaching was not part of the Oratorian vocation. Most of the London Oratorians were against anything to do with a boarding school, and some considered it against their Rule to have one. Their case rested on Decree 70, which declared that, lest anyone be taken away from the proper purpose of the Congregation, no Oratorian should commit or dedicate himself to running seminaries, colleges, and other universities, except in the case of grave necessity. Newman thought that an independent school would have been an infraction of the decree, as it entailed setting up 'a substantive body'; instead, he had intended to establish 'a mere dependance and function of the Oratory'.[29] The Birmingham Fathers considered themselves exempt because, in Newman's words:

[27.] Hope-Scott thought the comparison was invalid: 'To make a parallel with the Dublin University you must suppose an Oratory at Dublin – that Oratory to found an University, and to depute one of its members to be President, issuing such a Prospectus as you did for the School – A case very different from the real one.' (Hope-Scott to Newman, 13 January 1863, BOA.)

[28.] Bellasis to Newman, 11 January 1862, BOA.

[29.] Newman to Hope-Scott, 12 January 1862, *L&D* XX, p. 123.

1. the school is in no sense an *Universitatis*, or established body or corporation.
2. no one is or can be *abduci* [taken away], by means of it, from the institution of the Oratory – inasmuch as the Father, who is Schoolmaster, in fact does take his part, as any other Father, in all the duties, preachments, ceremonies, exercises etc of the House
3. the absence of any lay school in England is a *gravis necessitas*.[30]

Hope-Scott answered that Decree 70 technically spoke of corporations and therefore seemed to contemplate 'external and independent Societies, and not a dependent School without separate organisation'; thus it 'hits Darnell's theory and leaves yours untouched'.[31] Furthermore, he thought that the *gravis necessitas* of such a school as Newman's, and the absence of anybody else to undertake it, seemed to make a solid case and dispel any doubts on the question. A further point argued by Newman was that the *Brief of Institution* specified the educated upper classes as a special object of the Oratory's apostolate in England – but it had placed them in Birmingham, where that upper class did not exist. So, Newman argued, they were able to conform to the object the Holy See had given them, as best they could, by having a school for gentlemen's sons. Hope-Scott considered this an unsatisfactory argument for having a school; if the class to which they were sent did not exist in Birmingham, then there had been an *error loci*.

A separate matter concerned Decree 94, which effectively disallowed modifications to their constitution through *immutatio, derogatio* or *innovatio*. Newman enquired whether the compatibility of Decree 70 and their keeping school amounted to one of these, or whether it was just a *declaratio* of what was not clear; or whether in fact a choice of one of two interpretations, both of which were admissible. Hope-Scott did not answer; he thought Newman already had a good case. Given the circumstances, Newman concluded that the Oratory did

[30.] Newman's comments beneath a copy of *Decretum LXX*, BOA.
[31.] Hope-Scott to Newman, 13 January 1862, BOA.

not have to consult the Holy See about the matter, and summarised their reasons for carrying on as before: their *Brief* sent them to the upper classes – 'one special want of the upper class of Catholics just now is a lay school, there being no such thing, beyond our own, in England'; the care of boys was a 'special object of St Philip'; and their Rule 'not only admitted it, but had been altered in two instances from the Rule of the *Chiesa Nuova* in order to admit it'.[32]

The public school lobby

On the whole, reaction to the crisis was delayed as Newman had restricted its resolution to a small circle of friends. Besides, it was characteristic of him to wait for the true facts to surface without undue activity on his part. By contrast, Darnell was in close contact with his friends, all of whom stressed the public school dimension, and several reacted strongly to his departure and read into the changes a shift away from the public school model. The caretaker committee only became aware of this lobby among the school supporters after reading Scott-Murray's letter at their first emergency meeting, and it provided them with a disturbing view of the school's development which could not but influence their thinking.

Scott-Murray had been brooding over his last conversation with Newman, in October 1861, when he wrote it. He was disappointed, he said, because although the school had 'gentlemanly boys' and provided good teaching it no longer seemed 'to aim at the purpose for which it was founded, but to be quietly taking up the position of a large private school'. He had thought that the 'object was to creep on gradually into the Eton system', though he realised that Newman, 'to avoid courting opposition, was proceeding leisurely, especially as the boys were still for the most part young'. Newman had replied somewhat loosely that a reorganised Oscott might take the older

[32] Newman's comments beneath copies of *Decretum XCIV*, BOA and the *Brief of Institution*. The two alterations were the insertion of the clause *in gravis necessitate* in Decree 70, and the omission of the decree against having boys in their rooms; the latter was reinstated in 1858 because of an accusation against one of the Oratorians.

boys, but to Scott-Murray this prospect entailed

> throwing over all the objects for which the school was founded. The objections to the old Catholic English system were not so much that the learning was deficient (for I believe that could not be said of Stonyhurst) but that it partook of the spying or Jesuit system, and allowed of none of the independence and freedom of individual character, which seems to be so admirably cultivated in the Protestant public schools. Many old Catholics thought such liberty and such a system incompatible with Catholic training, but others thought that Catholic Superiors and the use of the Catholic Sacraments were alone wanting to make the English system of the Protestant schools available to Catholics. It was understood that Dr Newman and the Birmingham Oratory were of that opinion, and I thought that a plan for a short time entertained of beginning the school at the Oratory had been given up, because it was foreseen, that if the new school flourished, it must be independent of the Oratory as a body, and even possibly in lay hands.
>
> The mere suggestion of an improved Oscott being an end to be wished for, seems to me a falling off from the idea of establishing a public school, for Oscott improved would be at best but a College, and we want or did want a public school; and I must add Fr Darnell always struck me as the man cut out for forming one.[33]

Newman could not but agree with the substance of the letter, but he disowned the reference to 'the spying or Jesuit system', which he considered a great misconception of his meaning. He attributed the apparent divergence of opinion between them to his own, unintentionally misleading comments at their last meeting. Although Scott-Murray's sentiments expressed the ideal which had all along inspired Newman and his convert friends, that a Catholic upbringing and a public school education were not incompatible, the letter betrayed a fundamental

---

[33.] Scott-Murray to Bellasis, 22 December 1861, *L&D* XX, pp. 97–98.

and unvoiced difference between Newman and the likes of Scott-Murray: Newman 'dreaded lest it [the school] should become a mere Protestant School',[34] whereas they had no such fear. The difference manifested itself in the way Scott-Murray evidently considered the connection with the Oratory as detrimental to its ability to form boys in a spirit of freedom.

Mrs Scott-Murray, meanwhile, wrote at length to Mrs Wootten to persuade her to retire for a time on the grounds of ill-health, in order to prevent the resignations. While full of praise for Mrs Wootten's crucial contribution to the foundation, she reasoned that a sudden change of masters could bring about its destruction, 'to say nothing of the triumph it would give our enemies'. She implored Mrs Wootten to put 'the *public good*' above her private considerations, and to offer her resignation.[35] Although both the Thynnes wrote to Mrs Wootten after Darnell's overnight stay with them, neither so much as hinted that she ought to make way by resigning; they were simply distressed to hear that such a promising combination should have come to nothing. Darnell had 'so completely won the confidence of the parents, as well as the love of the boys', that he was irreplaceable.[36] Nevertheless, Thynne knew that Mrs Wootten was convinced Newman and Darnell 'represented *two* different systems of education, and that Fr Darnell was a fool in the hands of Mr Moody etc'; and that she felt it was her duty to counteract his influence and, 'constituting herself your shield, your eye and ear', had justified herself in interfering with the discipline of the school.[37] Lady Thynne thought that Darnell could have avoided the calamity by convincing Mrs Wootten how important it was that a headmaster should have supreme control and the support of all those under him. These letters indicate that the Thynnes had no notion of Newman's system of dual control, and that they took the conventional view that the powers of a public school headmaster were all-embracing – as indeed they were in all but the collegiate foundations at Eton and Winchester.

---

34. Newman, memorandum, 16 February 1862, *L&D* XX, p. 98.
35. Mrs Scott-Murray to Mrs Wootten, [5 January 1862], BOA.
36. Lady Thynne to Mrs Wootten, n.d., BOA.
37. Thynne to Newman, January 1862, BOA.

Thynne reacted sharply to the new list of staff, for it seemed to him to signal the abandonment of 'what is called the Public School system of Education'. He regretted the apparent return to the collegiate system which seemed so unsuited to the English character, and he reminded Newman that the promoters had originally decided to adopt a different model; the English public school system was the best to be found and suited their needs, 'if certain things necessary to Catholics were super-added'.[38] However, he finished by asking Newman to correct him if he had concluded wrongly. Both the Scott-Murrays and the Thynnes received explanations from Newman, and in both cases their sons remained at the school. In challenging the direction it was taking, under the perception that it was diverging from the original plan, they showed they had strongly identified with certain aspects of the scheme, while taking others for granted.

Acton had lost touch with the school, despite seeing Darnell and Oxenham regularly, and despite Bellasis urging him to take a greater interest in it. Initially unaware of the nature of the dispute, he guessed it concerned the connection between the school and the Oratory. The new buildings and the establishment of a dormitory on the top floor of the Oratory suggested to him that the school had become 'a regular appendage, almost a part, of a religious house', and that 'at the same time the secular character of the establishment is diminished, and the Protestant public school element so far as it consists in dames' houses and the absence of surveillance necessarily loses ground'. This would placate 'those whom the Protestant associations offended', but meant that the school was fixed on its site and that its fortunes were tied to the Oratory.[39] Acton wondered if these developments were connected to recent changes he had detected in Newman's views on education, such as his reply to Oxenham in *The Rambler*.

Besides the views of parents and promoters, it is also worth considering those of the resigning staff. To counter the impu-

---

[38.] Thynne to Newman, January 1862, BOA.
[39.] Acton to Simpson, 1 January 1862, *Correspondence of Acton and Simpson* II, pp. 247–48.

tation that they had conspired against Newman, a charge all the masters vehemently denied, both Marshall and Oxenham argued that their behaviour was consistent with that expected of public school masters. Marshall claimed that Mrs Wootten's interference had made it impossible to maintain school discipline. He had combined with the others because he had 'considered the point at issue to be a matter so essential to the very existence of anything in the shape of a Public School, that if the headmaster failed in carrying it, and was in consequence forced to resign, we had no course left but to do the same'. 'As a question of school discipline, or of behaviour due among gentlemen', he could not see how they could have done otherwise 'than make the cause of our head-master entirely our own, and abide with him in the results': there had been, he said, complete agreement among the masters as to the course of action.[40] Oxenham thought that while Mrs Wootten's presence had been useful to the school at the outset, it had become 'not only inconsistent with its professed claims as a public school', but an obstacle that made it impossible for Darnell to continue as headmaster. The crisis was one of the most bitter disappointments of his life and the destruction of 'my most cherished vision', but he felt unable to retract anything he had said or done, a stance he maintained over the following months.[41] Miss Ffrench, when offering her resignation as dame, explained that her inability to view the issue in any way other than Darnell's disqualified her from pursuing her duties with the loyalty required. Newman urged her to stay until Easter, but she gracefully declined. Meanwhile, the version of events going the rounds of neighbouring Edgbaston families was that Darnell had run off with Miss Ffrench.

Although Darnell had argued that Mrs Wootten's presence prevented the school from becoming a public school, later correspondence suggested to Newman that Darnell's battle with Mrs Wootten was of secondary importance, and that the point at issue was 'whether the school should be on an essentially private basis, or a public, as Eton and Winchester'.[42]

[40.] Marshall to Newman, 6 January 1862, BOA.
[41.] Oxenham to Newman, 17 January 1862, BOA.
[42.] Newman to Bellasis, 23 March 1862, *L&D* XX, p. 176.

Taking into account the school's Catholic dimension, it would appear – paradoxically – that it was Darnell's scheme, not Newman's, that was in some respects closer to the private school system. Unlike public schools, the nineteenth-century private schools were run by individuals for profit; their selling points were a greater flexibility in curricular and entry requirements, being unrestricted by custom or statutes. Endowed schools, while they often operated out of leased or rented premises and were heavily dependent upon the attributes of the head, were more likely to succeed, owing to the apparatus of an endowment and a governing body. It was no doubt possible to detect several private school characteristics at the fledgling school at Edgbaston, but they were not indicative of its status, for in their infancy a number of schools (such as, for example, Radley) began as private concerns, before later assuming the wherewithal of an endowed public school.

Having spent a fortnight listening to the woes of Darnell and Oxenham, Acton concluded that Newman had become frightened at the prospect of large changes as the school approached public school status, and had abandoned the whole idea of innovation: the three he had fallen out with – Darnell, Moody and Oxenham – were precisely those who championed the public school system. Acton was unsuccessful in dissuading Darnell from requesting temporary leave from the Oratory, but he did manage to restrain the other two from making a public protest; he urged them to write a short, matter-of-fact letter to the parents they knew best instead. In adopting this policy, Acton reckoned (with some truth) that he was rendering Newman an even greater service than when he had helped set up the school four years earlier. Uninterested in the personal side of the crisis, Acton was more concerned that his cherished dream of a Catholic university in England was 'trembling in the balance' with 'all the future of [Catholic] education at stake'.[43] The only hope he saw for the school was through Darnell's reinstatement, rather than setting up an opposition scheme, and it was to this end that to sought to cool the hot-heads around him.

[43.] Acton to Simpson, 13 January 1862, *Correspondence of Acton and Simpson* II, p. 254.

Darnell's draft circular blamed his resignation on Newman's refusal to carry out the public school system, to which he had originally committed himself. But in the end he decided not to issue it, as Flanagan pointed out that the public school question was not well understood among Catholics, despite Moody's insistence that it was the key to understanding their position. However, news that the correspondence between Newman and Darnell was being circulated by Bellasis and Hope-Scott persuaded Acton to concede that Darnell could now put forward a defence. Once Darnell's letter was issued, Oxenham followed suit and compiled his own circular which defended himself against three charges: entering the school under false pretences in order to force the public school system upon it, conspiring against Newman, and attempting to remove the school from Edgbaston. His letter referred to the Congregation decree which allowed Darnell to establish a public school on the model of Eton and Winchester, and it had the approval of Flanagan, one of the school's two spiritual directors.

As long after the affair as March 1862, Acton and Simpson still hoped for Darnell's reinstatement in the proposed upper school at a country location; but by then the Oratory School was in much better shape and the chances of this happening were virtually nil. Even after this Oxenham continued using every means at his disposal to encourage Darnell to leave the Oratory and, 'as soon as Newman's country school is opened, to set up an opposition shop'.[44] Rumours of the country school also led Moody to hope for 'a bonâ fide public school, say at Winchester'.[45] Meanwhile, Darnell was taken on as a private tutor for the eldest son of Prince Doria.

Acton considered the school's success to be vital for reforming the system of Catholic education and was willing if necessary to re-involve himself to save it; Darnell, he thought, had been treated roughly, having carried out all the work and having exercised all the day-to-day authority, while Newman had 'reduced himself to a nonentity in the school'. He wondered if Newman's 'liegemen' Hope-Scott and Bellasis

[44.] Simpson to Acton, 5 March 1862, *Correspondence of Acton and Simpson* II, p. 268.
[45.] Moody's diary, 21 February 1862, BOA.

recognised this, as it was plain, he believed, to all the masters and boys. And he felt that Newman needed to recover 'his own direct influence in the school not by Mrs W but by actually taking part in it, seeing the masters, examining the boys occasionally, and giving them occasional sermons. I hope somebody will tell him so.'[46] In fact, Bellasis and Hope-Scott had already done just this.

The previous December, when the Congregation had begun to resolve the dispute, Scott-Murray had declined to discuss matters any further with Bellasis, explaining that, like others, he had already presented his views at the promoters' meetings. Now the Oratory had to make up its mind, and it was 'for parents individually to decide whether they think the new arrangements likely or not to suit their views for their children'.[47] To judge by this criterion, it would seem that the vote of confidence in Newman and his school was unanimous. Moreover, as the dust settled, Newman observed that 'the more things are inquired into, the more the clear truth comes out, favourable to us'.[48]

A verdict on the crisis

It was the Oratorian Bittleston who was the first to reassure Newman that he had been bound to act as he had, out of justice to Mrs Wootten; 'by your obligations to the parents of the boys, and the friends and founders of the School'; and by his duty to the Congregation.[49] Insofar as there was written evidence of the dispute, it was contained in the documents that Newman had assembled and passed on to Bellasis and Hope-Scott. The two barristers confirmed that the contents were in complete agreement with all Newman that had told them, and confidence radiated out from them. Newman left perusal of the documents to their judgement; they were not circulated (as Acton thought), nor were they used in Newman's defence, on

46. Acton to Simpson, 5 January 1862, *Correspondence of Acton and Simpson* II, p. 250.
47. Scott-Murray to Bellasis, n.d., BOA.
48. Newman to St John, 16 January 1862, *L&D* XX, p. 129.
49. Bittleston to Newman, 2 January 1862, *L&D* XX, p. 103n.

the grounds that he needed no defence. They were only shown to those who were convinced that Darnell had been treated harshly, to reveal the extent to which he had assumed independence from the Oratory. At the point when Acton complained at being excluded, only five people had actually seen them.

The letters Newman received from parents provided proof of their confidence in Mrs Wootten. Gaisford wrote to say that he entirely approved of the measures Newman had taken, for he had bargained for two things at the school: that it would be under the control of Newman; and that a lady like Mrs Wootten would provide female care. The boys were of a more tender age than those sent to Eton and Rugby, and however much he wished for the school to 'take a Public School tone', such young boys needed 'a woman's superintendance'.[50] Captain John Hibbert, a convert married to the mother of the Earl of Shrewsbury, rejoiced at *'the change* in the management':[51] the return of one of his sons was delayed because of ringworm which had not been properly dealt with the previous term, a direct consequence of Darnell's having limited the boys' access to Mrs Wootten. Gaisford and Hibbert told Bellasis that the names of Newman and Mrs Wootten were essential for the school: without them they would not have sent their children. In Thomas Fitzgerald's letter, he noted that his two sons had originally been placed under Mrs Wootten's care and were content until told by other boys that Miss Ffrench 'gave a more bountiful supply of jam every evening'; he had yielded to their whim and allowed them to be transferred. Now he asked if they could be returned to Mrs Wootten's house, as he had 'unlimited confidence in her care and management of boys'.[52] The Hornyolds, well-known old Catholics, praised Mrs Wootten, as well as Newman's decision to support her; Mrs Hornyold claimed that nothing could exceed Mrs Wootten's kindness to her son.

This parental feedback assured Newman that if Mrs Wootten had gone 'there was a chance of half the school going – for her care of the young boys and popularity with the mothers have

[50.] Gaisford to Newman, 11 January 1862, BOA.
[51.] Hibbert to Newman, 11 January 1862, BOA.
[52.] Fitzgerald to Newman, 20 January 1862, BOA.

been the making of the school – as I know full well, if I did not know it before, by what the mothers have said to me since the row'.[53] No one was better placed than Bellasis to assess her worth, and he considered her 'one of the chief inducements to the great majority of parents'.[54] Looking back on the events of December 1861, we can see that it was on behalf of parents and friends of the school that Newman had pursued the course of action which had brought matters to a head; he had relied on them for backing, and had received it in good measure: 'My greatest support, after that of a clear conscience, is the verdict of my friends in this matter – and they go one way.'[55]

The tragedy of the crisis was that it occurred in a climate of goodwill, for everyone involved in the project was conscious that they were participating in an important development for Catholic education. All were working towards a 'Catholic public school', but since there was no consensus on what it entailed or how it was to be achieved, the promoters had decided to entrust the execution of the project to Newman. Nevertheless, in their enthusiasm, several promoters had begun to press for changes according to their own conceptions, doing so with a very superficial notion of what this new type of Catholic school entailed: they saw it as effectively a public school with a few Catholic elements bolted on. Thynne spoke of the Catholic elements being 'super-added', while Scott-Murray thought that 'Catholic Superiors and the use of the Catholic Sacraments were alone wanting'.[56] Newman realised that the task was by no means so straightforward, and desired a more organic combination so as to enable the Catholic element to be present in a vital way. It was inevitable that this would entail the sacrifice of certain public school characteristics.

Although Newman's scheme – Darnell, as headmaster, under Newman, as president – never looked like working, because Darnell acted and thought too much like a conventional headmaster, Newman too was at fault in not exercising his presiding role decisively in the crucial early stages. When it was evident

[53.] Newman to Ornsby, 31 January 1861, *L&D* XX, p. 143.
[54.] Bellasis to Darnell, 17 December 1861, BOA.
[55.] Newman to Pollen, 10 January 1862, *L&D* XX, p. 118.
[56.] Scott-Murray to Bellasis, 22 December 1861, *L&D* XX, p. 98.

that the school was developing along lines markedly different from those he had intended, his attempt to involve himself after having so fully surrendered control must inevitably have seemed like interference, and his defence of Mrs Wootten an unreasonable preference for her over Darnell and the masters. The alienation between Darnell and Mrs Wootten has been attributed to her knowledge of, and opposition to, his plan to move the school away from Edgbaston,[57] but the evidence suggests that she opposed Darnell on a broader front, to the extent that his policies deviated from those of Newman. The resigning staff (and Scott-Murray) strongly denied the charge of attempting to remove the school from Newman's control, and their position is borne out by the available evidence. Nevertheless, there had been a growing conviction, if not a working assumption, that the school was Darnell's and that it would soon move into the country.

The pursuit of conflicting plans for the school's development indicates a lack of communication and a failure on Newman's part to transmit the aims of the undertaking to the staff and parents; there was in fact no mechanism by which the views of friends and supporters could be incorporated into future plans for the school. The absence of communication is illustrated by the masters' defence of their act of resignation, which showed that they considered themselves to be conventional public school masters, and had not been led to think otherwise. Why should only Bellasis and Hope-Scott be involved in Newman's plans for the school, and not other promoters and the masters – not to mention Darnell, who complained at Bellasis's 'mischievous interference' and Hope-Scott's '*evil* part'[58] in resolving the crisis? The reason is that in Newman's eyes the initiative belonged to the parents, and Bellasis and Hope-Scott were, to all intents and purposes, their representatives. However, their roles needed clarification as the school was in the process of assuming a more public character.

The problem of the school's unsuitable location had no obvious remedy, yet like others it could have been eased by better communication. The conflict of interests in deciding

57. Ker, *Newman: a Biography*, p. 507.
58. Darnell to Newman, August 1862, BOA.

whether or not to move from an urban setting was one which afflicted other establishments, most notably the four great public schools in London – Charterhouse, Merchant Taylors', St Paul's and Westminster. At the Oratory School it was associated with the question of whether to cater for older boys, and, if so, how. The question had been foreseen from the outset but had come to the fore sooner than expected, as the school had not begun with eight- and nine-year-olds only, as originally anticipated, but a range of ages; and it was exacerbated by the addition of older boys from other schools.

These problems – the integration of Catholic and public school elements, the plans for development, communication with parents and staff, the school's location, and others – were ultimately Newman's responsibility, yet he found himself in a dilemma. How could parents or others be allowed to dictate terms while the Oratory was 'on trial' and supplying most of the finance, shouldering the financial burden that, in justice, belonged to the promoters and parents? So keenly did he feel it, that his immediate reaction to the plan to form a separate upper school was to warn Bellasis: 'you parents must turn your thoughts to the creation somewhere of a higher school – for at present it seems as if we could do nothing more than take boys under 13'.[59]

The connection with the Oratory was crucial to the school's identity, yet even the Oratorians were unclear about it. The matter had been discussed in 1858, but not fully clarified, as a fundamental difference of opinion had arisen. Then, Scott-Murray and others had pushed for a school in a rural setting under Newman's supervision; the connection with the Oratory was more or less tolerated, as it provided 'security for the religious element', but in Scott-Murray's opinion the link was 'not intended to apply to the *spiritual* supervision in any way'.[60] He feared that the school would forfeit its public school credentials and become simply another Catholic college if it attached itself to a religious body. The intertwining of school and Oratory buildings served to fuel these fears; Acton was uncertain

---

[59.] Newman to Bellasis, 27 December 1861, *L&D* XX, p. 89.
[60.] Scott-Murray to Bellasis, n.d., BOA. It is unclear what Scott-Murray thought the link with the Oratory *was* supposed to supply.

whether the object was to increase Newman's involvement with the school or to strengthen it with the Oratory's support. He thought the latter a mistake, as the school would stand after Newman's death by virtue of Darnell and his staff, not of the Oratory. On Hope-Scott's clear advice, Newman abandoned his former position – the school viewed as the private undertaking of two Oratorians – and opted for closer identification with the Oratory. The fact that the school reverted to a more conventional formula after the crisis does not prove Acton correct in judging that Newman's views on education had changed; instead, Newman's decision was eminently plausible as an emergency measure intended to provide a guarantee for what the converts tended to take for granted – religious security.

What *had* changed was Newman's view on the Oratory having a school at all, and it did so according to circumstances. His early thinking derived from a study of the beginning of the Oratorian Congregation in Rome, where youths were educated at the *Chiesa Nuova* and some had joined the Congregation; as many as fifty had attended, but most lived at home. When first discussing schemes for St Wilfrid's, a property inherited by the Oratorians in 1848, the Oratory was already taking boys who showed signs of becoming Oratorians, and Newman was prepared to relax the criteria – but not so far as to include those 'who are *certainly not* going to be ecclesiastics',[61] and he initially ruled out schemes for lay boys. He likewise turned down the chance to tutor the son of Lady Georgiana Fullerton, the convert novelist, on the grounds it was not an Oratorian task, and because they had no intention to set themselves up against the Jesuits. Newman eventually came round to the idea of running a school at St Wilfrid's because of the need to maintain the property and the likely supply of vocations, yet he insisted on a restriction: a school for small boys, a seminary, a noviciate, all these would be useful in supplying or training novices – but not a school for youths, for this entailed 'a work which is simply not Oratorian'.[62] What is clear from these schemes is that the good of the Oratory was uppermost in his

[61.] Newman to Ryder, 13 March 1849, *L&D* XIII, p. 85.
[62.] Newman to Hutchinson, 6 January 1850, *L&D* XIII, p. 367.

mind. When it became clear that only the school for youths was feasible, Newman insisted that it should be temporary and that they should look to dispose of it as soon as possible, along with St Wilfrid's. A decade later, in 1858, Newman again committed himself to a project he thought would only require temporary assistance, yet after the crisis he found himself having to water down his original assurance to the promoters that only two Fathers would be fully involved. The '*quotidiana sollicitudo* of the School' meant that it and the Oratory were becoming increasingly bound together.[63] This closer union compromised the school's secular character, yet it also compromised the Oratory's identity – in fact, Flanagan left the Oratory in 1865 blaming the effect the school had had on it.

The changing relation of the school to the Oratory is most clearly seen from the financial perspective. The school was initially sanctioned by the Congregation as a private undertaking of Newman, with Darnell as his representative and collaborator, and Newman's friends were to supply the funding: 'The Congregation was not to pay a farthing towards it.' Alterations to the church for the school's sake were supposed to be financed from a loan raised by the school promoters, and the interest paid from fee income. Instead, individual Fathers provided loans. (The same happened with later church enlargements, with the conversion of the top storey of the Oratory House into dormitories, and with the erection of new school building.) Then in February 1861 the liabilities for the school were transferred from Darnell to the Congregation. The logic of these changes was completed just after the crisis, when the Congregation formally made the school 'absolutely ours'; 'The whole management and control of the finances' now belonged to them.[64] Newman admitted it had become impossible to separate the school financially from the Oratory and that it had effectively become the property of the Congregation: because large sums had been spent on it that the school could never repay; because it was now placed on land belonging to the Congregation; because the school had

---

[63.] Newman to Hope-Scott, 8 March 1863, *L&D* XX, p. 419.
[64.] Newman, memorandum: 'Relation of the School to the Oratory', 7 February 1865, BOA, A.26.5.

appropriated a considerable part of the Oratory House; 'and because, if it does not belong to the Congregation, to whom does it belong?'[65] However, for internal accounting purposes Newman continued viewing it as a separate enterprise.

In assessing the damage the crisis caused the school, it is necessary to go beyond the immediate facts – the return of all the boys and the replacement of the resigning staff. For Catholic parents who wanted a public school education there were no other options available, so it was not surprising that the sons of Scott-Murray and Thynne remained.[66] On the other hand, parents who were worried about Catholic instruction and training did have an alternative. When a sixteen-year-old boy was withdrawn for a private tutor in September 1862, Newman anticipated an exodus of old Catholics – 'The old Catholics hold together like a bunch of currants; one go, all go'[67] – and losses of up to twenty. By October he reckoned the school had lost about ten boys, but mainly because of families changing their minds. In fact, despite a small decrease in admissions, school numbers remained buoyant after the crisis. As early as the previous Easter, Newman had been convinced that while Darnell's departure had been a blow for the Oratory, it had not been one for the school – indeed, it had benefited the school immeasurably. Although he admitted afterwards that he had never in his life had a severer trial, he also thought that 'never did things begin so soon to mend'.[68]

Nor should we forget the wider context. The evidence shows that Liberal Catholic influence also had its part to play in the crisis, since most of its prominent adherents were linked to the school in one way or other. When Darnell engaged Oxenham in 1861, Acton and Simpson began conferring as to how they might persuade Darnell to take on the Oxford convert Thomas Wetherell, the third proprietor of *The Rambler*. More revealing

[65] Newman, draft of a Congregation decree, n.d. [1864], BOA, A.26.5.
[66] In the case of Scott-Murray, he was indebted to Bellasis and Hope-Scott who had successfully supported and defended his appointment when High Sheriff of a Catholic priest as his chaplain; Bellasis with legal advice, and Hope-Scott with two letters to *The Times*.
[67] Newman to Neville, 30 September 1862 *L&D* XX, p. 282.
[68] Newman to Wilberforce, 26 January 1862, *L&D* XX, p. 138.

still was Simpson's suggestion, after Darnell's resignation, that Döllinger be asked to mediate in the dispute.[69] Ultimately, however, the crisis and its solution revolved around the tension between the apparently opposing aims in establishing a school that was both Catholic and imitative of the best Protestant schools. The attitude of the resigning staff in their single-minded pursuit of a public school revealed that they had failed to appreciate the delicate balance fashioned by Newman in his solution to the problem. To counterbalance this bias, Newman felt obliged to introduce a safeguard: a closer connection between school and Oratory. The public school lobby found it hard to appreciate what seemed like an unnecessary conces-sion, but to the majority of old Catholics Newman's compromise appeared eminently sensible.

Regime change

The success of the rescue operation was by no means assured when the school reopened in January 1862 and it was several months before it became clear that it had pulled through. The first few post-crisis terms were vital for restoring the confi-dence of parents, and much depended on how the staff performed. While Newman worked with Bellasis on matters external to its daily life, such as engaging new staff, it was St John who was entrusted with the day-to-day running of the school, and his role in the changeover period proved to be just as vital as that of Bellasis and Hope-Scott – more so, in fact, since he had to fill Darnell's shoes to the satisfaction of parents, boys and staff.

Newman could not have achieved the remarkable transfor-mation of the school without the assistance of his right-hand man at the Oratory. Ambrose St John had been a pupil at Westminster School and an undergraduate then Student

---

[69.] Simpson considered that Newman's position was plausible on only one of two counts: his ignorance of educational structures, 'not being a public school man', or 'that painful subserviency' to author-ity Newman regularly showed in yielding 'his own convictions to the supposed desire of Bishops or Pope' (Simpson to Acton, 4 January 1862, *Correspondence of Acton and Simpson* II, p. 249).

(Fellow) at Christ Church Oxford. Unlike Darnell, he was not a natural schoolmaster, but his friendship and mutual sympathy with Newman meant that Newman could rely on St John to turn his idea of the school into a reality. In 1843 he had gone to Littlemore to stay with Newman for three months, but he ended up spending the next thirty-two years by his side; the bond of friendship that developed between them was so strong that Newman declared: 'As far as this world was concerned, I was his first and last'. As with many famous friendships, they had contrasting personalities and interests: St John was genial and vivacious, fifteen years younger than Newman, large of frame and bustling in movement, and while Newman's interests lay in philosophy and patristics, St John specialised in Biblical studies and Semitic languages. He also had a good command of French, German, Italian and Spanish. It was after St John's death that Newman described how in typical fashion he had come to the rescue: 'When we suddenly wanted a Headmaster to our School, he, without a word, giving up his intended work on the Psalms, undertook the office.'[70]

They both found everything in the greatest confusion, for the sudden departures meant that they 'had the least possible assistance from the past to enlighten the present – so we had to learn to do every thing'.[71] Newman did not lay all the blame on the 'late regime, (for the School has been all along in a state of commencement)'.[72] But being a relatively new institution, there was no established pattern and this meant that everything had to be overseen, though the lack of continuity did present them with the chance to apply a new broom and give the school a fresh start. First Bellasis, then St John, and finally Marshall, Rougemont and the ushers visited Oscott to learn about arrangements there. St John made careful notes about their punishment system, their exam routine, the boys' library, dormitory arrangements, and the division of the playground and study between older and younger boys. What ensued was a burst of regulation. The duties of ushers, tutors and masters were discussed and clarified at several meetings with them,

---

[70.] [Tristram], 'The Oratory School', *OPM*, November 1932, pp. 191–92.

[71.] Newman to Morris, 26 February 1862 *L&D* XX, p. 157.

[72.] Newman to Bellasis, 5 February 1862, *L&D* XX, p. 148.

before being promulgated by Newman. Older boys had their privileges and duties specified ('1. Later hours. 2. More liberty about bounds. 3. Care of little boys'[73]), a new timetable was drawn up, and the school rules were clarified.

To judge from St John's diary, his major preoccupations were discipline and academic standards. As to be expected, the diary recorded many petty incidents of indiscipline and insubordination. St John introduced the Westminster practice of 'bricking on the hands' for some offences, while flogging was reserved for serious ones, and parents informed on these occasions. In March 1862 two boys were caught pistol-shooting, having obtained ammunition at school through trickery: one was stripped of his prefectship, while the main culprit was offered the choice of expulsion or flogging; he chose the latter and he received his punishment in the presence of the senior boys. On another occasion, after a riot by prefects at new regulations for their study rooms, during which windows were smashed, he sacked all of them; but after apologies and promises they were reinstated a fortnight later, and regained their privileges, for although St John could easily be roused to anger (or at least a semblance of it), he was tender-hearted and readily placated. Not intent on seeking out trouble, he advertised his presence by always carrying around with him a large set of jangling keys – on one of the rare occasions he forgot them, he was set upon by pillows as he entered a dormitory. His greater strictness in the enforcement of rules was balanced by the granting of half-holidays to mark special occasions. One such was St Patrick's Day, about which St John recorded: 'Evening. Gave punch. Made the boys very disorderly – threw ink about – The boy who did so showed himself up.'[74]

In the first half of 1862 Newman worked closely on staff recruitment with Bellasis, whose unflagging efforts were made despite heavy professional commitments and illness. Together they exercised an induction process for both new and returning staff. The process can be seen in the meeting of Bellasis with Richard Pope, at which he explained the origin of the crisis: that it had occurred because of the independent views of the head-

---

[73.] St John's diary, 3 February 1862, BOA.
[74.] St John's diary, 17 March 1862, BOA.

master which Newman could not tolerate, sparked off by a dispute over Mrs Wootten's position as dame. He also explained what the parents had asked for regarding Mrs Wootten and about the school's connection with the Oratory. Bellasis impressed upon Pope the importance and difficulty of Newman's undertaking and the need for all engaged to 'throw themselves heartily' into his view of the school. Bellasis listened carefully to what Pope had to say about his former school at Gibraltar: there the bishop acted as provost and exercised a constant superintendence; he presided at a weekly meeting of masters, 'when enquiries were made, and explanations given, and any question which might have arisen determined'.[75] Bellasis recommended the practice to Newman on the grounds that it might prevent the masters developing their own schemes, and remarked that Pope was used to the system of keeping silence in the dormitories. To judge from St John's diary, all this advice was quickly acted upon. And the general tightening-up is evident from the post-crisis dormitory rules, which stated:

1. Every boy is expected to kneel down at his own chair, and say his prayers immediately on reaching the Dormitory.
2. No talking or Play is allowed in the Dormitories.
3. All leave to miss mass or morning school must be received from the matron over night: in any unexpected illness boys must apply to the tutor.
4. It is forbidden to go to church in slippers.
5. No boy is allowed in the Dormitory during the day without leave from the tutor.[76]

Newman did his best to keep Bellasis fully informed of developments from his end. His reports about the masters were frank and incisive, indicating that he had his finger on the pulse of the school: 'Arnold and Pope promise well – and Fr St John'; but neither of the returning masters was satisfactory, for 'we cannot quite join the new and the old [...] and there are

[75.] Bellasis to Newman, 24 January 1862, BOA.
[76.] Dormitory rules, n.d., BOA.

signs of a party movement already'.[77] As the returning masters were men Darnell had appointed, it is not surprising that they did not meet Newman's more stringent requirements and that he wished to replace them. Marshall lacked stamina for the job and had difficulty enforcing discipline, while Rougemont had been kept on despite Newman's attempts to persuade Darnell that he was not up to the work. In fact Newman doubted whether Rougemont had taught the boys anything 'in arithmetic or mathematics [. . .] that they have not been taught by the *books* themselves', and he asked Bellasis to make discreet enquiries about it through his eldest son.[78] However, the task of finding suitable replacements proved to be more difficult than expected. On the school's behalf Bellasis engaged a young convert as a reading, writing and arithmetic master, but he turned out to be incompetent and broke down on the first day, and had to be dismissed. His replacement, Edmund Alleguen (known to the boys as 'Hex'), lasted longer – no less than thirty-two years. At Easter 1862 Miss Mitchell decided to leave, and, though she returned after the summer, she left for good in 1863.

The process of weeding out the unsatisfactory teachers was to take several years. At Christmas 1862 Newman removed La Serre's tutorship and confined him to his teaching duties; three years later he resigned and returned to France. The easing out of Marshall was begun, then postponed due to the pleadings of Arnold and Pope, and a compromise reached: Marshall remained as a 'master (i.e. *in* School) not Tutor (i.e. *out* of School)'.[79] His departure in the summer of 1866 was friendly, and at Newman's request Bellasis helped him into the legal profession, where he had a very successful career. Rougemont's activities could easily have put an end to the school as he turned out to be a thief and womaniser. He resigned in June 1862 but disappeared before the end of term. Items stolen from boys were found in his room, along with false moustaches, coloured neckties, love letters and linen betraying 'a bad disease', and investigations showed he had

---

[77.] Newman to Bellasis, 1 March 1862, *L&D* XX, p. 160.
[78.] Newman to Bellasis, 20 April 1862, *L&D* XX, p. 190.
[79.] *Ibid.*

slept out at night. He had also made off with a valuable gold watch belonging to a boy on the pretext of getting it repaired; it was never returned, and the boy's father preferred his son to think it was lost rather than that a priest could have been guilty of theft. Rougemont fled to Ireland, where he obtained a position as a tutor for a magistrate's family; he absconded with jewellery and other valuables, but was caught and received a six-year sentence. News of this was reported in the press in October, but his connection with the school was not spotted. Otherwise, it would have been devastating for the school, coming just six months after the Darnell affair.

Exactly a year after the crisis Newman composed a 'Circular to the Masters, Tutors, and Dames of the Oratory School' in which he thanked them for a successful year and re-emphasised their complementary roles. The Fathers (he meant principally St John and Neville) had 'at a word given up their own engagements and personal objects, in order to save the School'. He congratulated 'the Masters and Tutors on their magnificent success in attaching the boys to them, in setting their minds in the right direction, in teaching them what discipline is, in making them obedient, and in advancing them in their studies'. Lastly, he expressed gratitude for

> the assistance, so indispensable to our welfare, of the Matrons, for the unwearied vigilance with which they have watched over the bodily and moral health of the boys, have made school a second home to them, and have [...] shielded them from the illnesses which we hear of round about us.[80]

Newman praised the peace and harmony that prevailed among them all. His observations on the healthy state of affairs are corroborated by the memoirs of Marshall, who commented on 'the real fraternal love' among the masters, and on how fortunate it was they 'pull so well together'.[81] Such comments and the absence of staff squabbles after the recent mutiny would

[80] Circular letter, 19 December 1862, *L&D* XX, pp. 365–66.
[81] W.R.B. Brownlow, *Memoir of Sir James Marshall* (London: Burns & Oates, 1890), pp. 6–7.

seem to suggest that sound arrangements and wise management were now in place. Parents were not slow to notice the beneficial effects of the changes and approved. More importantly, the attitude of the staff provided Newman with the stability and cooperation he required in order to see his vision of the school come about.

1. John Henry Newman at the Bowden's during the Darnell crisis, 1861

2. James Hope-Scott, co-founder, in c. 1870

3. Edward Bellasis, co-founder, in c. 1865

4. John Acton, a leading promoter, in 1858

5. Nicholas Darnell,
headmaster 1859–61

6. Frances Wootten,
head dame 1859–75

7. Robert Moody,
master 1859–61

8. James Marshall,
master 1860–66

9. Ambrose St John,
headmaster 1862–72

10. Richard Pope,
master 1862–99

11. Thomas Arnold,
master 1862–65

12. Gerard Manley Hopkins,
master 1867–68

13. 97 Hagley Road, School House 1859–60

14. View across the Hagley Road of the Oratory House (right) and the main school building (left) with the schoolroom on the first floor

15. Part of the main schoolroom, opened in 1862

16. Cast of the *Andria*, 1886
J.B. Bowring, H. Belloc, F. Murray, R.O. Eaton, H. Pope, A. Wall,
B. Gaisford, A. Wall; C.S. Cocks, E. Pereira, (J. Norris), W. Mathew,
W. Tweedie, A. Tweedie; W.O. Eaton

17. Cricket pavilion at Ravenshurst

18. Billiard room, opened in 1881

19. Richard Bellasis,
pupil 1859–70

20. Augustin Scott-Murray,
pupil 1859–65

21. John Stokes,
pupil 1859–62

22. Duke of Norfolk,
pupil 1861–64

23. The school chapel, opened in 1873

24. Group of Oratorians, 1878: from top left, F.X. Morgan, former pupil; J. Norris, headmaster; H.I.D. Ryder; W.P. Neville, Prefect of houses; G.L. Teeling; R.G. Bellasis, former pupil; T.P.A. Eaglesim, former master; H.L. Bellasis, former pupil; from bottom left, H.A. Mills, school secretary; J.H. Newman, school president; H. Bittleston, school spiritual director; T.A. Pope, former master

Chapter 5

Newman's School

Having surrendered the initiative for forming the fledgling foundation at Christmas 1858 and not regained it until Christmas three years later, Newman oversaw its reorganisation and development thereafter with an energy that was all the greater on account of the troubles. The crisis provided him with an ideal opportunity for reviewing school practice and making alterations, and it is these changes which provide vital clues for identifying Newman's idea of an academic school that would prepare boys for university and the professions. The academic utopia described in his Dublin lectures had been intended to act as a stimulus for founding the Catholic University, but there was no equivalent for the school. Nevertheless the *Idea of a University* sheds light on Newman's idea of a school by implication, insofar as school education is the preamble to university education; so too do the chapters on disciplinary and pastoral matters in the *Rise and Progress of Universities* (the first section of *Historical Sketches* III). To see how this vision was translated into practice, however, it is necessary to examine school life after the Darnell affair.

When the school reopened in January 1862, its internal affairs were handled jointly by Newman and St John; together they undertook the crucial task of *forming* it. The partnership lasted until February 1872, when St John retired and was replaced by a young Oratorian, John Norris, who remained at the helm for the next four decades. Although Newman's presidency did not end in 1872, but continued until his death in

1890, the deaths of other key figures – Bellasis and Hope-Scott in 1873, St John in 1875 and Mrs Wootten in 1876 – mark out 1872 as the end of the main foundational period; by then the school had had a decade of Newman's close attention.

Newman's energetic oversight manifested itself in all school business; even in relatively minor matters he showed he was prepared to act decisively. When he discovered that a lottery had been organised by the boys, he alerted St John to the fact; a day later, after mulling over the matter, he asked St John to find out who had organised it: 'Nothing ought to be done in the School without our knowing it. Our permission ought to have been asked. [. . .] I should not have allowed it [. . .]. I trust so great a misapprehension will not occur again.'[1] There were occasions when Newman refused to cave in to parental objections, and even threats, against corporal punishment being employed. Such occurrences confirm that, after the Darnell crisis, he exercised his presiding role with a marked firmness of purpose.[2]

The crisis had forced Newman to exercise much more than a presiding role, and this was compounded by his own exacting vision of how the school ought to be. By April 1862 he was so overcome with fatigue and anxiety that he was confined to his room and, for the first time in his life, received Communion for the sick. Over the years his involvement diminished as the pattern of school life became established, but it did so only gradually, because as one problem receded others emerged. Continued uncertainties and difficulties undermined Newman's best efforts and kept school numbers below eighty during his lifetime. In vacations he was often left with school business while St John was away visiting parents, recruiting, or else resting – for schoolwork wore him out and brought on his asthma, and on several occasions Newman had to replace him in the classroom. After a life of high-profile activity and rewarding work, it was not easy for Newman to adapt and resign himself to the relatively humble and monotonous task of

---

1. Newman to St John, 14 July 1863, *L&D* XX, p. 493.
2. In 1881 Newman, as president, received complaints from masters and Oratorians about the headmaster, John Norris, and his tendency to centralise authority in himself; Newman's intervention with Norris seems on this occasion to have averted a crisis.

overseeing a small school, yet he entered fully into the spirit of schoolmastering. In response to friends who wondered why he now wrote so little, he declared:

> We are as yet very fortunate in our boys – and, if I could believe it to be God's will, would turn away my thoughts from ever writing any thing, and should see, in the super-intendence of these boys, the nearest return to my Oxford life – for, to my surprise, I find that Oxford "men" and schoolboys are but varieties of one species, and I think I should get on with the one as I got on with the other.[3]

It was during the decade after the crisis that the Oratory School was truly shaped by Newman, and it is chiefly from this period that his distinctive contribution to secondary education emerges. This contribution stands out most clearly when practice at the Oratory School is contrasted with practice elsewhere. The public schools were something of a moving target in the 1860s, as extensive reforms were being undertaken in response to criticism, first in the press and then in the Clarendon Report: about the neglect of pupils, the low master–pupil ratio, the narrow classics-dominated curriculum and the absence of more modern subjects, the over-emphasis on memory work and dearth of incentives to stimulate learning, the corruption in governing bodies and the misuse of endowments, and the run-down, inadequate facilities. Unlike the 1830s, when the controversy had centred on moral inadequacies, the reforms of the 1860s were inspired by the system's intellectual and economic failings. Immorality and bullying were largely over-looked, while the notion that a 'wholesome neglect' encouraged self-reliance gained official approval. Meanwhile, in a world apart, the daily routine at the Catholic colleges continued in its time-honoured fashion, largely unaffected by the upheavals elsewhere. The colleges were shielded from the influence of public opinion and, as they shared few of the public school defects, there was little stimulus for change from within – except from converts.

The influence of Newman's own school background on the

[3.] Newman to Miss Bowles, 13 February 1864, *L&D* XXI p. 51.

pattern of life at the Oratory School should not be underesti-
mated; nor should it be forgotten that the man chosen to begin
a public school for Catholics had never attended one himself.
After an early education at home, Newman had been sent at
the age of seven to Ealing School, a large and very successful
private boarding establishment. And although it was principally a preparatory school for Westminster and Winchester, he
had chosen to remain there until he was fifteen, against his
father's preference for Winchester. Ealing was quite unlike the
public schools at the time: it was blessed with first-class facilities, a homely atmosphere, a broad curriculum, specialist
teachers and small classes. Newman excelled in his studies and
participated enthusiastically in school life, acting in Latin plays,
taking part in debates, playing the violin, leading a boys'
society and editing several school magazines. Fifty years later,
he drew extensively upon his Ealing days when establishing the
pattern for education at Edgbaston.

A liberal education

Everyone associated with the Oratory School expected the boys
to receive a liberal education, since the idea was central to the
educational process Newman had elaborated in his Dublin
lectures, a process whose foundations were laid at school. At the
heart of his concept of a liberal education was the principle that
knowledge is its own end; that is, it need not be pursued for
immediate tangible benefits but for its own sake, for the cultivation and perfection of the intellect. Although these ideas
predated his experience of running a school, Newman had
already heard of their acceptance at Eton from one of the
masters there, William (Cory) Johnson, by repute a brilliant and
inspiring teacher. Johnson told Lord Thynne that Newman's
Dublin lectures[4] had been well received at Eton, and had given
masters and boys 'a new feeling about universities altogether:

[4.] The first set of lectures were published as *Discourses on the Scope and
Nature of University Education: Addressed to the Catholics of Dublin*
(1853); together with *Lectures and Essays on University Subjects* (1859),
they came to form *The Idea of a University: Defined and Illustrated*
(1873).

and that no book had ever come out which created so great and good a sensation amongst the boys and men at Eton'.[5]

Newman endorsed the traditional view that the study of classics was the best instrument for mental cultivation and the best guarantee for intellectual progress. For Newman, as Ian Ker has emphasised, what makes a liberal education is not the liberal arts themselves, but the discipline and mental cultivation arising from them; it has more to do with learning how to think than reading great books.[6] Nevertheless Newman favoured a broader curriculum than the public schools, as can be seen by a breakdown of the Oratory School curriculum:

First form – algebra, geometry, Latin, English history, scripture and French, plus practice in reading, writing and spelling;
Second form – geography added and elementary subjects dropped;
Third form – Greek and German added;
Fourth form – Latin composition begun;
Fifth form – elementary Greek prose begun.[7]

It was similar to the curriculum Newman had experienced at Ealing, but contrasted markedly with the Harrow curriculum in the early 1860s, where classics consumed eighteen of the twenty-two hours of a boy's weekly class-time. Though close in content to the curriculum at the Catholic colleges, Newman's choice was inspired by his own convictions and schooling rather than by practice elsewhere. Despite the breadth of the Oratory School curriculum, classics was the staple diet; Latin and Greek grammar and, to a lesser extent, mathematics occupied a special place in encouraging accuracy of thought, for Newman held strongly that 'the first step in intellectual training is to impress upon a boy's mind the idea of science, method, order, principle, and system; of rule and exception, of richness and harmony'.[8]

[5.] Thynne to Newman, n.d. [1858], *L&D* XVIII, p. 519n.
[6.] I.T. Ker, *The Achievement of John Henry Newman* (London: Collins, 1990), pp. 5–7.
[7.] Jackson, 'Newman', p. 196.
[8.] Newman, *The Idea of a University: Defined and Illustrated* (London: Longmans, Green & Co., 1873; 1907), p. xix.

The initial absence of science from the curriculum was due to Newman's contention that science at the time was insufficiently developed as a subject to act as a suitable training-ground for the intellect at school level.[9]

Assuming – though from what evidence is unclear – that Newman had altered his views on education some time after the Dublin lectures, Acton suspected he now inclined towards the abbé Gaume, whose writings on the place of pagan authors in classical studies had ignited a lively controversy in France. Gaume's exaggerated thesis argued that the revival of interest in pagan antiquity during the Renaissance had paved the way for the Revolution and other social ills. He wanted the pagan authors excluded from the greater part of the curriculum and replaced by Christian ones, even though the pagan authors had had a secure place in the colleges for three centuries. The Gaume controversy had begun just as Newman started his Dublin lectures, and he used them to refute the new theory: 'the Church's true policy is not to aim at the exclusion of Literature from Secular Schools, but at her own admission into them. [. . .] She fears no knowledge, but she purifies all; she represses no element of our nature, but cultivates the whole.'[10] The way this was put into practice at the Oratory School was by using the classical authors extensively, though selectively. While Acton doubted Newman's liberal credentials, others suspected him of a contrary disposition – yet another manifestation of Newman's pursuit of that delicate balance between two opposing tendencies. By contrast, the Protestant public schools adopted an ambivalent attitude towards classical literature, whose choicest pieces were frequently at odds with Christian doctrine and morals.[11]

9. The first entries in the school examination mark book (1873–88, OSA) show that 'natural philosophy' (physics) was taken by all fourth formers, and that four of the seven fifth formers studied chemistry. Of the nine schools investigated by the Clarendon Commission, science was only taught at Rugby.

10. *Idea of a University*, pp. 233–34.

11. The Oratory School's dilemma over classical texts was repeated in the search for suitable history books: the school began by using *The Student's Hume* but it was, in Newman's opinion, 'so flippantly irreligious' it had to be abandoned, and he even considered writing a history of England himself to fill the vacuum. More generally, Newman thought the whole question of schoolbooks and prizes was a great difficulty for Catholics.

It was in the *teaching* of classics that the Oratory School differed from the ecclesiastical colleges, and it did so by placing a greater emphasis on classical authors rather than works of the Church Fathers. At Oscott the curriculum had a more religious bent, being a preparation for priestly training (and for a foreign university system), while at the Oratory School it was humanist and geared to Oxford and Cambridge. Teaching in a way 'consistent with Catholic habits and requirements', as the prospectus advertised, implied a careful selection of texts, and expurgation where necessary. Newman objected strongly to the lewdness of the texts he was forced to use when coaching the eldest Bellasis boy for the London University exams, because the immoral thoughts introduced by Lucretius, Plautus and Terence were likely to enkindle immoral desires and actions; some of the books were steeped in indecency and impurity and one involved 'unnatural liberties between boys'.[12] Newman wrote to the authorities to complain, but without success. On Hope-Scott's advice, Bellasis sent Newman's letter to Lord Granville, Chancellor of the University of London, and it was shown to the Senate, but Bellasis was told candidly that there would be no changes unless the authorities were shamed into them. Bishop Grant advised Bellasis to pursue the matter himself by taking it up as the father of a family, so Bellasis wrote to the *Pall Mall Gazette*, enclosing Newman's letter, but it was not accepted. Despite the apparent futility of the protest, the University of London decided to adjust their syllabus the following year and did so along the lines requested.[13]

The declaration in the Oratory School prospectus that the curriculum would be that of an English public school was no glib advertisement or idle boast. Genuine academic excellence was aimed at, as testified by masters, boys and parents. St John's diary records his constant concern and that of the other masters for academic matters, and their (frequent) disappointment when progress fell short of their expectations. Parents showed no signs of being fobbed off with the trappings of a public

[12.] Newman to Bellasis, 25 January 1868, *L&D* XXIV, p. 19n (Section added in June for publication).
[13.] H. Tristram, 'London University and Catholic education', *Dublin Review* 199, October 1936, p. 278.

school, and their requests confirm that there was a real demand for scholarship. A measure of their self-confidence and commitment was that they were prepared to badger Newman about the curriculum, teaching methods and textbooks. When, for example, Simeon complained that the English pronunciation of Latin was not used, Newman explained that he had been outvoted by Arnold and St John in favour of the Italian pronunciation (which had been adopted throughout the Catholic Church). Challenged on the system for teaching Greek, Newman explained that formerly books such as the *Eton Grammar* had assigned ten declensions to nouns, whereas more recent books – those most serviceable for the boys – relied on different declension-theories; the school had chosen to move with the times rather than rely on old-fashioned books.

When Simeon complained that his son was backward, and – owing to the low standard among Catholics – unconscious of his incompetence, Newman firmly countered this impression; having taken the boy for Terence, he was able to vouch for his progress and he identified the problem as the boy's poor retention. However, Newman did admit that he and St John were concerned about the difficulty of drumming grammar into the heads of the weaker boys; Pope and St John brought the boys on in their grammar but it was neglected when they moved up to Arnold. This concern for academic standards at the Oratory School needs to be considered in the context of the times, when the teaching of Latin and Greek achieved very modest results with the majority of boys, even at the great schools; among the leading schools, only Shrewsbury was serious about the teaching of classics before the Clarendon Commission. Simeon had also complained about the lack of private tuition, which the school was unable to provide because of the expense – though *extra* tuition could be, and was, arranged on request. In 1864 several parents complained that no work had been set for the long vacation; it had in fact been set in previous years, but was remitted on this occasion because of an outbreak of measles. The dilemma Newman then faced, as on other occasions, was that some parents did not want holiday work, while others did; the ideal solution, he thought, was to set each boy separately the work his father wanted. All in all, the level of interest in scholarship compared very favourably with schools like Eton, where there was little incentive from home to study; to the extent that there was an academic elite there able to benefit, it was to the exclusion of the majority, for whom school was more a socialising rather than educational experience.

If a gauge of the academic seriousness of a school is the state of its library, then the Oratory School fares well, for it was well established by 1864, with senior and junior sections, a boy librarian and three assistants, and an elaborate system of rules (and fines). It indicates the existence of a culture of reading – and this despite Newman's concerns about the negative effects post-school examinations were having on school work, which fostered a modern, un-Oxford 'system of cramming and shallowness'. The school, he felt, ought to make good scholars out of good boys, 'and it is not simply our aim, but our passion to do so. If there is anything I detest, it is the superficial knowledge of many books.'[14] His maxim was ' "a little, but well"; that is, really know what you say you know'.[15] Applied to the teaching of classics, it was better to have a thorough understanding of how Latin syntax works, 'how the separate portions of a sentence hang together', than to have read through many classical authors. Newman's principle (applied to higher studies) was that 'A thorough knowledge of one science and a superficial acquaintance with many, are not the same thing; a smattering of a hundred things or a memory for detail, is not a philosophical or comprehensive view.'[16]

A clue to Newman's views on study habits is provided in his reply to a father's request for his son to have a single room. Besides the practical ruling that such rooms were reserved for senior boys paying higher fees, the request was turned down on educational grounds: Newman argued that there were considerable advantages in boys having to gain the power of abstraction by studying with other boys, and he cited the example of Dr Arnold, who in later life attributed his powers of concentration amidst distractions at home or elsewhere to having gained this habit in the schoolroom at Winchester. Newman thought that, for the boy in question, a separate room

---

[14.] Newman to Simeon, 22 August 1864, *L&D* XXI, p. 205.
[15.] *Idea of a University*, p. 335.
[16.] *Idea of a University*, p. 144.

NOTE.

ORATORY SCHOOL LIBRARY.

RULES.

1. The Senior Library to be open to boys of the 6th, 5th, 4th, and 3rd forms. The Junior Library to be open to the remainder of the School.

2 The terms of admission to be 2s. 6d. for the Senior, and 2s. for the Junior Library. This is to be paid before admission.

3. No book or periodical to be admitted which has not been passed by the Prefect of Discipline.

4. All books to be registered before being taken. The days of registration are Sunday, Wednesday, and Friday, from 5 to 6, and 6.30 to 7 o'clock.

5. New books are registered to subscribers for one week only—old ones for a fortnight. When read, they are to be returned, and all damage done to be pointed out to the librarian. Fine for not doing so to be 4d.

6. All books lying about the library to be confiscated for the use of the library, unless redeemed within a fortnight by paying a fine of 3d. each book.

7. All damage to books, furniture, or anything appertaining to the library to be compensated for according to its value.

8. The Masters (who subscribe) are alone to be permitted to have a book or periodical out of the library.

Library rules and fines, 1864.

9

FINES.

—

1. Leaving door open ... ... 1d.
2. Talking above a whisper ... ... 1d.
3. Putting a book in its wrong place ... ... 1d.
4. Moving chairs or benches from their places... ... 1d.
5. Standing before the fire ... ... 1d.
6. Sitting round the fire ... ... 2d.
7. Leaving books out ... ... 2d.
8. Eating or bringing in eatables ... ... 3d.
9. Non-Subscribers entering the Library ... ... 6d.
10. Taking an unregistered book ... ... 6d.
11. Taking books or periodicals out of the Library ... 1s.
12. Disturbance ... ... from 2d. to 1s.

At the discretion of the Librarian.

G. SHERSTON BAKER,

1864.

(A framed copy of these Rules was placed in each of the two rooms
constituting the Library. I was authorized to appoint sub-librarians to
assist me, and I appointed three concurrently, Charles Scott-Murray, Hubert
Hibbert, and Charles Riddell.—Note from Sir G. S. B.)

would be a temptation to read books that were not relevant to his school studies: as he had written in the *Idea*, it was a common mistake 'to fancy that the gratification of a love of reading is real study'.[17] On another occasion he discouraged a parent from engaging a private tutor as his son was not backward, and advised him: 'He will learn more thoroughly and steadily, when he learns with others, than when he had to learn by himself, as would be the case with a private Tutor. [...] I think it best to let things take their course, and to be patient'.[18] Newman greatly admired the existence of 'a sort of self-education in the academic institutions of Protestant England', whether in the public schools or ancient universities, which explains why he stressed the importance of schoolboys gaining habits such as diligence, regularity and persevering application.[19] A major error of the day, he felt, lay in considering that 'our true excellence comes not from within, but from without; not wrought out through personal struggle and sufferings, but following upon a passive exposure to influences' outside. It entailed 'the theory that diversion is the instrument of improvement, and excitement the condition of right action'.[20]

Partnership with parents

While Newman is acknowledged as a champion of the idea of a liberal education, it is less well known that he stressed that a school's *main* task is to assist parents in their duty to care for and educate their offspring. This underlying conviction was not explicitly stated in school documents but manifested itself in practice by shaping the Oratory School's attitude to boys and their parents. It surfaced frequently in Newman's correspondence and was expressed in utterances like the following: 'It is a tremendous thing to be intrusted with the hopes and loves of so many Mamas.'[21] And there is evidence that parents were

17. *Idea of a University*, p. 341.
18. Newman to Colyar, 27 September 1862, *L&D* XX, p. 278.
19. *Idea of a University*, p. 147.
20. Newman, 'The Tamworth Reading Room', *Discussions and Arguments on Various Subjects* (London: Longmans, Green & Todd, 1891), p. 266.

grateful for the attention lavished on the school by Newman: among the addresses to mark Newman's cardinalate in 1879 was one from mothers of schoolboys, past and present, who thanked him, 'as parents, for the character and tone with which your personal influence has invested the Oratory School'. In reply to a separate address from former pupils, Newman acknowledged the burden of responsibility he had assumed, declaring that the care of schoolboys was 'a pastoral charge of the most intimate kind'. Parents, he said, had made a great sacrifice and 'an act of supreme confidence' in committing their sons to a boarding school; the 'sense of the great trust' made the school anxious to respond faithfully to its duties. 'No other department of the pastoral office requires such sustained attention and such unwearied services', because those with pastoral responsibilities lived with their pupils, saw them grow up, and 'are ever tenderly watching over them, that their growth may be in the right direction'.[22] On an earlier occasion, when Bellasis told Newman that the school had been a great success for his sons, Newman replied that it could only take a 'due portion of the credit [...] seeing the patterns and guidance they have at home'[23] – in other words, a school had to rely and build on the education received in the family. By contrast, Woodard had little sympathy for the conception of education as a partnership between parents and school; he aimed to substitute the degradation of family life with the moral and religious atmosphere of school, and therefore, unlike Newman, brooked no interference in school affairs by parents or others.

Foremost among the duties of a school acting *in loco parentis*, Newman was convinced, is care for the religious formation of its pupils, a task that he considered perfectly compatible with a sound academic education. To repair the neglect of the school's spiritual health under Darnell, Newman carried out a complete overhaul of arrangements. Just before being appointed headmaster, St John had already remarked on the

[21.] Newman to Bloxam, 24 October 1863, *L&D* XX, p. 542.
[22.] *Addresses to Cardinal Newman with His Replies*, ed. W.P. Neville (London: Longmans, Green & Co., 1905), pp. 121–22, 124.
[23.] Newman to Bellasis, 4 September 1865, *L&D* XXII, p. 42.

'tremendous uphill work to get back [a] habit of prayer',[24] and his diary entries for 1862 confirm the laxity of the previous regime, as well as describing the efforts made to reform it:

Sat. 1 Feb.	Opened school. Disorder before school in Schoolroom. Very bad attendance in Chapel. Not more than 28 boys.
Sun. 23 Feb.	Some boys shirk the catechism.
Sun. 2 Mar.	Bad attendance at Mass. 6 boys [given] impositions for being late.
Wed. 5 Mar.	All noise and confusion in school [...] At evening prayers spoke to the boys about their devotions – only 5 boys at Rosary.
Sun. 9 Mar.	Many boys late at Mass. Mass Prefect didn't do his duty. The Father [Newman] preached to the boys on inattention in church. [...] Some boys behaved badly at night prayers.[25]

Under Newman and St John the timetable was properly enforced: on weekdays the boys rose at 6.30 a.m., said their prayers at 6.50 a.m., either at their bedside or in church, and at 7.00 a.m. attended Mass; the Angelus was recited at the end of morning school. At night the younger boys went to bed at 8.30 p.m. and at 8.50 p.m. there were joint prayers and then a reading from a spiritual classic such as the *Garden of the Soul*, after which they remained on their knees for a few minutes for private prayers; the older boys followed this routine an hour later. In Holy Week all the boys made a three-day retreat, preached by a priest invited for the occasion and sometimes attended by masters. Although the school timetable resembled those in use at the Catholic colleges, it was more flexible; attendance at the Rosary after tea, for example, was optional. By contrast, there was nothing similar at the ancient public schools, not even for those intended for ministry in the

---

[24.] St John to Newman, 16 January 1862, BOA.
[25.] St John's diary, BOA.

Established Church; indeed the atmosphere at Eton has been described as one of 'pleasant heathenism'.[26]

Foremost among the duties of the two spiritual directors was hearing the boys' Confessions, besides being available in their rooms for boys to chat to; and, as part of the general tightening up, Newman asked the confessors to give him a monthly return of the boys going. From anecdotal evidence it can be seen that the sacrament was an integral part of school life. In 1865 the school's second theft occurred when a large sum of money was stolen from a boy's desk; the boys knew of it and, as the money was still missing after three weeks, the Oratorians took action by declaring it was a matter of humiliation for the whole school. With the day for monthly Confessions approaching, it was announced that the whole school should go with the theft especially before them, and that nothing would be done if, after the Confessions, the money was returned. Everyone went and the money reappeared, while the culprit's identity remained a secret. 'The boys took it in the best spirit, and the whole School with Fr Ambrose [St John] said some Hail Marys for the penitent.'[27]

The comments of one of the masters, John Walford, about Confession are particularly revealing, since he had taught at Harrow and Eton. A friend still teaching at Eton received letters from him 'full of the difference between Catholic schools and those of which he had experience, and he was greatly struck by the simple faith of the lads'. Walford was particularly impressed by

the manliness of the Edgbaston boys and the fervent piety of many, the combination not having been frequent in his previous experience. The bearing of the Sacrament of Penance, not only on individual souls, but on the discipline and purity of school life, came to him like a revelation.

Walford was convinced that 'for boyish needs and for boyish sins confession and frequent communion were the only safe-

26. Chandos, *Boys Together*, p. 270.
27. Newman to Bellasis, 26 November 1865, *L&D* XXII, p. 112.

guard and cure'.[28] A major factor in his conversion was his conviction that the sacrament of Penance was administered in an inadequate fashion within the Established Church. Woodard had argued in a similar vein, that regular spiritual direction and the availability of Confession were essential for avoiding the dangers public school boys were exposed to, and in particular helping them in the virtue of chastity.[29] It should be pointed out, however, that Woodard's attitude was exceptional, because at the time the public schools were generally incapable of providing any teaching or guidance on sexual matters.

Arrangements after the crisis show that religious instruction had been completely transformed: boys were taught to recite their prayers properly, they learnt their catechism thoroughly and tested each other in pairs every week in the presence of Newman or St John. There were instructions and sermons for the whole school, and Scripture was studied in English, Latin and Greek. Newman himself gave the catechetical lectures to the older boys, and he carefully marked and annotated the essays they were required to write afterwards; no doubt the subject matter was carefully chosen to avoid any hint of dullness, in line with his contention that 'Youths need a masculine religion, if it is to carry captive their restless imaginations, and their wild intellects, as well as to touch their susceptible hearts'.[30] Newman had always anticipated that the Oratory would stimulate the piety of the boys, but under Darnell its influence was stifled. Now Newman was able to involve the boys in devotions throughout the liturgical year: Stations of the Cross on Fridays in Lent; devotions to Our Lady in May; a Corpus Christi procession (accompanied by a band) within the school grounds; a novena of prayer for St Philip's Day; Forty

---

[28.] C.K. Paul, *Memories* (London: Kegan, Paul & Co., 1899), pp. 235, 238.

[29] Boys at Lancing were seen individually for spiritual direction every six weeks, but Confession was voluntary and required the prior consent of parents. In the mid-1850s about a quarter of the school went, but by the early 1860s the proportion had dropped to around ten per cent.

[30.] Newman, *Sermons Preached on Various Occasions* (London: Longmans, 1870; 1898), p. 14.

Hours' adoration of the Blessed Sacrament; and 'spiritual entertainments', consisting of stories about saints interspersed with music. Regarding the practical aspects of worship, Newman maintained that a handsome church was essential for the proper establishment of a boys' school, as 'children and boys take in religion principally through the eye',[31] so that the church was to be 'one main instrument of religious and moral training'.[32] The financial sacrifice entailed in adapting the Oratory church was considerable – £3530 before the crisis – but parents happily acquiesced. When Francis Ward understood that the building works for the school would not include a private chapel, he argued that it was too important to omit and worth the sacrifice; as all the existing schools had private chapels, he pleaded, how could they do without one? He need not have doubted Newman's priorities, because Newman had personally overseen the building of the University Church at Dublin. In both cases – school and university – the architect was Pollen, who had previously worked with William Morris and Edward Burne-Jones.

For Newman's idea of partnership with parents to work, communication was essential. Reacting to complaints about lack of information from Darnell, Newman acknowledged that 'one deficiency has been that we have not let parents know enough how their sons were going on. This I hope will be henceforth set right.'[33] To this end, he sent them twice-yearly reports, in the form of individual letters written by himself based on information supplied by the staff; he would only consider himself excused from the task if he met the parents at the end of term, or if St John called on the family in the holidays. However, the operation proved to be very time-consuming and by 1865 had been simplified by using a pro-forma. Besides report writing, Newman personally undertook the burden of dealing with parental demands, which usually concerned petty school matters and kept him busy in term and out.

Newman complained to Major-General Sheil, an old

[31.] Newman to Bellasis, 13 April 1858, *L&D* XVIII, p. 319.
[32.] Newman to Bellasis, 23 April 1858, *L&D* XVIII, p. 332.
[33.] Newman to Allies, 26 January 1862, *L&D* XX, p. 135.

Stonyhurst boy, that he could not be expected to provide a written reply to all parental requests. Sheil had asked for his son to have extra lessons in 'penmanship' from the writing master, but implementation of his request had been delayed. Newman asked Sheil to be 'more merciful in future', for 'if you knew enough about the conduct of a School, you would understand that the directions of 60 or 70 parents cannot be carried out at once [...] as a footman answers his master's bell'.[34] He was all too aware that parents could expect too much of a school and, at times, wondered if the schoolmaster had a more onerous task than someone like his father, a banker.

> Bankers had all the responsibility of all pursuits and traders upon them, for, whenever any one was in pecuniary difficulty, he went to his Banker. And so a schoolmaster has the anxieties of all the parents of his boys – and more so – for parents would not blame themselves, if their children fell ill at home – but they are naturally disposed to think that school-carefulness [...] might be greater than it is.[35]

An instance of this was the way the school had been obliged to re-paper and wash all the bedrooms in one house merely because a boy, who had left school well, had fallen ill at home. It would seem that Newman was wary of assuming responsibilities that naturally belonged to parents. When, for example, a parent asked the school to assist in organising a collection from British youth to mark the twenty-fifth anniversary of Pope Pius IX, Newman replied that he thought it should be done at home by parents, not by schoolmasters. In the school's interests, and therefore the boys', Newman reciprocated with his own demands; he tried laying down rules about vacations, though this turned out to be problematic as parents had such varied preferences. In January 1862 he received two letters

---

[34.] Newman to Sheil, 2 March 1865, *L&D* XXI, pp. 426–27. The state of affairs was, to Newman's thinking, worse at Oscott, where the president was assailed by the parents of a hundred lay boys who paid low fees, yet expected first-class teachers, while his first duty was to the twenty church boys (*ibid.*).

[35.] Newman to Mrs Mozley, 2 January 1864, *L&D* XXI, pp. 3–4.

about the Christmas holidays: one from Sheil, insisting that they were too long as, by the end of the three weeks, the boys were tired of home and ready for school; the other from Gaisford, who wanted an extension to allow his boys a few more days' hunting. Newman dealt with them in a novel way: he cut off the signatures from each letter and sent them to the other, after which no more was heard from either of them!

When parents came to collect or take away their sons at the beginning and end of term, Newman used the opportunity to speak to them at length. If alone, mothers could stay overnight at Mrs Wootten's and fathers at the Oratory; otherwise couples took rooms at the Plough and Harrow inn. Such in-depth discussion of children was not a common practice, either at the public schools or at the Catholic colleges. In days when term-time visits from home were infrequent, letter-writing was the best substitute, and the younger boys were all expected to write home once a week; some did so daily. Mrs Wootten supervised the operation until a parent complained; thereafter it became a school matter, and all boys were given an hour a week, in school time, for the purpose. Although Newman realised that the privilege was sometimes abused, he preferred to trust, rather than check, that the boys complied.

Under Newman's guidance the dames continued making school a second home to the boys, particularly the younger ones, and Mrs Wootten remained a powerful figure in their eyes. In fact the dame's role, as well as her title, remained fully intact, for Newman spoke of each dame being 'supreme in her own place',[36] and he applied the same division of labour as he had in 1858. 'There will always be *some* opposition between Masters and Matrons', he wrote in the spring of 1862, 'for their duties lie in different directions; the one wish to bring on the boys in their studies, and the other have to take care of their souls and bodies.'[37] He readily admitted to one father that a conversation with Mrs Wootten about his son was worth many with himself. Such was Mrs Wootten's continued and crucial contribution that Newman could say that she and St John had been 'the life and the making of the School'.[38] If this seems to

[36.] Newman to Hope-Scott, 22 June 1863, *L&D* XX, p. 478.
[37.] Newman to Miss Hallahan, n.d. [1862], *L&D* XX, p. 146.
[38.] Newman to Miss Bowles, 4 December 1875, *L&D* XXVII, p. 390.

imply that it was the *person* of Mrs Wootten rather than her *role* as dame that mattered, an incident in 1882 indicates otherwise: a convert who taught briefly at the school before becoming an Oratorian recorded a discussion he had with Newman about a new school prospectus; at first Newman wanted only those with degrees named on it, but he gave way and agreed to listing all the masters *provided* that the dame, Mrs Holden, was also included; and Newman 'went on vigorously to insist upon the importance of this speciality of ours – a lady-matron'.[39]

Along with attending to the boys' spiritual needs, the dames were responsible for their bodily health, a concern of considerable importance, since the risk of contracting contagious diseases or illnesses was ever-present (as it was at all boarding schools). When an epidemic of scarlet fever hit Birmingham in 1862, an infirmary was immediately set up far from the school buildings in case there was such an outbreak, or one of measles or whooping cough, and a nurse was sought. Oscott was so badly hit that the boys were sent home, and one died. Newman attributed the Oratory School's success in escaping a serious epidemic to the great care of the dames, who exercised the utmost vigilance in dealing with boys who showed symptoms of illness. Parents were asked not to return their sons from holidays unless they were in good health, and rumours of illnesses in families were investigated – delicately, but firmly. Fears of individual parents were assuaged individually, but at times it became necessary to send out circular letters. One in 1863 announced that a master had contracted scarlet fever but that he had been separated from the school before it had fully developed; another the following year informed parents that the boy Horace Gaisford had come from home with scarlet fever but had been sent back home at once, and that sufficient time had elapsed as quarantine for parents to receive their sons home at Easter without risk of infection. On a lighter note, the 1862 prospectus declared that special attention was to be paid to the diet, as well as the health and comfort of the boys, and to this end parents were requested to have all jams and sweetmeats handed in, as medical advice warned of the dangers of miscellaneous eating (known in school as 'grubbing') upon the health of

[39.] Eaglesim's diary, January 1882, BOA.

the boys, if for no other reason than that of taking away their appetite for meals. The prospectus also proclaimed that water and baths were supplied in abundance, and that good medical advice, including the homeopathic variety, was within call.

Knowing the boys

The tone Newman set by his example at the school was a manifestation of his lifelong insistence on the pastoral role of the educator. Though a great lover of books, Newman was first and foremost an advocate of direct and personal teacher–student interaction; and he held personal influence and oral tradition in higher regard than books and the written tradition. The emphasis he placed on the role of personal influence in education can be traced back to his early formative days at Ealing, where the scholarly and cultured headmaster, Dr Nicholas, befriended Newman from the start and accorded him special privileges; and where one of the classics masters, Walter Mayers, deeply influenced him through sermons, conversations and suggested reading. After Newman's 'seven years of plenty' at Ealing, Trinity College Oxford was a chastening experience, as he learnt little from his tutors and suffered from a lack of guidance – though it taught him the value of a good teacher–pupil relationship by its absence. As a tutor at Oriel he had changed the lecture system to favour the more serious students, and had found time for the more worthy ones; 'With such youths he cultivated relations, not only of intimacy, but of friendship, and almost of equality', Newman later wrote of himself, 'seeking their society in outdoor exercise, on evenings, and in Vacation.'[40] To Newman's thinking a school was like a university, 'an Alma Mater, knowing her children one by one, not a foundry, or a mint, or a treadmill'.[41] After the crisis there was a significantly greater investment in pastoral care, which cannot be attributed solely to the school's struggle for survival – although Newman did recognise the advantage of the school's being on trial as a

[40.] Autobiographical memoir, 13 January 1874, *AW*, p. 90.
[41.] *Idea of a University*, pp. 144–45.

stimulation, for he reckoned that 'A long established school grows callous'.[42] The detail and incisiveness of his termly letters to Oratory School parents was symptomatic of his concern for the individual and of the way his mind instinctively recoiled from systems requiring identical treatment of people.

To compile the school reports, Newman pulled together observations and opinions from the whole staff to provide a balanced overview: the depth of analysis and the insights they contain lead to the conclusion that Newman had both a gift for judging individual boys and a keen understanding of the genus 'boy'. Some of these characteristics are brought out in Newman's first report on Cyril Allies, who seems to have been a difficult boy. All boys are wayward, he told the father, but in Cyril there was a lack of $\pi o v$ $\sigma \tau \omega$ (basis to work from) that made it difficult to stimulate him. As with most boys, religious principle or a sense of duty did not act energetically enough to motivate him, and attempts to encourage him to sit the entrance exam for Woolwich had failed because he had dropped out of the special mathematics class: an example of his shortcomings was supplied in the shape of a sum he had been given and his solution. Cyril had been excused Greek to do more mathematics, 'but how can he do algebra unless he can work figures correctly?' His lack of grounding in various subjects made progress difficult; 'his heart is not in his work, and his influence in the school is not good'.[43]

A theme Newman repeatedly emphasised to parents was the need for patience with their sons. He calmed their eagerness for quick gains, insisting that the phases of growing up be respected and that irritating passing habits be overlooked. Boys could not be forced like plants; each would bear flower and fruit in his own season. Newman showed considerable understanding and patience for the fitful process of adolescent maturation, as can be seen from his comments on the young Duke of Norfolk:

> He has fits of negligence when every thing goes wrong, and then we are perplexed with the number of impositions which fall upon him from every quarter – and we

[42.] Newman to Bloxam, 24 October 1862, *L&D* XX, p. 542.
[43.] Newman to Allies, 15 April 1862, *L&D* XX, pp. 186–87.

have to release him from the weight of them, as best we may.

There are boys who do him harm by encouraging him to make game of these magisterial corrections – and he sometimes comes up for the imposition, as if it were good fun. (Pray, do not hint this to him.) He will become more manly in a little time. I think on the whole he is better in getting up – but here too he has fits of dawdling. In spite of all this, he is exact and methodical in his habits – and it is amusing to see how well he keeps his books and clothes. [...] As to ourselves, the only fear is that, from extreme anxiety about him, we should meddle with him too much, and make too much of little things.[44]

Lack of patience arose from anxiety and not having 'confidence enough in God's mercy', he told the Duchess. 'We ought in the first place to put him into the hands of Divine Love – and then do our part carefully and calmly.'[45]

Newman was keenly aware that lack of success at school was no indicator against future success.

[...] boys at school look like each other, and pursue the same studies, some of them with greater success than others; but it will sometimes happen, that those who acquitted themselves but poorly in class, when they come into the action of life, and engage in some particular work, which they have already been learning in its theory and with little promise of proficiency, are suddenly found to have what is called an eye for that work – an eye for trade matters, or for engineering, or a special taste for literature – which no one expected from them at school, while they were engaged on notions.[46]

As the purpose of education was 'to prepare for the world',[47] it

44. Newman to the Duchess of Norfolk, 16 April 1862, *L&D* XX, pp. 187–88.
45. Newman to the Duchess of Norfolk, 30 December 1863, *L&D* XX, p. 572.
46. Newman, *An Essay in aid of a Grammar of Assent* (London: Longmans, Green & Co., 1870; 1898), pp. 75–76.
47. *Idea of a University*, p. 232.

was vital to cater for the individual as far as possible. The school was for the boys, not *vice versa*: studies were tailored to suit individual needs; rules were waived for good reasons; expectations varied according to the individual – more, for example, was expected of Bellasis's sons as Newman felt they should turn out as 'patterns of Oratory education'.[48]

Newman was not satisfied with an acquaintance with the boys; he aimed to know them well and make their personal friendship. While the monthly tests he had established enabled him to monitor each boy's academic progress, the introduction of termly 'characters' had a broader sweep. After the end-of-term exams, boys went individually to receive their characters; St John read out an account of the boy's progress and behaviour, after which Newman gave a few words of encouragement, approval, or remonstrance. Newman attached great importance to this termly engagement and gave it priority over all other business, refusing to depute the task to others; at the age of eighty-nine he was still conducting the personal interviews of school leavers.

A clue to Newman's ability to relate to boys comes from Oscar Browning, the well-known educational reformer; he stayed overnight at the Oratory in 1866 and was 'struck with Newman's marvellous copiousness of language and his abundant fluency, also with his use of harmless worldly slang, that he might not appear priggish or monkish'.[49] Browning himself, during his years as an Eton housemaster, placed great emphasis on trust in boys, continuing the cult of friendship between master and boy that had been introduced at Eton and Harrow. His approach reflected (and inspired) a gradual change at the time towards a better master–pupil relationship and less reliance on corporal punishment. Newman was also influential in this change of attitude. In *Historical Sketches* (first published in 1856), he had ridiculed with devastating effect 'the reign of Law without Influence, System without Personality', and had remarked: 'An academical system without the personal influence of teachers upon pupils, is an arctic winter'.

---

48. Newman to Bellasis, 30 December 1863, *L&D* XX, p. 571.
49. O. Browning, *Memories of Sixty Years at Eton, Cambridge and Elsewhere* (London: John Lane, 1910), p. 269.

I have experienced a state of things, in which teachers were cut off from the taught as by an insurmountable barrier; when neither party entered into the thoughts of the other; when each lived by and in itself; when the tutor was supposed to fulfil his duty, if he trotted on like a squirrel in his cage, if at a certain hour he was in a certain room, or in hall, or in chapel, as it might be; and the pupil did his duty too, if he was careful to meet his tutor in that same room, or hall, or chapel, at the same certain hour; and when neither the one nor the other dreamed of seeing each other out of lecture, out of chapel, out of academical gown. I have known places where a stiff manner, a pompous voice, coldness and condescension, were the teacher's attributes, and where he neither knew, nor wished to know, and avowed he did not wish to know, the private irregularities of the youths committed to his charge.

By contrast, Newman described how at Oxford those like himself who united rule and influence 'gained the hearts and became the guides of the youthful generation'.[50]

Several decades later his venerable age and status meant that this approach was less feasible, although it was still his aim. Reflecting on his schooldays in the 1880s, Arthur Pollen recalled that nothing pleased Newman more than making friends with the boys, and the many opportunities they had of personal contact with him made their friendship a real one. On the other hand, another old boy, Lord Edmund Howard, considered that neither Newman nor St John were on particularly familiar terms with the boys – a fact which merely indicates how the chemistry of friendship only worked in some cases. However, both Newman and St John were generally regarded with schoolboy affection, and in their different ways they each made a profound impression on the boys. Newman's movements about the school were very different from St John's: he glided by with rapid noiseless steps without looking about him, seemingly oblivious to the boys who stood up and raised their caps in his presence. The contrast in their preach-

---

50. Newman, *Historical Sketches* III (London: Longmans, Green & Co., 1872; 1909), pp. 74–76.

ing styles was just as extreme. St John declined to use the pulpit and instead paced up and down the front of the altar, eyeing the boys and addressing them in a vigorous fashion. The younger boys found Newman very quiet and apt to quote at length from Scripture, but they were held spellbound by his readings from the Bible after Mass, and at times his silvery voice and beautiful intonation reduced them to tears. Half a century after Newman's death, one old boy could still recall the distinct, deliberate manner in which he intoned the *Pater Noster* during Mass, so full of deep devotion.

In spite of their contrasting styles, Newman and St John had much in common, above all a strong devotion to their founder St Philip Neri, whose temper coloured the activities of the Birmingham Oratory. The qualities of this saint had a profound influence on the school, too, and this influence also worked through someone like Mrs Wootten as well as the Oratorians themselves. Among his most notable qualities, St Philip is known for his sympathy for others, his honesty and good humour; his preference for eliciting the cooperation of others through affection rather than by force or command; his love of spontaneity and his dislike of pretence of any kind – characteristics that strongly influenced the Oratorians in the way they dealt with the boys.

As for the masters, only a few clues survive about their dealings with the boys and whether they were able to exercise a personal influence in the way Newman intended. James Marshall spoke of the 'openhearted affectionate standing' of the masters with the boys;[51] Henri La Serre described himself as 'easy and playful' in the playground, but 'pretty stiff in study time';[52] while Gerard Manley Hopkins felt 'as if they [the boys] were all my children'.[53] More revealing still is a letter home from Hilaire Belloc in which he wrote:

> a new master came the other day and he understands me, he opened the way and though the battle is there, it is

[51.] Brownlow, *Sir James Marshall*, p. 7.
[52.] La Serre, 'Memoirs', p. 16.
[53.] Hopkins to Coleridge, 26 October 1867, *Further Letters of Gerard Manley Hopkins* (London: OUP, 1954), p. 45.

possible to fight it and a great weight is off my heart. Why I hated everything was because no-one had broken the ice for me, now it is all right. I am in a truer, happier state of things than I ever was before.[54]

By all accounts it was Richard Pope who best fulfilled Newman's idea of the master who is kind and sympathetic to boys. 'Pa Dick', as he was known, had the rare knack of gaining their confidence and affection, while remaining a strict disciplinarian. He regularly took boys in twos and threes for walks – different ones each time – and used the opportunity to give words of advice by steering the conversations onto serious topics, yet without appearing to preach. Remembered as a fatherly figure, he managed to combine his enormous contribution to school life with raising eight children, a task made especially difficult by his being widowed twice.

As some of the masters were also tutors, it is worth bearing in mind the distinctive role of the tutor, though its form at the Oratory School can only be ascertained indirectly through Newman's commentary on the distinction between college and university. The conventional division of labour at the two ancient universities concerned teaching methods (professorial at the university, tutorial at the college) and determined purpose (the pursuit of knowledge at university, the formation of character at college). This division was also recognised at the public schools in the distinction between the masters, who taught, and the tutors or housemasters, who had pastoral duties. The same system was employed at the Oratory School, with the added refinement that it was not just tutors but also dames and spiritual directors who were involved in character development. Just as Newman argued that 'the office of a Catholic university is to teach *faith*, and of Colleges to protect *morals*',[55] so masters and Oratorians (it seems) concentrated on giving religious instruction while tutors, dames and spiritual directors focused on religious training. Unfortunately, there is no record of the tutor's duties and how they dovetailed with

---

[54.] M. Belloc-Lowdnes, *The Young Hilaire Belloc* (New York: Kennedy & Sons, 1956), p. 73.

[55.] Newman to Dalgairns, 23 July 1852, *L&D* XV, p. 134.

those of spiritual director and dame; only the dame's role is transparent. Nevertheless, three principles emerge from Newman's conception of the tutor's role at the collegiate houses in Dublin which undoubtedly he sought to apply at the school: that the pastoral function was more easily undertaken when relieved of the disciplinary element; that it required 'a sustained solicitude, and a mind devoted to his charge'; and that it is best exercised with flexibility.[56] Ideally Newman would have wanted a system of private tuition at the Oratory School; it had long been talked of, the plan being, 'if possible, to combine the advantages of a large school with those of private tuition', but it was decided against as the cost was prohibitive.[57] In theory, if not in practice, the full Oxbridge tutorial system nurtured intellectual and moral growth: it had been an essential ingredient at the Catholic University, but due to its expense it was beyond the reach of Edgbaston, and could only be employed in schools like Eton and Harrow.[58]

Inside and outside the classroom

Although the timetable at the Oratory School was not a permanent fixture but was altered whenever necessary, the timetable of 1863 is as representative as any other in showing what a boy's daily routine was like:

7.45–8.30	Class
8.30	Breakfast, then play
9.30–12.00	Classes
1.00	Dinner, then play
2.30–5.00	Prep, then classes (Monday, Wednesday and Friday)

[56.] Newman, *My Campaign*, p. 119.
[57.] Newman to Lewis, 26 August 1860, *L&D* XIX, p. 398.
[58.] In the tutor system at Harrow, which had been imported from Eton, the older boys spent an hour or two a week reading classical texts with their tutor, and were set reading by him — independent of form work. The tutor sent monthly reports to the housemaster, who added comments about behaviour in the house before sending them to parents.

5.00–6.00	Play
6.00	Tea
7.00–8.30	Prep
8.30	Supper.[59]

On Tuesday afternoons the boys had two hours of drawing, music practice, prep or letter-writing; on Thursdays there were games; and on Saturdays Confessions followed by an hour's military drill. For both teaching and boarding purposes the school was divided into two: the first and second forms, each with upper and lower halves, constituted the Lower School, and the third, fourth and fifth forms the Upper. In the mid-1860s the Lower School was taught in the old schoolroom in the Oratory House, while the older boys used the large purpose-built schoolroom, which was divided up in the usual Victorian fashion into smaller self-contained units. As the masters had great difficulty in supervising prep, a rearrangement took place in 1867, when at Newman's suggestion they adopted the practice he had known at school: instead of splitting school hours between classes and prep, the two were combined and a master alternated between teaching a class and seeing boys individually with their difficulties. The aim was to free the masters from noon to 6.00 p.m. to enable them to take private pupils, as well as prepare lessons and correct work. Even so, young masters like Hopkins found that school duties took up all their time. Besides the teaching and the marking (which he found very taxing), he was required to take games – first hockey, then football – but he found time to relax by listening to the school chamber quartet. St John noticed how overworked he was and took pity on him, rearranging his duties to allow him time for private reading. According to Hopkins, the school had a reputation for working the boys hard, but it seems that the masters were worked harder still.

One of the key founding ideas of the school had been to provide a better academic education than the Catholic colleges by using the higher fees to attract first-class schoolmasters, so it is not surprising that the main source of masters was the pool of well-educated converts: as products of the public schools and

[59.] 'Some old memories', *OSM* 36, December 1904, p. 5.

the two ancient universities, they provided one of the vital credentials for status as a public school. Some of them were recommended by promoters or friends, some volunteered, while others were sought out; and after the crisis Newman was able to carry out the selection himself. No-one was better placed to tap this pool, but even he found that 'public school men are rare'.[60] And unfortunately for the school, the converts taken on were, for the most part, birds of passage who sought a temporary refuge after becoming Catholics until they decided on their future. Some became priests; others entered the professions.

As might be expected, Newman chose men who were not only educated but scholarly; several of them had even published. However, scholastic aptitude had its drawbacks, for Newman realised that 'a very superior man' like Arnold was unsuited for teaching the younger boys because he could not control them. It is recorded that on one occasion 'Tommy' (as the boys called him) decided to crack down on misbehaviour and took a cane into class with him, but he was pelted with peas and paper pellets and the boys became very disorderly. Even with the older ones he tended to teach above them and neglect their grammar; but he had his strengths, and Newman recognised that he was like his father in the way he 'opens a boy's mind'.[61] The name of Arnold had helped rescue the school, but ultimately the school could not meet his demands for greater remuneration, which became more acute after the publication of the Clarendon Report. Against Arnold's £400 per annum plus accommodation for his family and places for his three sons at the school, the Report revealed that his equivalents at Rugby, the four senior classical masters, each received £120 from the foundation, about £600 from boarding profits, and £870 from the tuition element of fees. Arnold acknowledged that the Oratory School did not have Rugby's economies of scale, but nevertheless requested a considerable addition to his salary, as well as a means by which it might increase in line with pupil numbers. Permission to boost his income by taking in boarders was denied, though this was offset to some extent by his appointment as an examiner for the Indian Civil Service. At the time

[60.] Newman to St John, 26 August 1863, *L&D* XX, p. 512.
[61.] Newman to Simeon, 22 August 1864, *L&D* XXI, p. 205.

Arnold was drifting away from the Catholic Church, encouraged by his vehemently anti-Catholic wife. A critical moment arose when Newman and St John prevented him from giving a boy a translation of Döllinger's *Kirche und Kirchen* (later placed on the Index of prohibited books) as an extra school prize, and he was encouraged to leave at Easter 1865. He went on to become a private tutor at Oxford.

Newman realised that Arnold's relatively enormous salary was more than the school could afford, and had only been justified by the special circumstances of the crisis and the prospect of a significant increase in school numbers. In the term before the Darnell crisis, the annual salary bill was £800: Moody receiving £300, Darnell £150, Marshall, Oxenham and Rougemont £100 each, and La Serre £50. After the crisis the bill rose by £200, excluding the paid services of the drill sergeant, the singing master and the drawing master. By the academic year 1869/70, however, the bill for a full complement of seven masters had dropped to £525 (although this excluded the considerable amounts earned from private coaching and tuition in extra subjects). By then stagnant numbers had limited the financial inducements that it was possible to offer; and the school had become accustomed to employing young converts who usually moved on after a few years' teaching. No significant evidence survives to tell us how these donnish men taught and whether they attempted to pitch their lessons to the level of the boys; no doubt some quickly acquired the knack and others struggled. There is, by contrast, abundant evidence that Newman was brutally frank in rejecting applicants whom he felt would be unsuited to the classroom; and by relying on interviews and references he was able to ensure that new staff would identify with his vision of the school.

Immediately after the Darnell affair Newman introduced a more rigorous system of testing. Whilst he disliked cramming, he maintained that regular tests had a specific use in training the intellect: 'they impart self-confidence, they serve to bring home to a youth what he knows and what he does not, they teach him to bring out his knowledge and to express his meaning clearly'.[62] In February 1862 the school began a system

[62.] Newman to Northcote, 23 February 1872, *L&D* XXVI, p. 26.

of monthly 'repetitions', oral exams in which boys were examined, a form at a time, on work completed the previous month, and which took place in the presence of Newman, St John and the form-master. From Lord Edmund Howard's account of the ordeal, it seems that the formidable presence was St John's, but the disconcerting questions usually came from the old man with the gentle voice; and when St John and the form-master got carried away with linguistic niceties, Newman would sometimes dispel the gravity of the occasion by interposing a mischievous remark. Great emphasis was placed on learning by heart, since Newman insisted on perfect accuracy and readiness in the repetitions, which reflected his stress on developing the memory at school. But he was no Gradgrind, as can be seen from the *Idea*, where he strikes a balance between the 'storehouse' or passive function of memory and its 'digestive' or active role.

End-of-term exams were conducted with more solemnity than they had been under Darnell; and they were presided over by Newman, who set aside two or three days for the purpose. Not content with these changes, he further emphasised their importance by bringing in visiting examiners, mainly from the Catholic University in Dublin – though ideally he wished for examiners from Oxford: public schools at the time engaged their own examiners privately, using their university contacts, and in 1863 Newman sounded out a Fellow of Trinity, but without success. Naturally, besides exams, the school used prizes to stimulate academic endeavour. The prize-list for 1865 shows they were awarded for classics (one for each of the lower forms), mathematics (four), and drawing (two); and, as a matter of course, printed class lists (exam classifications) and prize lists were sent to parents with the school bills. On leaving the school, the Duke of Norfolk endowed an annual prize (the Norfolk Prize) worth £20 in books. The competition comprised of six parts (Greek, Greek Testament, Latin, written Latin, Euclid and learning by heart) and was something of an ordeal: when Hilaire Belloc entered for it in the mid-1880s it lasted for six days, at five hours a day.

While emphasising the importance of study, Newman was equally sensitive to the boys' need for play and free time, and his automatic reaction to parents who asked for extra lessons was to remind them of the boys' reluctance to forfeit time outside classes. The complaint that under Darnell the play-hours were too broken up was accommodated, and evening prep or classes were moved to the early afternoon in the summer to allow time for longer cricket matches. Major feast days and special occasions were marked with half or whole holidays, and celebrated with a festive meal and after-dinner toasts. Special occasions included Newman's birthday (21 February) and one-off events such as a visit by Hope-Scott, or the bishop's visit to examine the school on their catechism. Once a term, when the weather was fine, classes were cancelled and the whole school spent the day at Rednal.

One of the reasons Newman gave to friends for writing only two books in fifteen years was 'the time I have given to the Schoolboys, especially in preparing and editing four Latin Plays for their use'.[63] The custom of an annual Latin play became established in 1865, with three performances in the days leading up to St Philip's Day (26 May): the first attended by the boys, children from the Oratory orphanage, and members of the Oratory; the second – known to the boys as 'Brum night' – by the church congregation and local trades-people; and the last by parents, old boys and dignitaries. After the final performance, many families stayed overnight and next morning attended High Mass; then they all went off to Rednal in carriages for lunch in a large pavilion. In the after-noon there was cricket and croquet, while parties of Oratorians, staff, parents and their sons and daughters strolled round the gardens or in the neighbouring countryside.

The inspiration for the Latin play came from Newman. He had acted in such plays as a boy at Ealing, where performances had similarly taken place on three successive nights. The four plays Newman selected for the Oratory School were the *Andria* and the *Aulularia* of Plautus, and the *Phormio* and the *Eunuchus* (renamed the *Pincerna*, or 'Cup-bearer') of Terence. Prepar-ations began in September, when the plays were read in class; afterwards Newman took the actors alone or in small groups, construed the Latin, made the boys construe it, and then heard them repeat it by heart. He helped them deliver the Latin

---

[63.] Newman's diary, 14 October 1874, *AW*, p. 272.

verse and advised them on how to act their parts (though most of the guidance on acting came from St John, who operated as stage manager). Newman's infectious enthusiasm was manifested in discussions with St John about casting, and in detailed instructions for scenery; even in old age he could be found at dress rehearsals. For each play Newman had a specially expurgated edition printed, with his own translation, detailed grammatical notes and a Latin prologue. The idea of publishing adaptations was copied at other public schools, first at Radley, whose 'curtailed' *Phormio* and *Andria* appeared two and four years respectively after Newman's, and then at Westminster, where the custom of an annual Latin play had been established back in Elizabethan times. (The Jesuits, on the other hand, composed their own Latin plays for acting, though they used expurgated classical texts for their teaching.)

As the Oratory School prospectus stated, there were no extra charges. Music, drawing and other studies that were usually considered as extras in other schools came as standard, but at the headmaster's discretion: only he was at liberty to decide if, and when, a boy should start. If parents disagreed, these studies became extras. The policy on music reflected Newman's view that it was a common mistake to begin learning an instrument too early: young boys were reluctant to practise, as it entailed sacrificing playtime, and masters begrudged giving their free time just for supervision of practice – and without practice little progress could be made. Newman thought that music, unlike drawing, was 'an important part of education, where a boy has a turn for it. It is a great resource when they are thrown on the world – it is social amusement – perfectly innocent – and what is so great a point employs their thoughts.'[64] A considerable amount of music-making, both choral and instrumental, took place at the school; much of it was employed, in true Oratorian fashion, in divine worship. Newman sometimes joined boys in their recitals by playing second violin, and other masters joined in too.

As the proportion of older boys increased during the 1860s, so school life benefited from activities of a cultural or academic nature. One of these was journalism. The first magazine

64. Newman to Bellasis, 4 September 1865, *L&D* XXII, p. 42.

'published', *Stale News*, appeared in the winter of 1863/64. In the Lent term of 1868 the weekly magazine, *The Tuesday Tomtit*, edited jointly by a young master and two fifth formers, claimed the first published poem of Gerard Manley Hopkins; although each issue was limited to three hand-written copies, it inspired some fourth formers to produce a rival magazine, *The Weekly Wasp*. Meetings of the debating and essay societies took place on alternate Sundays; the debates in particular were of a high standard, and masters were regularly called upon to address meetings. The motions recorded in the anonymous *School Boy's Diary* (possibly by Bellasis's second son Edward) give an interesting insight into the burning issues of the day, as well as the concerns of the earnest schoolboy: they include whether a good speaker or good writer has more influence; whether the printing press or the steam engine has done most for mankind; the good and bad effects of athletics; the advantages and disadvantages of the monitorial system; classical *v.* general education; voluntary *v.* compulsory education; pleasures of hope *v.* pleasures of memory; town *v.* country; was Hannibal or Alexander the greater general?; is emigration a good thing for England?

Naturally enough, outdoor activities abounded, some run by masters, others by boys. The younger boys were taken for walks, 'botanizing', making bonfires, skating, fishing, swimming, rowing and gymnastics; they were allowed to keep small pets, on the express understanding that they would keep and feed them well, and to cultivate small garden plots. Outdoor games included rounders, prisoner's base and paper-chases, though the main organised games – besides a two-day annual athletics competition – were cricket, football and hockey. In days before the proliferation of 'foreign' (inter-school) fixtures, the sides for matches were chosen from an ingenious variety of subdivisions of the school: older *v.* younger boys (and other form-related permutations), boys *v.* masters, Darnell's boys *v.* St John's boys (i.e. pre-crisis *v.* post-crisis boys), north *v.* south, gospel *v.* epistle, 67 and 68 Hagley Road *v.* Oratory House, first refectory table *v.* rest, first half of alphabet *v.* others, English *v.* foreigners, actors *v.* non-actors, and flogged *v.* non-flogged (usually won by the former).

It was during the 1860s that the cult of games emerged as a characteristic feature of public schools. The ideology of athleticism, which lasted until the Second World War, conferred upon games the capacity to inspire virtue, develop manliness and form character; it developed into a simple-minded belief in the value of organised outdoor exercise for producing captains of industry and leaders of empire. In this climate academic activity became unmanly and a virulent anti-intellectualism set in, leading a master at Eton to observe how the boys 'toil at games and play with books'.[65] Certainly there was considerable enthusiasm for games at Edgbaston, too, and it is conveyed by an article in *The Weekly Wasp* which decried the ease at which boys could be excused games by 'humbugging the authorities that they have a *headache*'; the schoolboy journalist hoped 'that the boys will soon show a spirit *akin* to that of Eton and Harrow for the improvement of their public games and that next football season the field will be as thronged as it is now empty'.[66] Although games featured prominently in the lives of most Edgbaston boys, the school was sheltered from the worst excesses of the tyranny of games because they were worked hard, and also because of the abundance of other extra-curricular activities (quite unlike the majority of public schools). Nevertheless a cricket professional was hired by the Oratory School boys; and in the school cricket photographs it is possible to detect the swagger of the 'bloods'. Though Newman had no interest in games of any sort, he admitted that 'It is almost as good a thing to be a good player as a good classic[ist] or anything else';[67] and he followed the fortunes of their games and always watched the match against the old boys, which became a regular feature of the celebrations for St Philip's Day. The prestige fixture was against Beaumont, the Oratory School's new Catholic rivals. It was established in 1867, and in 1895 the venue was switched to Oxford; in 1926 it took place at Lord's itself.

[65.] J.A. Mangan, *Athleticism in the Victorian and Edwardian Public School* (Cambridge: CUP, 1981), p. 111.
[66.] 'Boscoe', *The Weekly Wasp* 4, 1886, pp. 9–11.
[67.] Newman to the Duchess of Norfolk, March 1862, Jackson, 'Newman', p. 211.

Balancing the books

It was during the climax of the Darnell affair that Newman had pressed Bellasis one last time on the matter of parental responsibility in shouldering the school's financial burden, reiterating the familiar arguments: that the parents had the whole advantage of the foundation, the Oratory the risk; that the parents had provided little, just £1050, while the Oratory had invested heavily, £3530 on the church and £8503 on other buildings and land; and that the Oratory had given time, labour and thought. Only at this point did Bellasis reveal to Newman the difficulties he had encountered in obtaining financial backing for the school: the £1050 collected had come only after 'a hard canvass and many refusals'; most parents were not in a position to contribute, and of those who were, many had had to be coaxed into sending their sons, had grumbled at the expense of doing so, and were not yet sufficiently convinced of the benefit.[68] At the time, he had exhausted all the possibilities open to him, and was unable to contribute more personally; he felt at a loss to see what more he could do.

Did this revelation cause Newman to re-think his conception of parental responsibility? It would seem so, to judge from the absence of any further mention of the matter to Bellasis. But other evidence suggests an alternative explanation. Before the crisis was even fully over, Newman confided in his bishop that 'after such a catastrophe, we must be for some time on trial even in the minds of our friends';[69] effectively the clock had been turned back and the trial period extended. Many more years of stability were needed to restore confidence and put the school in a position of strength from which Bellasis could make extra demands on parents. It seems that the propitious moment never did arrive. New uncertainties arose and hovered over the foundation, and then time ran out; Bellasis and Hope-Scott retired, and declining health due to overwork led them to winter abroad.

All along Newman had worked to the principle that the Oratory ought not to subsidise the school. Accordingly, the

---

[68.] Bellasis to Newman, 26 December 1861, BOA.
[69.] Newman to Ullathorne, 31 January 1862, *L&D* XX, p. 144.

debt due to capital expenditure (except on the church) was serviced by interest payments from the school's current account. Realising that Darnell could not keep accounts and was losing money fast, Newman had replaced him as bursar in January 1861; but it was only after the crisis that he had the freedom to tackle the situation properly. Thereafter he was constantly on the lookout for measures to cut the running deficit. A payment of 1 guinea was levied for each church sitting (this charge was commonly made by schools with no endowment); the rule on music lessons was enforced; a previous decision not to charge for Bass ale was reversed, as it cost considerably more than common beer and many boys had it; an extra charge was introduced for boys who had meat or eggs for breakfast; and the wastage on employing servants in the vacation was reduced. Such measures provide confirmation of a financial responsibility in Newman that was lacking in Darnell. Yet in spite of them all, Newman had to admit: 'The truth is the school cannot be done at £80 – in the way we do it', and he regretted not starting with higher fees.[70] Just over a year after the crisis he told a parent that

> to my extreme distress, though I started with the firm resolution that the Oratory should not lay out a penny on the School, because we began it, not for *ourselves*, but as a good work which would please St Philip and do good to the Catholic body, and though I know well how great vigilance it required to hinder the Congregation being compromised in its financial concerns, I say, to my extreme sorrow, we are involved to the extent of thousands.[71]

The school's finances were delicately balanced: with eighty boys it would flourish, but every boy below seventy represented a loss. Rarely did numbers rise above this critical point during Newman's time, and there were terms when outbreaks of measles, mumps or other illnesses reduced numbers to dangerously low levels. Paradoxically, a major saving was achieved

---

[70.] Newman to Wilberforce, 31 July 1862, *L&D* XX, p. 249.
[71.] Newman to Wilberforce, 13 February 1863, *L&D* XX, p. 408.

when Miss Mitchell left and a replacement could not be found, because it allowed Newman to close one of the three kitchens and to cut costs considerably. Before her departure, the two dames' houses had operated as independent units with their own kitchens and servants, in addition to the kitchen in the Oratory House; now the boys from 67–68 Hagley Road joined those from the top floor dormitory and ate in the former schoolroom in the Oratory House. As female care for younger boys was part of the founding ideal, the remaining dame's house was not abandoned: when Mrs Wootten died in office in the Christmas holidays of 1875/76 she was succeeded by Miss Emily Bowles, a convert whose brother had joined the Oratory.[72]

During the brief period in which pupils had been taken in as boarders by Moody, the school had lost about £500. After the crisis the question of masters taking boarders was again raised by those anxious to boost their income. The Oratorians decided to allow it, but only in exceptional circumstances: to prevent boys leaving, or to attract new boys. In such cases, day fees (thirty-nine guineas per annum) were charged by the school, leaving the master to make his own arrangements with parents. The decision was based primarily on financial considerations: the school needed the full fees to meet its running costs, because it was not yet in a position to imitate Eton or other public schools; 'for *we* are not *established*, nor have a tradition – and arrangements might be dangerous to *us* which are harmless in such old and recognised institutions'.[73] There was also the risk that a master might leave and take his boarders with him (a common occurrence in mid-Victorian times). Elements of the housemaster system were present, since each dame's house or dormitory was looked after by a tutor; but the absence of the full-blown system meant losing a main inducement for attracting and retaining first-rate masters – a fact recognised at Marlborough where the governors reversed the founders' decision to begin without a house system.

Newman was fully aware of the school's main difficulty: 'The

[72.] There were two further replacements in Newman's time: Mrs Holden in 1881 and Mrs Keysell in 1882.
[73.] Newman, memorandum, 9 September 1862, *L&D* XX, p. 269n.

Oratory *must* be in a *town*, and a school *ought to be* in the *country*'. The school's expenses were all much greater because it was sited in a town; the only advantages were easier access to medical aid and the proximity to New Street railway station. Edgbaston was rapidly becoming a populous neighbourhood, and this was acting unfavourably on the interests of the school. A partial solution that was considered seriously in 1865, and again in 1872 and 1885, was to build a summer school on the eight acres of ground at Rednal, and to move the 'whole school establishment (not the Oratory) to this place from St Philip's Day (May 26) till the Long Vac (July 20) and from September 10 to the end of October'.[74] But the scheme was estimated at £3000 and would require an additional ten to fifteen boys to enable it to break even, and so the risk of the extra investment was judged to be too great.

In 1867 Hope-Scott tried to persuade Newman to alter his conception of the school and to view it as a charitable enterprise rather than one that aimed to be self-sufficient. Annual losses up to then (after deducting £274, the interest on sums invested in buildings) averaged about £340, in spite of Newman employing every means at his disposal – except using Oratory money as a subsidy. Besides what the Oratorians might leave to the school, the only prospect for recovery was the expectation of a further £4000 from Mrs Wootten, who had made out her property to the Oratory in 1862, to meet the school's debts, in return for an annuity. Hope-Scott advised Newman to cease paying the Oratorians for their services to the school (such as the £100 per annum to St John), as old boys and others would soon be in a position to help; if they knew the Fathers were paid 'it would damn the whole concern'.[75] He argued that if the school was an Oratorian work it ought to be done gratuitously since they would not be paid if otherwise engaged – but Newman continued to pay the headmaster. As Hope-Scott anticipated, the school soon began to receive bequests. Most of those who had subscribed to the Oxford Oratory fund in 1866/67 agreed that the money could be used for school purposes, once it became clear that the Oxford

[74] Newman to Hope-Scott, 28 April 1865, *L&D* XXI, p. 453.
[75] St John to Newman, 24 April 1867, *L&D* XXIII, p. 174n.

project was doomed; it amounted to just over £2000 – and almost all of it came from school promoters and parents.

In the decade after the crisis no new buildings were erected. Newman declined to venture beyond what was strictly necessary, for there was neither money nor land for expansion. One minor addition was the construction of the 'tin passage' which connected the front of the top floor of the Oratory House with the back, increasing its capacity from twenty-eight to forty-two; along with accommodation for twenty-six at 67–68 Hagley Road and fourteen at 21–22 Plough and Harrow Road, the total boarding capacity was eighty-two. Between these buildings was a gravel playground boasting a tennis court, a pair of parallel bars and a fly-pole, and an adjacent field with cricket nets, but for matches the boys had to walk to grounds elsewhere: initially at 'Bosco', a rough field half a mile away; then 'new Bosco', a mile away; and from 1873 Ravenshurst, a site with two pitches and an old farmhouse, but at a distance of two miles. (In these manoeuvres, the boys were not marshalled to playing fields but put on their honour not to dawdle in shops or break away into town.) Newman realised that the school's poor sporting facilities belied its claim to be a public school, all the more so in view of the growing obsession with team games, which meant that, irrespective of how dingy the classrooms were, a school could stand or fall by the quality of its wickets and the extensiveness of its sports fields. It was partly with a view to encouraging games at the Oratory School that an old boys' society was established in 1874; the first of the past *v.* present matches took place the same year.

After a decade without building activity, the school resumed its expansion westwards in 1872 with the acquisition of three more adjacent houses on the Hagley Road, and work began on completion of the cloister. In part this was the result of the Oratory reclaiming its rooms to accommodate new vocations, but it was mainly due to the success of a fundraising campaign. Since 1869 the small schoolroom had been used as the school chapel; now funds were raised to provide the school with a purpose-built chapel, separate from the main Oratory church. The Duke of Norfolk and Hope-Scott each gave £1000 for the expansion, and other contributions amounted to another £2000. A decade later, in 1882, a new school library was added using a gift of £3000 from the Duke. All these improvements were on a modest and unpretentious scale, and fell short of Newman's early aspirations. He had originally wanted the school to have more imposing buildings so as to give it 'consequence in the eyes of the boys', as he thought that 'if it is to flourish at all, they must have visible objects, to make them venerate it, to engage their affections, to make them proud of [it], to lead them in after life to look back with pleasure on their school days'.[76]

Arrivals and departures

The Oratory School's policy on admissions underwent considerable change after Darnell's departure. Eager to boost numbers and without a proper appreciation of Newman's conception of a school, Darnell had no special reason to be cautious about whom to accept. Newman regretted the effects of this conventional policy, as individuals had arrived whose negative influence could have been anticipated and an influx of older boys, unaccustomed 'to our particular rules and ways', had had a detrimental effect on discipline.[77] Newman's policy was more rigorous, because his sights were set on a more ambitious goal: as his priority was to promote and protect the healthy growth of the nascent school, he tried to ensure that new boys were capable of being grafted on to the school body. Before the crisis, Newman had envisaged the school growing naturally as word spread: interested parties would apply as a result of contact with parents or friends of the school, thereby supplying some guarantee of suitability. But how was this to be adapted to those outside this extended school network? Early in 1862 Newman asked Allies: 'What is done at Eton or Harrow in the way of *introduction* of the parents of boys, candidates for admission, to the Head Master? Does he admit the son of any one who presents himself? At Oxford, a father applies to the Head of a House *through some common friend*.'[78] As Newman

---

[76.] Newman, memorandum, 30 May 1860, *L&D* XIX, p. 348.
[77.] Newman to Darnell, 29 August 1861 *L&D* XX, p. 39.
[78.] Newman to Allies, 10 February 1862, *L&D* XX, p. 151.

began to formulate a policy, he had frequent recourse to Allies, Bellasis and Hope-Scott.

One requirement for admission was a guarantee of character – and the older the boy, the greater the need for this assurance. Applications were vetted not only on grounds of character but on suitability; boys requiring a commercial education, or who were unlikely to fit in, were turned away. The recommended age for entry was eight or nine, provided a boy could read and spell English adequately, but apart from the barrier of fees and social adaptability there was no restriction on grounds of class per se. One enquirer was told to 'be under no apprehension about the class of boys who come to us. All boys need teaching and training, and any boy is respected and makes his way who is diligent, obedient, and manly and amiable to his companions.'[79] Applications for concessions in fees were dealt with by the Congregation, as they had been before the crisis, though options were severely restricted since there were many equally deserving cases (typically sons of convert clergymen) and the school was already losing money, even on its operating costs. Scholarships were therefore beyond the school's resources. Nevertheless, reductions and free places were given on an *ad hominem* basis; and from 1868 fees for brothers were reduced.

The admission of foreign boys was problematic on account of the difficulties in obtaining references and the risk of a negative effect on the school. Newman had heard about the harm done when Spanish and Portuguese boys were taken at St Edward's College Liverpool, while South Americans were considered to be 'for a time the ruin of Oscott'.[80] In the summer of 1862 Newman asked Bellasis for advice, and the latter discussed the question with Hope-Scott. Hope-Scott's suggestion was that foreign boys over a certain age should not be taken, that a letter of introduction from a reliable person be obtained, and that the fees remain the same but be insisted on in advance. Although these precautions were adopted, and boys over fourteen were only taken exceptionally, many foreigners were accepted: twenty-two out of the ninety-nine

[79.] Newman to Mrs Sparrow, 25 August 1863, *L&D* XX, p. 511.
[80.] Newman to Bellasis, 24 July 1862, *L&D* XX, p. 243.

admitted in the five-year period 1867–72. However, these figures are by no means exceptional if compared with the statistics from the Catholic colleges. When the history of St Edmund's was being written in the late 1890s, the author had the list of past pupils analysed, but the results had so undermined St Edmund's claim to be a great *English* Catholic school that they were not included. The proportion of English to foreigners to Irish at St Edmund's was in fact 1:1:2 – Stonyhurst's figures were little different, 'the English being in a sad minority', while Oscott had nearly fifty per cent English but, like Ushaw, was losing ground fast. Sedgley Park, being a preparatory school, had the highest proportion with seventy-three per cent either English or Welsh.[81] Analysis of the background of Oratory School pupils for the period 1859–72, on the other hand, yields an approximate proportion of 4:1:1 for English (or Welsh) to foreigners to Irish. The evidence thus suggests that, despite the modest number of boys on the Oratory School books, Newman was wary about boosting the rolls by accepting foreigners.

Unlike Darnell, Newman was prepared to adopt whatever measures were necessary to protect the atmosphere in the school and avert the danger of even just one undesirable boy. He feared that precocious foreign lads who acted like 'little men' could bring about the school's destruction – 'it would be a moral scarletina' – and so was very wary of accepting the fifteen-year-old Prince Imperial, the son of Napoleon III, who was in exile in Chislehurst. In tune with Newman's thinking, St John raised two problems about him: whether he would keep to the rules and thus satisfy the masters, and whether he would join in with games and so be popular with the other boys – and in the end he was not admitted. It appears that the only boy Newman actually expelled was Prince Camporeale, the spoilt half-cousin of Acton. Mrs Wootten had noticed how he operated on other boys while a pupil from January 1861 until July 1862; and not long after his return in 1867 he was removed for foul language.

It was because Newman was interested in imparting a full

81. F. Roberts, *A History of Sedgley Park and Cotton College* (Preston: privately printed, 1985), p. 113.

intellectual and spiritual formation that he laid great stress on boys starting young; by the time they were fifteen or sixteen, such boys 'were of great use to us, set a good example, and acted with much zeal and steadiness as prefects of the school'.[82] A separate dilemma arose over whether the school should continue accepting 'home' boarders or day-boys, because parents objected to them being unsupervised out of school hours. Newman decided to follow Bellasis's advice: the rule allowing them was removed from the prospectus to avoid criticism, on the understanding that exceptions could be made. As with other issues, the negotiations relied on Bellasis acting as a buffer between Newman and the parents.

Just as at other public schools, the majority of Edgbaston boys did not go on to Oxford or Cambridge, even though studies were tailor-made for the transition. (Only a third of the boys at the seven leading schools went on to university.) Of those who did go from the Oratory School (about ten per cent of pupils), the vast majority went to Oxford. Contrary to what might have been expected, Newman did not press boys to apply to Oxford or Cambridge colleges, but instead worked to parental wishes. Immediately after the crisis, the main demand for specialist coaching happened to be in mathematics in order to prepare for the entrance exams of the Royal Military Academy at Woolwich; in 1863 a Woolwich 'grinder' was engaged to tutor four boys for five hours a day, his remuneration being met by higher fees, but this temporary arrangement was quickly superseded by a system of extra tuition staffed by the permanent masters. Pope undertook the mathematics and drawing required for Woolwich, Sandhurst and London University, and his services were later extended to cover mathematics as far as the London University B.A., English history and literature, and general geography, as well as preparation for the Indian Civil Service, including Sanskrit and Tamil![83] Newman coached in classics and English literature for the London University Intermediate Examination in Arts, while St John undertook the Hebrew tuition.

[82.] Newman to Lady Fullerton, 9 April 1871, *L&D* XXV, p. 312.
[83.] Far-fetched though this may seem, Pope was fitted to the task as he had, whilst still an Anglican, spent time in India as a missionary for the Society for the Propagation of the Gospel.

The school bagged an early success at Woolwich and two at Oxford, but the latter two had left early and been coached by Darnell, who hoped to turn the tutoring establishment he had set up at Grassmere into a public school. Newman discussed with St John whether they should make peace with Darnell and arrange for him to act as a private tutor for parents who insisted on sending their sons to Oxford, the aim being to keep such boys at school for at least another year. He recognised that Darnell's tutorial establishment had the advantage of offering parents a less regimented environment than school, although it laboured under a disadvantage when it came to motivating boys. The discussions came to nothing, but when Darnell's father died in 1865 it was feared he might risk his large inheritance on his establishment; this did not happen, though two years later Newman found himself competing with Darnell for masters. The pattern of boys leaving early, to prepare for Oxford under a tutor, was changed when Newman persuaded Colonel Towneley to keep his son at the school. Newman undertook the tutoring himself and coached Towneley nearly every day of the 1865/66 Christmas vacation, sticking at the task even when he was unable to say Mass and confined to bed. The result was a double success: Towneley was greatly praised by the examiners; and he was entered for Christ Church rather than Balliol, where his father had originally intended him to go. The switch was important as there was known to be a good deal of sceptical opinion at Balliol, whereas Christ Church had the largest number of Catholics and its size made it easier for a young man to choose his company.

The career destinations of Oratory School leavers in Newman's time is revealing. Of the 170 that have been traced, thirty-eight reached the rank of lieutenant-colonel or higher in the army, twenty-two became lawyers, six entered the diplomatic service and eleven occupied leading positions in political life. In the 1904 elections four old boys were returned as M.P.s, and Belloc joined them after the 1906 elections.[84] The figures show that the ranking of career destinations closely matched those of Rugby and Harrow, where the armed forces were the

[84.] Mohnen, 'Pre-university education', pp. 140–41.

most popular destination, followed by law, then administration. Preference for the army was due to its popularity among Catholics – they comprised about a third of the army in the second half of the nineteenth century – and the large number of military converts. Naturally, the destinations of Oratory School pupils also reflected parental professions: as studies of the period have shown, choice of career in the period was affected chiefly by family background.

Whether they were leaving for university or the working world, the school sought to prepare its boys to survive in a non-Catholic environment and hold their own in a Protestant society. The converts' desire for a greater stress on the natural or human virtues had met with Newman's full approval, and the statement in his draft manifesto that the Oratory School was intended 'for youths whose duties are to lie in the world' incorporated this concern and signalled an important shift in emphasis. It is possible to detect this emphasis on 'facing the world' in the advice Newman gave boys who suspected they had a priestly vocation, for he invariably urged them to be patient and avoid narrowing their options too early. When John Marie Stokes returned to the Oratory with the priesthood in mind, a year after leaving the school, Newman was concerned that if he changed his mind later he would lose those years 'for the purposes of any secular pursuit, and have to begin life again.' In accepting him at the Oratory, Newman assured his father he would 'take care to advance his education while he is with us, so that he will not have lost even for secular objects so important a portion of his youth'.[85] Stokes taught at the school for several years, but in the end he did not become a priest; instead he married and made his career in the Post Office. The tale of Robert Froude is equally instructive. He was sixteen when Newman received him into the Catholic Church, and on finishing a retreat at school he set his mind on the priesthood; but his non-Catholic father wanted him to prepare with a tutor for a degree in mathematics and natural science at Oxford in order to become an engineer like himself. Newman encouraged him to consider doing as his father wished, and the outcome was that the boy worked under his father in the

---

[85.] Newman to C.S. Stokes, 8 February 1864, *L&D* XXI, p. 45.

Admiralty Experimental Works at Torquay and succeeded him as Superintendent, a post he held for forty years; he wrote on naval architecture and other scientific subjects and became a Fellow of the Royal Society. These two stories show that Newman regarded preparation for the world on the same footing as for the priesthood and one calling for a serious and appropriate training. At the same time, the proportion of leavers going into the priesthood – twenty-three from Newman's time, two of whom became bishops – vindicated Newman's belief that a curriculum consisting mainly of secular studies would not deter those truly called to Holy Orders.

Newman's pastoral concern for the boys did not cease the moment they left school, for just as he laid stress on their welfare as pupils and on a working partnership with parents, so a continuing contact with past pupils formed part of his overall educational vision. Naturally, he welcomed the establishment of the Oratory School Society for 'old Oratorians' (as former pupils were known); and the club enlisted St John as its first chaplain, with the duty of saying Mass for its deceased members.

A Catholic Eton?

The Darnell affair had been a stern test for the school, yet Newman and his friends stuck to their founding ideal: a school with a lay character, a liberal education, first-class teachers, the feminine influence of the dames, a high premium set on spiritual values, and partnership with parents. But the lack of an endowment placed huge constraints on the school's development and rendered impossible promising proposals such as extending the dame system, allowing masters to take boarders, acquiring a country location (at Rednal), and attracting and retaining able masters. Most Victorian foundations of note started with solid capital – Glenalmond with £25,000, Lancing with £30,000 and Hurstpierpoint with as much as £40,000; the Oratory School began with just £900. Although Newman was convinced that a Catholic public school was workable, the ability to acquire public school characteristics was hampered by inadequate financial backing and conditioned by the imperatives of Catholic morality. Acton was mistaken in thinking that Newman had come round to opposing the idea of a public school; the only cradle Catholic among the most active promoters, he was less familiar with life at the public schools and therefore their deficiencies. From W.G. Ward's perspective it was clear that the Oratory School differed greatly from the colleges, being 'like our public schools and universities – with great freedom of life'.[86]

Originally Newman had spoken of setting up a school like Eton or Winchester: Eton customs, such as the dame system, had been blended with those Winchester traditions favoured by Darnell. But after the crisis Newman began to speak not of a Catholic Eton but of 'a miniature Winchester or Westminster',[87] and indeed of the fact that the school had started on the plan of Winchester and Rugby. Acton's description of the school as following a 'Winchester model'[88] appears accurate because it matched exactly the expression of an ex-pupil from the 1860s who recalled that 'Winchester was the chief English Public School held up to us as a model'.[89] Further confirmation of its Winchester credentials can be found by noting the background of key personnel: Darnell, Arnold and Neville came from Winchester, St John from Westminster which had been founded on the model of Winchester. Undoubtedly it was these four who helped nurture the school's prefect system, a distinguishing public school feature which is first mentioned in 1862. Though pupil power was often abused at the public schools, there was an unshakeable belief that character training was enhanced by a delegation of authority to the boys themselves – an assumption flatly rejected by the Catholic colleges. As well as instilling virtues, self-government had two practical advantages: it made the headmaster's job easier, and it prevented rebellion by uniting some of the most influential boys with the masters. At Edgbaston the prefect system was

[86] F. Rogers to E. Rogers (from a dinner-table conversation with W.G. Ward), 1863, F. Rogers, *Letters of Lord Blachford*, ed. G.E. Marindin (London: John Murray, 1896), p. 249.

[87] Newman to Crawley, 9 April 1863, *L&D* XX, p. 428.

[88] Memorandum, n.d., Cambridge University Library, Add. MS 4988/227.

[89] 'Reminiscences of an old boy', *OSM* 98, July 1940, p. 3.

incorporated in its entirety, and senior boys were appointed not only to play their part in the smooth running of the school but also to set the younger boys an example. They were granted privileges for their pains and occasionally treated to special suppers by the masters. Although the Oratory School prefects were appointed (as prefects of school, bounds, hall, chapel, library and the three boarding houses) Newman allowed the boys to elect the school captain directly.[90]

Newman's knowledge of the great public schools was undoubtedly enlarged by the Clarendon Report, which he acquired as soon as it appeared. If the Oratory School did not approximate more closely to the great schools, it was in part because Newman was inspired as much by an idealised form of the public school as by the reality. His concerted bid to occupy the academic high ground and willingness to modify public school practice showed he was no slavish imitator. Unlike Darnell, he felt no need to introduce corporate traditions or rituals (such as the *Dulce Domum*) that smacked of social posturing and corporate self-consciousness. This unusual approach explains why historians have generally erred in their studies on the Oratory School, by misunderstanding what was novel and idiosyncratic and categorising the foundation either as a large private school, or a straightforward, conventional public school.

Newman's active involvement after the Darnell affair ensured that masters and dames could work in their respective spheres without clashing, according to his original conception. A year after the crisis he told a friend:

> It was *quite possible* to lay down rules by which the Masters and the Dames could keep the peace with each other – and this the event has shown, for there has been no quarrel or shadow of quarrel between them throughout the past year – each side has kept to his or her own department.[91]

---

[90]. The list of school captains on the boards in the entrance hall of the Oratory School goes right back to 1859.

[91]. Newman to Miss Giberne, 24 December 1862, *L&D* XX p. 371.

The development of the school in the decade after 1862 followed Newman's lines. His sensitivity to the ways of boys – foibles and all – enabled him to pitch his demands with precision, and so with success. He placed great emphasis both on attention to the individual and on liaison with parents; but these striking features were established only by dint of enormous personal effort, writing *all* the reports and seeing *all* the boys, individually, after exams. Unlike the great nineteenth-century headmasters, Newman's influence derived from dealing with boys separately or in small groups rather than addressing them *en masse*. One pupil described 'Jack', or 'old Jack' (as Newman was irreverently if affectionately known), as a gentle, understanding and approachable figure for whom nothing was too trivial to attend to. When the editorial of *The Weekly Wasp*, a magazine run entirely by boys, criticised the school administration for providing inadequate facilities, such as the lack of equipment in the gymnasium or the solitary washbasin in the lavatories, Newman saw to it that their grievances were met. Given the importance he attributed to the religious dimension of the school, it comes as no surprise that he turned a deaf ear to their complaints that chapel services were too long and should be made voluntary.

Darnell had appeared to possess all the qualities necessary for undertaking the headmastership, yet for all his qualities turned out to be unsuitable, as did the masters he appointed. McClelland has drawn attention to an apparent contradiction concerning Darnell: his reputation as a tough disciplinarian, and his wish to grant boys the freedom given at Eton.[92] But this was in fact the norm: both characteristics were present at Eton, where endless floggings coexisted with an extremely lax regime.[93] Newman approved of neither, though he valued

---

[92.] McClelland, *A Catholic Eton*, p. 13.
[93.] public school laxness was typified by the custom of 'shirking' at Eton, which permitted the flouting of rules provided deference was shown to authority: thus a boy contravening rules on bounds was ignored when seen by a master, provided he made a gesture such as stepping inside a doorway or entering a shop. Such a system, in which 'nothing is permitted [...] but everything is winked at', inspired Gladstone to describe Eton as 'the greatest pagan school in Christendom'.

school as a place for toughening up boys through discipline and contact with their school fellows. He disliked 'the notion of corporal punishment' and the threat of it too, and he once objected to a boy's ears being pulled, because 'their persons should be sacred'.[94] Under him there was no fagging, and corporal punishment was rarely administered, and then only by the headmaster or 'Prefect of discipline'. Nevertheless, Newman maintained that 'the good old punishment of flogging, is, in due moderation as to severity and frequency, the most efficacious of all punishments', being 'the most prompt and summary, and the least irritating and annoying to the subjects of it. It is done and over – there is nothing to brood over, nothing to create a grudge, at least to English boys.'[95]

Newman strove for a new balance in that precarious transition from boyhood to manhood by placing a premium on trust. Experience of university life had taught him that 'nothing is more perilous to the soul than the sudden transition from restraint to liberty. [. . .] boys who are kept jealously at home or under severe schoolmasters till the very moment when they are called to take part in the business of the world, are the very persons about whom we have most cause to entertain misgivings'.[96] He was more concerned about the quality of education offered than the length of the school roll, and felt that if numbers picked up (as he hoped they would), it would be because the school lived up to his own standards. A year after Darnell's departure he was convinced that the school was 'more orderly, more religious, more cheerful, and more studious' than previously.[97] His verdict was that 'The school flourishes, except in numbers';[98] it 'really prospers internally' and 'really has fulfilled (if we dare speak without boasting) the problem of combining a good intellectual education with Catholic morality'.[99]

[94]. Newman to Faber, 6 February 1849, *L&D* XIII, p. 27.
[95]. Newman to Taylor, 15 February 1869, *L&D* XXIV p. 216.
[96]. Newman, *My Campaign*, pp. 36–37.
[97]. Newman to Miss Giberne, 24 December 1862, *L&D* XX, p. 371.
[98]. Newman to Miss Bathurst, 21 January 1866, *L&D* XXII, p. 135.
[99]. Newman to Hope-Scott, 28 April 1865, *L&D* XXI, p. 454.

Chapter 6

Against the Odds

The buoyancy of numbers in the years immediately after the Darnell crisis showed that the school had successfully weathered the storm, while the testimony of masters and parents from the same period confirms that it also grew stronger internally. These facts lead inevitably to the question: if the experiment of forming the first Catholic public school was so successful, why did it not become the undisputed 'Catholic Eton'? Why did school numbers remain stagnant? McClelland has argued that the crisis was entirely to blame, explaining that the Catholic aristocracy soon began to drift back to the older and more stable Catholic foundations:[1] but the argument is unconvincing. In the first place the Oratory School's strongest competitors proved to be two younger foundations; and secondly, the school list reveals that relatively few of the old Catholic families had tried the school to begin with. In fact the school's limited success can be explained by other, more serious reasons.

One major reason was the 'university question'. The 1862 prospectus claimed that the school embraced 'the same variety of destinations in life, as are met with and provided for at Eton, Winchester and Rugby'; in other words, one of its main purposes was preparation for a university education along the lines of Oxford or Cambridge. But in 1865 English Catholics received an official warning from Rome against attending

[1] McClelland, 'A Catholic Eton', p. 14.

Oxford or Cambridge; the warning was strengthened two years later, and only revoked in 1895.

A second reason was a campaign of gossip and calumny orchestrated by supporters of the Catholic colleges, in which the school was 'almost "done to death by envious tongues" ' (as Newman put it).[2] The campaign reached a climax in 1867 when Cardinal Barnabò, Prefect of Propaganda Fide, threatened to close the school for flouting Church policy on attendance at Oxford; St John had to go to Rome to clear Newman's name and the school's.

The third reason militating against the school was the competition within the Catholic system, which intensified with each new foundation. In 1861 the Jesuits began Beaumont Lodge, which soon became the Oratory School's main rival. Worse was to come in 1877 with the foundation of a Catholic public school at Woburn Park by William Petre; although it lasted only seven years, Woburn was during that time a formidable rival to the Oratory School.

The fourth reason was the climate of opinion in ruling ecclesiastical circles, which looked unfavourably on lay involvement in educational matters and was deeply suspicious of Newman's influence upon the Catholic laity of England.

The university question

A major reason for Newman's wishing to involve himself in the founding of the Oratory School was to feed the Catholic University with suitably prepared boys; the prospect must have looked promising, since seven of the thirty-eight students in the university's first cohort (1854/55) had previously received tuition at the Birmingham Oratory.[3] But despite his connection with the university and the English presence there, Newman received no support whatever in his strategy from the school promoters or parents, not even from those who had previously taught at Dublin; not one boy from Newman's time fulfilled his

---

[2.] Newman to Simeon, 10 April 1867, *L&D* XXIII, p. 140.
[3.] C. Barr, *Paul Cullen, John Henry Newman, and the Catholic University of Ireland, 1845–1865* (Gracewing: Leominster, 2003), p. 131.

wish, even though a good number came from Ireland. Nor was much interest shown for following the Catholic colleges which used their affiliation to London University to provide tertiary education. Two Bellasis boys were among the few who took the London University exams, although in this case their father had intended them to go to Oxford before the episcopal warning of 1865. In fact Newman was hardly likely to recommend London to parents, for it had been a principal subject of attack in the *Idea of a University* on account of being founded along expressly secular lines, with a constitutional ban on the teaching of religion; besides, it violated another of Newman's principles, since by its non-residential and professorial character it emphasised 'the imparting of information rather than the forming of minds'.[4] In any case, for the vast majority of Oratory School parents, the only university education they cared for was that provided at the ancient universities. Church policy, however, was one of opposition to what was called 'mixed education'; the policy had recently been fortified, so 'the school was left in something of a limbo, its basic purpose, to give the pre-university part of a liberal education, being frustrated'.[5] Moreover, unlike the Catholic colleges, it was unable to offer a philosophy course for lay boys.[6] This combination of circumstances meant that the school suffered from the absence of a university far more than any of the Catholic colleges, even though the majority of boys (as in the Protestant public schools) were not expected to make the transition to higher education.

Newman realised the problem would become more acute as the boys approached university age, and by 1865 the effect was

---

[4.] A.D. Culler, *The Imperial Intellect: a Study of Newman's Educational Ideal* (New Haven: Yale University Press, 1955), p. 99.

[5.] Nash, *Newman's Idea of a School* (Woodcote: Oratory School Association, 1990), p. 4.

[6.] Tertiary education was most developed at Stonyhurst which had up to fifty young men aged between seventeen and twenty-one in its 'philosophy department': some studying philosophy proper, some following London University courses, and others completing their education under private tuition. The latter were mainly wealthy foreigners who dominated to the detriment of the academic tone. For more, see H.J.A. Sire, *Gentlemen Philosophers: Catholic Higher Studies at Liège and Stonyhurst College, 1774–1916* (Worthing: Churchman, 1988).

evident: 'Our boys go on well till they get near the top of the School – but, when they are once put into the fifth or sixth form, they languish and get slovenly – i.e. for want of a *stimulus*. They have no object before them.' Newman complained to Hope-Scott that he felt at a loss how to answer parents who asked him: 'What *are* we to do with Charlie or Richard? [. . .] Is he to have a taste for any thing beyond that for shooting pheasants? is he to stagnate with no internal resources, and no power of making himself useful in life?'[7] A Catholic university in England would have provided a solution, and before the crisis Acton, Bellasis and Darnell had discussed how one might be started. As one might expect, Darnell entertained grand plans for a university, while Acton envisaged it growing out of the school and proposed beginning with a philosophy faculty for the liberal arts. He thought that 'the school must ultimately decide' the university question, 'either by setting up a Catholic university [. . .] or by getting a college at Oxford [. . .] or [. . .] by the abolition of the sectarian character of the university'. But he also realised that 'When the first generation of boys has been trained to the university level and turned out of Edgbaston – unless one of these alternatives is provided, it will break down – for no fruit can ripen if the year ends in June.'[8]

It was hoped, almost assumed, that with so much convert talent and energy available the university question would soon be resolved one way or another. However, given the greater complexities at the level of higher education, there was no equivalent to the commonly shared aspiration for a public school, and instead various different schemes were proposed. In 1861 the Cambridge convert Frederick Paley opened a house for Catholics at his old university and acted as a private tutor for them. Newman, meanwhile, persevered with the Catholic University connection, though he began to realise that its only chance to attract Englishmen was by 'the establishment of an English College in it with English revenues'. A more feasible, though less attractive, alternative was to set up a college in England, affiliated to the Catholic University in Dublin, just as

---

[7.] Newman to Hope-Scott, 28 April 1865, *L&D* XXI, p. 453.
[8.] Acton to Simpson, 1 January 1862, *Correspondence of Acton and Simpson* II, p. 248.

the Catholic colleges were affiliated to London University; although it would of course be *'practically* not a University', Newman thought that a sufficient number of boys from 'Stonyhurst, Ushaw, Oscott, ourselves, and other places' would be enough to give it 'a sort of University character'.[9] He felt that such a college was feasible, 'if only the great Catholic schools would interest themselves in the subject';[10] but even his own friends remained unconvinced. Hope-Scott's preference was for a proper Catholic university, and he hoped that Newman would lay the foundations for one by establishing a centre for higher studies at Edgbaston. Acton thought along similar lines:

> The Edgbaston school is striking root, and the youths who complete their course so far as it extends will create both supply and demand: they will feel more than the others the want of a University education and they will furnish one necessary portion of the materials. Here is a basis and an opportunity for the growth of something like a Catholic university such as did not exist in Ireland.[11]

He offered first Newman, then Peter Renouf (an Oxford convert teaching at the Catholic University), property and a library so that a start could be made, but without success.

Acton had already consulted Newman on the university question, as pressure was mounting for coverage of it in his *Home and Foreign Review*. He had even withheld an article that proposed allowing Catholics to go Oxford so as to give the university scheme precedence. The question was certainly a live one; the first issue of the *Dublin Review* under W.G. Ward's editorship (July 1863) contained an article entitled 'The work and the wants of the Catholic Church in England', in which a Catholic university was identified as the third of five 'wants'. The author, no less a figure than Manning, declared that the Catholic university was no Utopian dream, as all the elements

---

9. Newman to Acton, 24 April 1862, *L&D* XX, p. 193.
10. Newman to Wynne, 12 September 1862, *L&D* XX, p. 270.
11. Acton to Renouf, 14 November 1862, *The Letters of Peter le Page Renouf (1822–1897)* III, ed. K.J. Cathcart (Dublin: UCD Press, 2003), p. 152.

were present in the English Catholic body which 'naturally lead up to and demand a University for their completion'. His enumeration of these elements included four 'greater colleges' (Oscott, Stonyhurst, Ushaw and Ware) and eight lesser ones (Ampleforth, Beaumont Lodge, Downside, Mount St Mary's, St Beuno's, St Edward's, Sedgley Park and Ratcliffe) but, amazingly, omitted the name of the Oratory School.[12] Despite the bold policy advocated in print and Manning's personal desire to find a solution, his scheme was not adopted by Wiseman; nor were others that were discussed, such as a Catholic academy in Rome. Meanwhile, a former vice-principal of Jesus College, Edmund Ffoulkes, had begun promoting a plan for a Catholic hall at Oxford. Although only an M.A. could open a private hall there, the rector of Lincoln had offered to assist Ffoulkes by sponsoring a hall exclusively for Catholics; Ffoulkes wanted Newman to join his organising committee, which drew mainly from the Catholic aristocracy, but Newman felt unable to support the scheme publicly. Nor was he willing, when asked, to help Ffoulkes with addresses of Oratory School parents who were likely to support his scheme.

The schemes of Paley and Ffoulkes were only possible because in the mid-1850s the religious test barriers at Oxford and Cambridge were removed, except for the M.A. at Oxford, though, as access to the colleges was unaffected, only a few began to accept Catholics. Despite the small numbers (about twenty at Oxford in the first decade after legislation), between 1863 and 1867 a heated debate raged in Catholic circles over the university question, and it was focused on Oxford. Catholics were agreed that Oxford (as well as Cambridge) presented a danger to the faith. The university was, after all, an Anglican seminary: in the first half of the nineteenth century as many as two-thirds of Oxford graduates went into Anglican orders. So long as the Protestant upper classes predominated, the atmosphere there was bound to be Protestant. Nevertheless, the converts felt that the real danger to young Catholics was not exposure to High Church views but to intellectual liberalism; the Tractarian Movement, which most of them had supported, had attempted to stem the tide of

---

[12.] H.E. Manning, *Miscellanies* I (London: Burns & Oates, 1877), p. 59.

liberalism, but it had now been on the retreat for two decades. The dilemma that presented itself to this social group was that they wished their offspring to mix with the future leaders of English society, but without endangering their faith. Many of the converts took their lead from Newman. He had concluded that the ideal solution – a Catholic university – was unworkable, both for practical considerations and due to his increasing awareness that most English Catholics were unable to understand a university in his sense of the word. But he felt that the plan for an Oxford hall had its own drawbacks: while it had the merit of securing a liberal education, the measures likely to be put in place to safeguard faith and morals would make it 'so isolated as not to have the influx of Oxford opinions', and this would encourage Catholics to opt instead for the ordinary Oxford colleges, so that the scheme was unlikely to gain ecclesiastical approval. 'The best plan practically' was to continue 'to suffer still young Catholics to go to Oxford' and to introduce a religious body 'to counteract the irreligious spirit of the place'.[13] While Newman acknowledged that Oxford was dangerous for young men, he argued that it was hardly more so than the Royal Military Academy at Woolwich or the University of London, both of which were open to Catholics. The advisability of attendance depended on individual circumstances, and Newman was as much against a general prohibition on Catholics going there (as it would be too great a trial of obedience to some parents) as he was against a positive and general permission.

The prevailing ecclesiastical view was that attendance at the old universities could not be justified, as the intellectual atmosphere and the social nature of undergraduate life would render all safeguards useless. This view was fortified by the strong stance of highly influential converts such as Manning, George Talbot (a canon of Westminster and papal chamberlain), W.G. Ward and some of the London Oratorians. But many of the educated laity, particularly converts, inclined to the contrary opinion: that having the opportunity to enter fully into the life of the nation could justify the risk, provided suit-

---

[13.] Newman to St John, 26 August 1863 (to which Newman added comments in 1875), *L&D* XX, p. 512.

able precautions were taken. At their Low Week meeting in 1864, the bishops decided to reject Ffoulkes's project of a Catholic hall at Oxford; they also agreed that the Catholic university scheme was impractical, and that the clergy should dissuade Catholic parents from sending their sons to the universities.

The following summer Ullathorne offered the Catholic 'mission' (i.e. parish) at Oxford to Newman, who coincidentally had just been given the option on a large central site. Besides wishing to open an Oratory there, he now began to give serious thought to the feasibility of a Catholic hall. As usual he sought the advice of friends. While Gaisford favoured the plan for a Catholic hall, Hope-Scott urged Newman to tread cautiously and test the principle by starting with private houses for a tutor and students; Scott-Murray, predictably, said that he would send his sons to Christ Church rather than to a Catholic hall. Newman was minded to follow Hope-Scott's advice, but when he sounded out his bishop, Ullathorne was quick to inform Newman that he would only countenance the plan for an Oratory; and he reminded Newman that he had joined the Irish bishops in asking Rome for a warning against attendance at Oxford and Cambridge, at the time the Catholic University was being founded.

Alarmed at these developments, Manning appealed to Rome for an instruction to prevent more Catholics going to the universities; Rome, however, responded by instructing the bishops to meet again. Prior to their doing so, a questionnaire was sent to a number of graduate converts (not including Newman); it was to Newman's eyes so tendentious that he felt it could be summed up in just one question: 'Are you or are you not one of those wicked men who advocate Oxford Education?'[14] Nevertheless, at the bishops' meeting in December 1864 it transpired that only two of them favoured an outright ban on attendance at the universities; most preferred to issue a caution on the dangers of attendance.[15] Newman had already warned Bellasis that 'Manning will decide [the matter], I think, [for] both the Pope and the Cardinal; that is, unless the

14. Newman to Gaisford, 16 December 1864, *L&D* XXI, p. 343.
15. Ker, *Newman: a Biography*, pp. 565–67.

Catholic laity through England express strongly an opposite view'.[16] Allies felt that the bishops were unsympathetic to the predicament of married converts like himself. Reflecting on the fact that not one of the thirteen bishops advising the Holy See on the Oxford question had had an English university education, he complained to Newman: 'How many of them care sufficiently for mental culture to give an adequate consideration to the motives determining parents to send their sons to Oxford?'[17]

The converts' reaction to this educational problem bore similarities to their approach to the school question: keenly aware of their parental duties and responsibilities, they were eager that their sons should not forfeit an education that would provide access to mainstream national and social life. Their attitude was typified by the letter Gaisford sent Bishop Grant which complained that the questionnaire had been framed unfairly. Gaisford explained that, on becoming a Catholic, his hardest cross was the thought that his son would lose the advantage of a public school and university education, for Catholics were not accepted in London society on account of their different background. The dangers of Oxford were indeed *less* than elsewhere: 'the bane of the old Catholics has been lying about idle at their parents' houses, or lounging on the Continent'. As legislation had opened up Oxford, he was determined to send his son there, if provision could be made for religious instruction and spiritual direction – and an Oratory in charge of the Oxford mission promised just this. Gaisford declared he was responsible for ensuring that his son was brought up, firstly, as a Catholic Christian, and, secondly, as an English gentleman; he was willing to take advice from wiser men but would not shrink from his responsibility.[18]

Other laymen were acting individually or collectively, both at home and abroad. Bellasis, who was wintering in Rome, began to lobby energetically against a positive prohibition, visiting Barnabò and Talbot and encouraging friends to help him. Back in Britain, Simeon summoned a meeting of influential

---

[16.] Newman to Bellasis, 24 January 1864, *L&D* XXI, p. 28.
[17.] Allies to Newman, 3 December 1864, *L&D* XXI, p. 327n.
[18.] Gaisford to Grant, 11 December 1864, *L&D* XXI, p. 512.

laymen (the majority of whom were connected with the school) in order to draw up an address to Propaganda Fide, though they realised that to succeed it was necessary to widen the base – as in the school foundation – and to attract signatures of old Catholics. Wetherell took the petition to Rome and, together with Bellasis, presented it to the authorities there. Meanwhile the laymen began searching for a permanent representative in Rome who could lobby on their behalf. While Newman's scope for involvement was severely restricted on account of his earlier policy and connection with the Catholic University, he nevertheless felt the question was one which the laity ought to face squarely; the initiative, he believed, would be more effective if it came from those who were immediately involved in the decision. St John was instructed to convey this view to school parents who expressed their wish for provision at Oxford for Catholics.

In February 1865 Propaganda Fide instructed the English bishops to dissuade Catholics from attending non-Catholic universities. Ullathorne put Rome's instruction into effect by telling his clergy 'that Parents ought to be in every way dissuaded from sending their children to pursue their studies at such Universities.'[19] From this Newman concluded that 'no School, as ourselves, can educate with a professed view to Oxford', or indeed Cambridge, London University or Trinity College Dublin. However, from his interpretation of the directive, it was evident '1. that each case of going to Oxford is to be taken by itself. 2. that leave is to be asked by parents in the *Confessional.*'[20] Although Newman anticipated that no great fuss would be made about youths going to Oxford, as no alternative was being provided, he began telling school parents he could take no direct part in sending their sons there and he refused to obtain introductions or provide references, though naturally enough he regretted the unfortunate consequence – that the directive would hit hardest the only school attempting to educate Catholics boys in a way that would enable them to cope with Oxford. Two years earlier he had agreed with a friend that on 'Catholic boys, educated as Catholics educate

[19] *L&D* XXI, p. 440n.
[20] Newman to Pollen, 31 March 1865, *L&D* XXI, p. 441.

them, Oxford life will not act happily – but it *ought* not to be so, and we trust we are educating our own boys here in a better way'.[21] In dealing with the matter Newman undoubtedly drew upon his own experience of going up to Oxford, when his classics teacher at school warned him of the dangers there, and wrote to encourage him to stand firm amidst the dissipation of student life and to be prepared to endure ridicule for doing so. There is evidence that Oratory School parents were also alive to the need for preparation for undergraduate life: Thynne, for example, asked if his son could be given some idea how 'our religion is controverted by Protestants and how to meet their arguments'.[22]

Despite the bishops' latest decision, Ullathorne again offered the Oxford mission to Newman, and in June 1866 the Birmingham Oratory accepted, on condition that the warning against Oxford was not strengthened. Newman realised that the provision of a strong Catholic presence in Oxford was likely to be considered by many parents as 'a pledge that their children would be protected against the scepticism and infidelity which too notoriously prevail there just now'.[23] It was to avoid this that Propaganda Fide sanctioned the proposal of an Oxford Oratory dependent on the Birmingham Oratory – with the specific proviso that Newman himself should not reside in Oxford: the purpose was to grant Newman sufficient scope to influence Protestants there, but not enough to attract Catholics. Ullathorne, however, withheld the 'secret instruction' from Newman, believing he could get it rescinded. Friends of Newman launched an appeal for the new church, and within months about £2000 was pledged, mainly from the school promoters; on this occasion it was Gaisford who led the initiative, as Hope-Scott and Bellasis were wintering at Hyères. Then in April 1867, when Newman's own preparations were well under way, the secret ban on Newman was made public in the press. It was a great blow, and after agonising long over the matter, Newman decided to let the plan lapse. Shortly afterwards Propaganda Fide issued its

21. Newman to Orsnby, 6 July 1863, *L&D* XX, p. 486.
22. Thynne to Newman, n.d., *L&D* XXI, p. 379n.
23. Newman to Jenkins, 12 December 1867, *L&D* XXIII, p. 383.

strongest warning yet, declaring that English Catholics sending their sons to the national universities would be guilty of exposing them to a proximate occasion of grave sin; the bishops were charged to communicate the decision to the faithful through pastoral letters. Pondering the implications for the school, Newman considered lowering the upper age to fourteen or sixteen and emphasising their care of young boys; but, on Hope-Scott's advice, the school continued on its former course. However, an addition had to be made to the prospectus, stating that in accordance with their bishop's pastoral there was no preparation provided for the examinations at Oxford and Cambridge. One remedy to the situation suggested by Hope-Scott was to begin a centre of higher studies at Rednal: the scheme was carefully considered, but had to be dropped owing to the expense and for want of a suitable tutor.

Asked by anxious parents for guidance in interpreting the official strictures, Newman's replies reveal his deep sympathy with the aspirations of youth. He explained to Lady Simeon that the declaration was not an outright prohibition but the gravest of warnings, thus a general rule admitting exceptions for very strong reasons.

> It does not do to beat the life out of a youth – the life of aspiration, excitement and enthusiasm. Older men live by reason, habit and self-control, but the young live by visions. I can fancy cases in which Oxford would be the salvation of a youth; when he would be far more likely to rise up against authority, murmur against his superiors, and (more) to become an unbeliever, if he is kept from Oxford than if he is sent there.[24]

The goal of Oxford might be the sole motivation for a youth to work, and avoid idleness and despondency; 'It may make all the difference between his being a useful member of society through life and employing his talents to God's glory, or not'.[25] Newman realised that by adopting this line he was laying

---

[24]. Newman to Lady Simeon, 10 November 1867, *L&D* XXIII, p. 366.
[25]. Newman to Simeon, 9 December 1867, *L&D* XXIII, p. 381.

himself open to the charge of complying with the letter of Propaganda Fide's instruction while ignoring its spirit – an accusation some of his contemporaries (and later historians) were quick to seize upon. In a memorandum he wrote at the time, he recorded that his 'appearance of having in some respect adopted a shuffling course' was due to being pulled in opposite directions: by his duty of obedience on the one hand, and his private judgement on the other.

> Thus, as to youths going to Oxford, a parent may never have spoken to me on the subject, much less asked my advice, I may not know him or his son, whom he has sent to Oxford – that son may be going on well there – he may have got honours – I may judge from his career that he has gained very much good, and no harm, from being there, and, since I have ever felt that there *are* those who will gain good from going there, I may be glad he has gone there. Now, suppose I express this satisfaction, it is easy and obvious for a hearer to assert that I am "disobedient", I am going against authority, as approving that which authority has discountenanced.[26]

But more than his words, it was certain facts that Newman's accusers pointed to; and it was difficult to resist their inference, for of the forty-seven Catholics who matriculated at Oxford during the two decades after the warning, thirteen had passed through the Oratory School. The leakage from other schools was minimal: Stonyhurst and Beaumont supplied four, Oscott and Woburn three each, and Ushaw one. At first glance this suggests that the Oratory School flouted the episcopal ban; but a more careful consideration of the school's special circumstances casts a different light on the facts. For one thing, several of the boys going to Oxford went via Darnell or other tutors; more significantly, it must be recalled that the Oratory School was the natural choice for converts whose educational convictions were unaltered by their change of religion. It would be harsh to blame Newman for decisions which were not his; and it is easy to sympathise with the predicament of

---

[26.] Newman, memorandum, 5 September 1867, *L&D* XXIII, p. 332.

Oxford converts who were being told in the strongest terms not to risk sending their sons to the university which, in a sense, had made them Catholics![27] That said, Oxford was no longer the place it was in its Tractarian days. In 1868 Newman received a frank appraisal of the dangers there from Arnold, the former master of the Oratory School, who sent news of two former pupils at Christ Church. To the extent that they worked hard and aimed at an honours degree, they were brought into contact with influences that would sap their faith, and even their Christianity; but if they kept apart from the 'intellectual race' they were safer. However, Arnold considered that the main danger lay elsewhere. He pointed out that

> the chief mischief, and a real one, is the *discontinuity* in their education which is involved in capping the edifice begun at home and carried on at the Oratory [School] with a Christ Church coping stone. At the Oratory [School] all was work, order, and duty; at Ch. Ch. all is play, license, and amusement. It is not the Protestantism but the idleness of Oxford that is to be dreaded for them.[28]

In response to repeated promptings from Propaganda Fide, the English bishops decided to re-consider the question of establishing a Catholic university, and in 1871 they appointed a committee to investigate the prospects. Newman was included among the eight hundred individuals invited to respond to the committee's questionnaire, but, as with the 1858 questionnaire about the school, Newman found himself unable to do so properly on account of differing fundamental assumptions about the nature of education. To the first question, which asked whether there were any perceived deficiencies in the provision of liberal education for young Catholic laymen of the higher classes,

---

27. In the decade after 1887, however, as many as 116 Catholics matriculated but only fifteen were from the Oratory School (and fifteen from Woburn). One of these was James Hope (Lord Rankeillour), the only surviving son of Hope-Scott, who was exceptionally given permission by his bishop.

28. Arnold to Newman, 2 February 1868, *Letters of Thomas Arnold the Younger, 1850–1900*, ed. J. Bertram (London: OUP, 1980), pp. 162–63.

Newman answered that there was *no* provision: there was nothing at all available deserving the name of a liberal education. The other replies the committee received were equally revealing, for they showed that the laity, unlike the committee or the bishops, had clear ideas about what they wanted. After an Oxford or Cambridge college, the next most acceptable proposal was for a centre of higher studies under Newman: in the words of one of the committee members, 'to turn your present *school* into a College for such a purpose exclusively'[29] – a proposal which Newman thought was 'simply impossible'.[30]

In the event, it was Manning's scheme that was adopted and the Catholic University College was opened at Kensington in 1875. However, it survived only seven years. In the first place Manning's choice of rector, Thomas Capel (a prominent figure in London society), was unfortunate as he turned out to be an incompetent administrator, and he was forced to resign in 1878; four years later Manning suspended him from priestly duties for moral reasons. The college also failed because it lacked support: the Jesuits gave the scheme no assistance, the bishops lost interest once it had been opened, and the laity showed their preference for Oxford and Cambridge over Kensington. When Manning invited Newman to participate he turned the offer down, officially because of the connection with London University, privately because he feared it would be under too close clerical control. Three years after the demise of Kensington, the warning about Catholic attendance at Oxford had to be reiterated; but a decade later, after the death of Manning (and Newman), the policy was jettisoned. Although there had been mounting pressure from the laity, the official reason given for the reversal of policy was the assessment that conditions at the universities had changed: Catholic residence was now possible as the moral condition had improved and the Anglican monopoly had been broken.

'Continual cannonadings'

The rejection of the Oxford hall scheme, the ambivalence towards the plan for an Oxford Oratory, and the warnings on

29. Northcote to Newman, 25 March 1872, *L&D* XXVI, p. 50n.
30. Newman to Northcote, 25 March 1872, *L&D* XXVI, p. 49.

university attendance were all indications of the prevailing wind. Rome would not countenance mixed education; and under Wiseman and then Manning, that policy was resolutely implemented in England. This climate goes a long way towards explaining the campaign of opposition to the school that arose almost from the beginning, for the perceived allegiances of Newman allowed the school to become a serviceable target for those with strong Ultramontane views. Newman's inclination was to lie low and let the storm blow over; it was with great reluctance that he found himself forced by circumstances to counteract tales told about the school

At first, opposition took the shape of 'prophecy'. It was said – and by priests – that although the Oratory could give intellectual training, it would prove unsuitable for the religious and moral training of boys: to rebut these allegations, Bellasis recommended issuing a circular, or else publishing Newman's catechetical classes. In a reference to the dame system, it was reported that women were to be allowed into the Oratory building – a scandal for a religious house such as the Oratory. These and other such stories circulated even before the school had opened.[31] Later, gossip fed off every aspect of the school: disputes among the staff, misdemeanours of boys, school arrangements. The circulation of damaging stories has always attended educational establishments, especially new ones, but in the case of the Oratory School they were particularly virulent: both in the extent to which the exaggerations and falsehoods were persistently repeated, despite the explanations provided, and in the way they were embroidered. It was said that the boys were allowed out into Birmingham unaccompanied (contrary to what was stated in the school prospectus); later it was alleged that they went to public houses, dancing rooms and even brothels. The boys were said to swear; then it

---

[31.] Some opposition emanated from the London Oratory, reflecting both its Ultramontanism and the contention of some London Oratorians that it was against the Oratorian Rule to run a school. There, Newman recorded, a 'thousand whisperings [...] have succeeded in prejudicing the Catholic body to a great extent against me'; and he noted that the whisperings, 'since we began the School, have been both increased, and directed against it' (Autobiographical memoir, 21 January 1863, *AW*, p. 256).

was said they were so profane that, instead of saying a man 'swore like a trooper', he would say, he 'swore like an Edgbastonian'.[32] Birmingham was bad for the morals of the boys; later it was said to be bad for their health too, so that, unlike the Oscott boys, they were puny and unhealthy (an opinion which Moody willingly aired).

Some Catholics had entertained doubts about the school for another reason: Newman's supposed incompetence in organisational affairs, as illustrated by Oratorian disputes and the apparent failure of the Catholic University in Dublin. These misgivings seemed to be only confirmed by the Darnell affair. Moody gave out that the affair demonstrated Newman's singular incapacity for government; for Simpson it represented the 'destruction of the last refuge of the would be believers in Newman's practical ability', and he hoped Newman would 'give up attempting to rule men by his command, instead of exerting an almost omnipotent influence over them by his teaching'.[33] In such a hostile climate, it was assumed in many Catholic circles for some time after the crisis that the school was on the point of collapse.

Newman knew that the gossip had the effect of 'frightening people with the suspicion of our being crypto-heretics'[34] – a reference to *The Rambler* (and its successor, the *Home and Foreign Review*), which had become since the time of Newman's brief editorship an outlet for the German school of historical criticism due to Acton's links with its most representative figure, Döllinger. In 1862 Manning had asked Propaganda Fide to include *The Rambler* on the Index because of the rationalist principles which inspired it. A mother with three boys at the school became so worried by rumours from Church authorities about excommunication and schism that she wrote to Mrs Wootten for reassurance that the school was not about to be closed because of its links with Liberal Catholics; and it was partly with a view to protecting the school that Newman felt obliged to distance himself from them and their publications.

[32.] Memorandum, *L&D* XXIII, p. 116.
[33.] Simpson to Acton, 4 January 1862, *Correspondence of Acton and Simpson* II, p. 249.
[34.] Newman to St John, 25 October 1862, *L&D* XX, p. 328.

Newman has been described as at the time 'an isolated figure
[...] at the periphery of the institutional Church'[35] – a predicament that so intrigued Acton that he compiled several lists of
reasons to explain Newman's gradual estrangement and
marginalisation. Newman personally felt that his influence was
undermined by the opposition and distrust of other converts;
and he was keenly aware that the school received no support
from the bishops, other than Ullathorne. Bishop Brown of
Newport gave out that the school was unacceptable because,
being modelled on Eton, it allowed the boys to roam around
town; Bishop Brown of Shrewsbury maintained that religion
was not taught properly at the school and that its spirit was not
Catholic – and indeed that since the school was staffed by
converts, it was *unable* to impart a proper catechetical instruction.[36] Newman complained that Bishop Grant said 'quite
atrocious things of our school', and that he repeated them in
spite of being given explanations to the contrary.[37] The school
may have been flourishing internally, but such 'continual
cannonadings'[38] meant that it could show no external signs of
success.

   Under Wiseman, the bishops' policy was to maintain cordial
relations with Newman but to keep him out of all schemes
involving tertiary education.[39] However, insofar as the school
prepared boys for Oxford, it became implicated in the
bishops' policy; and this was one reason why they chose not to
support the school. Another reason was their perplexity as to
whether Newman's ideas were fully compatible with Catholic

[35.] Norman, *English Roman Catholics*, p. 313.
[36.] Brown called 'catechetical instruction the *real Tradition* of the
Church – those who have never received it can never deliver it'
(Brown to Bellasis, 5 November 1862, BOA). He expressed this
view in an exchange of letters with Bellasis after a chance meeting
on a train journey, during which they had had a heated discussion
about religious education at the Oratory School.
[37.] Newman to Monsell, 8 October 1863, *L&D* XX, p. 534.
[38.] Newman to Bellasis, 19 October 1862, *L&D* XX, p. 314.
[39.] Nevertheless Wiseman once confided to Bellasis that he considered
Newman the person to begin a Catholic university in England, and
that he would have preferred to have seen the nucleus of a university, rather than of a school, at Edgbaston (Bellasis to Newman, 23
April 1864, *L&D* XXI, p. 98n).

teaching. This was unfortunate for the school, as Newman reckoned that just a little episcopal support would have brought the extra ten to twenty boys it needed to break even financially.

Unlike the bishops, Manning chose to ignore the school. Its glaring omission from his enumeration of Catholic schools in England was either a deliberate oversight to avoid giving the school any public echo, or perhaps more likely an indication that Manning had come to think of it as a temporary measure: 'that the School had been opened to gratify a whim of a generation of converts [...] and [...] would in the natural course of events pass with their passing'.[40] Alternatively, it is possible that Manning viewed the Oratory School as part of a separate system of education, alien to the college system, and thus not part of the substructure of his prospective university. Whatever the reason, Manning's stance also reflected his conviction that Newman had not acquired Catholic instincts and therefore lacked the Catholic spirit; had it not been for this, Manning would surely have favoured the school, since he viewed the dismantlement of mixed education as a step towards one of his primary objectives, the improvement of clerical education.

Newman's reputation in Rome had been severely damaged after his *Rambler* article of July 1859 was delated for heresy; years later, Talbot continued to fan the flames and cite it as having encouraged the laity in a wish to govern the Church in England by public opinion. Talbot was Manning's agent in Rome and, together with Herbert Vaughan (Manning's successor at Westminster), furthered the cause of the Roman party with stories against Newman: that he had twice refused to see the Pope, that he contributed money to Garibaldi's cause, that he was associated with a dangerous party in England. Pius IX heard from Vaughan that Newman was unreliable, being a representative of the liberal and national school of thought, while Propaganda Fide received complaints from Grant and Talbot of a more precise nature: that Catholics at Oxford had made a shipwreck of their faith and morals, and that despite this Newman was preparing boys at his school for Oxford in

40. [Tristram], 'Oratory School', *OPM*, February 1933, p. 27.

defiance of papal policy.[41] In fact, the Pope already knew that boys from the school aspired to Oxford, because two of them (probably Bellasis's sons) had expressed their desire to go there in an audience with him.[42]

While Newman was busy preparing to establish an Oratory in Oxford in the spring of 1867, unaware of the secret instruction to keep him out, Barnabò wrote to him to complain that he was actively preparing a number of youths for Oxford, and was doing so in spite of the declarations of the Holy See that it was imprudent; and the cardinal added that the Pope was upset at the 'recent unhappy perversion' of Catholics at Oxford and had asked for the English bishops to discuss the matter, and for Newman 'to abstain altogether from any activity or deed which may have the appearance of directly or indirectly favouring the entry of Catholic youths' to Oxford.[43] Newman replied that only two boys were being prepared at the school for Oxford, one at the insistence of his father, the other sent by a bishop in New Zealand; it was his understanding that the matter had been left by the bishops to the prudent discretion of confessors, in some cases to dissuade, in others to provide safeguards, sometimes reluctantly acquiescing, where parents were rashly but obstinately determined. Besides, he went on robustly, he had heard of no loss of faith at Oxford; and the Oratory School was only doing as Oscott and Stonyhurst were, by preparing boys for Oxford. And he finished by promising Barnabò that he would obey, while expressing surprise 'that, after my twenty years of most faithful service, your Eminence reposes so little confidence in me in the matter'.[44]

The feeling of Oratory School parents towards these proceedings can be gauged from a letter that Sheil (an old Catholic) sent Newman. Sheil considered it 'lamentable that the Propaganda should interfere in a matter so political and so English as education', particularly as the direction of the interference seemed to indicate that Propaganda Fide was entirely

---

41. *L&D* XXIII, pp. 3, 89n, 137n.
42. [Tristram], 'Oratory School', *OPM*, May 1933, p. 67.
43. Barnabò to Newman, 11 March 1867, *L&D* XXIII, p. 91.
44. Newman to Barnabò, 21 March 1867, *L&D* XXIII, p. 94.

blind to the downtrodden position of English Catholics, and to 'how unfit they are to come forward in public life, how unable to impart the least benefit to their co-religionists', largely as a result of their incomplete education. 'I assume to myself an absolute independence in the management of my secular affairs,' said Sheil, 'in which I include education: my son shall learn fractions and the Greek Grammar where and under whom I choose'. And he added that Propaganda Fide might just as well dictate that, because of dangers to faith and morals, his sons could not be soldiers or lawyers.[45]

Several weeks before the release of the secret instruction, Ullathorne had revealed to Newman that there had been a strong complaint from Grant, Manning and Talbot after Propaganda Fide had granted permission for an Oratory in Oxford, and that Vaughan spoke in Rome about Newman having established a school whose purpose was to prepare boys for Oxford. Newman knew that Vaughan's version was not difficult to disprove; yet he could not but recognise that the force of the objection to the school was the ease with which it could send boys to Oxford. As he confided in Hope-Scott,

> We must be ready to give up the school and *I think it will come to this*. For how can we say that we do not *indirectly* prepare for Oxford, *while* we teach classics and mathematics, and *those* parents send their children to us especially *who will not* pledge themselves *not* to send their boys to Oxford?[46]

As the pressure continued to mount, Ullathorne urged Newman to go to Rome to clear his name and resolve the whole issue of the school. But instead St John was chosen to undertake the mission since he was headmaster and, besides, could speak Italian. In order to avoid the suspicion that he was playing a game with the Holy See over Oxford, Newman gave St John a lengthy memorandum he had prepared, 'Notes for a Statement to be presented to Propaganda in behalf of the School of the Oratory by Fr Ambrose St John', together with a selection of letters for use as evidence, should the need arise. At

[45.] Sheil to Newman, 27 March 1867, *L&D* XXIII, pp. 102–3.
[46.] Newman to Hope-Scott, 29 March 1867, *L&D* XXIII, p. 113.

the Congregation meeting to ratify his brief, St John was told:

> You must boldly say, that we must give up the School,
> unless we are allowed to teach in our own way, both as
> regards *subjects* and *method* of teaching, whatever be the
> subjects and method of other educational bodies, and
> whatever be the animus and intentions of parents who
> place their sons in our charge.[47]

In other words, the academic dimension of the school's public
school identity was not to be surrendered.

The memorandum described the salient features of the foundation: how the initiative came from parents; how some bore
the financial responsibility; how they had petitioned Newman
to start the first 'purely lay school'; their objections to the
college system in wanting Greek taught better, older and more
educated masters, and feminine care for young boys; and their
willingness to pay extra to gain these advantages. It explained
that Newman's intention had been to prepare boys not for
Oxford, but for the Catholic University in Dublin, which he
had just left; only the previous year he had petitioned Monsell,
who was working in the government ministry that was granting
privileges to the Catholic University, to ask that they might be
drawn up in such a way as to allow boys from the school to take
examinations and degrees at it while in England.

The memorandum provided a summary of the 'series of
calumnies [...] persistently circulated against our School'. The
latest form of slander had turned 'the very excellence of our
teaching into an offence': because they taught so successfully
that boys were succeeding at difficult competitive examinations, it was rumoured that 'the system of education has been
formally and intentionally' designed to prepare boys for
Oxford. The memorandum attributed opposition to the school
to three causes: 'the strong feeling of the adherents and parti-
sans of the existing Catholic Colleges' – not the colleges
themselves – against any new rival institution; 'the fears of
pious but narrowminded men, who cannot comprehend how
intellectual excellence and moral can be compatible [...] and

---

[47.] Newman to St John, 2 April 1867, *L&D* XXIII, p. 121.

who think that a good secular education must be a bad moral one'; and a jealousy of the Birmingham Oratorians, together with a suspicion that because they worked silently and without fuss, they must therefore be 'deep and crafty, and be pursuing some secret object of our own'. As the school had been accused before the authorities in Rome, the memorandum asked that the accusations be disclosed so that the charges could be answered.[48]

Following Ullathorne's advice, Newman ended the memorandum with three questions. Would they be wrong to teach classics with great attention to accurate grammatical knowledge, knowing that Oxford demanded such knowledge of its students? Would they be at fault if parents of their boys decided – without consulting them, and without their knowledge or encouragement – to send their sons to Oxford? And if it were possible, would it be permissible for the school to affiliate to Oxford University, on the same conditions as the colleges affiliated to London University?[49]

On 3 April 1867 St John set off for Rome via Hyères, where he was to liaise with Bellasis and Hope-Scott. Three days later news of the secret instruction became public when the Rome correspondent of the *Weekly Register* claimed that the Pope was to reverse Propaganda Fide's decision and stop Newman going to Oxford, on grounds of suspected heresy. At this point Ullathorne was forced to reveal to Newman that he had been instructed by Barnabò to prevent him from taking up residence in Oxford. The news, and manner of its revelation, shed a new light on proceedings: 'now they have thrown off the mask and attack, not the school, but me and my teaching', Newman concluded.[50] After conferring with Bellasis, Hope-Scott and St John on how to proceed, he decided that neither the memorandum nor the questions should be presented to avoid the possibility of new conditions being imposed on the school, for they feared it could be put directly under a bishop; as this was contrary to the privileges of the Oratory, St John was instructed to say they would rather close it than submit to a

[48.] Newman, memorandum, 30 March 1867, *L&D* XXIII, pp. 115–17.
[49.] *Ibid.*, p. 118.
[50.] Newman to St John, 6 April 1867, *L&D* XXIII, pp. 129–30.

transfer of control. Instead they decided that St John should concentrate on defending Newman, and that all he should request for the school was that it be treated like others. Bellasis composed a long defence of the school for Talbot; following Newman's suggestion, it was sent instead to Cardinal Reisach, Prefect of the Congregation of Studies.

The article in the *Weekly Register* provoked a public outcry. The Stafford Club, founded by members of the Catholic aristocracy in 1851, adopted an address expressing sympathy for Newman which declared: 'we feel that every blow that touches you inflicts a wound upon the Catholic Church in this country'.[51] The address, framed by Monsell and F.R. Ward, attracted 184 signatories (only six of whom were school promoters); they included all the Catholic M.P.s, nearly all the Catholic peers and a host of other Catholic laymen of standing. Several Catholics refused to sign on the grounds that it would be interpreted as an act of defiance or disapproval of Manning, and a few like Simpson and Wetherell were persuaded not to sign on the grounds that it would deter others from doing so. Inevitably the address revived tensions with the clergy and it was interpreted by some clerics as confirmation that the laity had absorbed Protestant attitudes.

The principal achievement of St John's trip to Rome was the partial lifting of the cloud of suspicion hanging over Newman, caused by his supposed refusal to answer the Holy See about his delated article. During St John's interviews with Barnabò and the Pope, it became apparent that the Holy See was principally intent on upholding its policy of opposition to mixed education and that it was uninfluenced by gossip in Rome. At St John's meeting with Reisach, it was clear that the cardinal was aware of the need for provision of higher education; with Talbot, St John had to convince him that the school was not trying to prepare its older boys for Oxford. In an attempt to secure written assurance from Barnabò that the school would be treated like all the others, Newman wrote to thank him for the verbal assurance he had given St John, but Barnabò's reply gave yet another twist to events. The colleges were approved establishments, the cardinal pointed out, whereas

---

[51.] *Weekly Register*, 20 April 1867, p. 250.

the Oratory School was still on trial; and it was, he mused, a remarkable coincidence of on the one hand a new school starting up 'professedly founded on the type of Protestant public schools, and on the other a desire to send to Oxford springing up in the minds of Catholic parents'.[52] To Newman this seemed to imply that there was a policy to block any connection he might have with Oxford, whether it was a question of his attracting Catholics through his presence there or his sending boys there from the school. It was a clear warning that the school could still be closed down, for even if its boys went to Oxford via a tutor, the school could be accused of obeying the letter but evading the spirit of the directive from Propaganda Fide. The prospect of endless troubles, dwindling school numbers and eventual closure seemed all too possible. Yet there were good reasons for carrying on: closure would be a victory for the school's opponents and a betrayal of its friends, and besides, the prospect of better times ahead could not be discounted; moreover, Newman was convinced that 'We are doing direct good to the next generation by setting up an educational system such as ours – and indirectly by our action on other Catholic schools.'[53] Hope-Scott's advice was to carry on, and so they did. But in the circumstances in which they found themselves, prudence became the order of the day in all matters relating to Oxford: parents who announced that they were contemplating Oxford for their sons were immediately asked to withdraw them from the school; others were warned not to mention Oxford on visits to Edgbaston; and Newman refused to comment on possible exceptions to the bishops' warning.

The numbers game

A decade earlier, when the Oratory School had been about to open, there were six main Catholic boarding establishments. In order of size they were Stonyhurst (over 200), Ushaw (also over 200), Oscott (about 130), Ware (about 100), and then

---

[52.] Newman to Hope-Scott, 9 September 1867, *L&D* XXIII, p. 334.
[53.] *Ibid.*, p. 335.

Ampleforth and Downside (both about 80 each); but in terms of social class and fashion, the pecking order was headed by Oscott and followed by Stonyhurst. Inevitably the newcomer threatened the dominance of the leading three, but the colleges were unsure how to respond to the challenge: whether by emulation of its principles, or rejection of them, or a combination of the two. In his memorandum for Propaganda Fide, Newman claimed that the Oratory School's most marked success was 'indirect, but immediate, viz. the effect we have had on other places of education'[54] – by which he meant improvements at Oscott and Ushaw, and the foundation of Beaumont. And he also mentioned to friends the Oratory School's example 'in making the other schools, even the Jesuit schools, less continental in their ways and more English, as in trusting boys and giving up *espionage*'.[55] Acton, too, boasted that 'Edgbaston has revived studies in all our colleges'.[56]

These claims are almost certainly valid, but it is hard to find direct evidence to back them up. Certainly there was no *immediate* realignment of the collegiate system along public school lines, as some historians have claimed: this realignment did not begin until the early 1900s. [57] Newman's boast to Propaganda Fide that 'we have led the way in a system of educational improvement on a large scale through the Catholic community'[58] was no doubt valid, but it is far from clear that the colleges actually followed: the deciding factor which led the

---

[54.] Memorandum, *L&D* XXIII, p. 117.

[55.] Church to Mozley, 13 June 1865, *The Life and Letters of Dean Church*, ed. M.C. Church (London: Macmillan, 1894), p. 170.

[56.] Acton to Renouf, 14 November 1862, *Letters of Renouf* III, p. 153.

[57.] The prefect system was introduced at Beaumont in 1901, and within seven years blossomed into a full system of duties and privileges, completely supplanting the surveillance system. Downside was remodelled along Wellington lines from 1902 by an Oxford-educated convert, who introduced a prefect system and the house system, and boosted games; numbers trebled in his sixteen-year reign. A parallel development occurred at Ampleforth, where extensive reforms modelled on Winchester were begun in 1912. Last of the leading colleges, Stonyhurst did not begin to adapt until 1921.

[58.] Memorandum, *L&D* XXIII, p. 117.

colleges to realign and mimic the public schools was probably not the example of the Oratory School but the hierarchy's decision in 1895 to allow Catholics to attend the universities. It is likely that at first the example of the Oratory School was dismissed, for Acton spoke of the 'advocates of the Seminary System' who deprecated the competition, seeing in it 'an implied censure of their methods; a complaint of their results'.[59] Nevertheless the tide soon turned. Old Catholics met Ullathorne's surprising but enlightened appointment of James Northcote (a former editor of *The Rambler*) at Oscott in 1860 with hostility and suspicion, but the cultivated convert friend of Newman soon raised academic standards and instituted wide-ranging reforms. The curriculum was revised and the classical side strengthened; formal college exams were introduced; new staff were appointed; and the use of clerics as tutors for lay boys was discontinued. However, although the changes at Oscott introduced elements of public school practice, it remained essentially an ecclesiastical college; in fact, the distinction between the colleges and the public schools remained until Ampleforth, Downside and Stonyhurst ceased educating boys and training clerics together.

Was the Oratory School the catalyst for the changes at Oscott and elsewhere? It is difficult to gauge its influence as a 'beacon school', not least because the evidence is so fragmented. Doubtless the dispersion of Oratory schoolmasters such as Hopkins, Moody, Ransford and Walford accelerated dissemination of school practice. It is known, for example, that after teaching at Harrow, Eton and the Oratory School, Walford trained as a Jesuit and introduced reforms while teaching at St Francis Xavier's College, Liverpool and at Beaumont. At the same time, the leavening effect of the converts was in proportion to their presence in the system, and though there was a practically undiluted concentration of them at the Oratory School it could not claim a monopoly over their influence. Besides, it has been argued that the changes the converts inspired were not all to the good, since they were influential in narrowing the curriculum at the very time when social pressures were beginning to favour a broader and more practical emphasis.

[59.] Acton, n.d., Cambridge University Library, Add. MS 4988/227.

There is an element of pious exaggeration in the claim that Beaumont resulted from the Oxford Movement and the desire it inspired in Catholics for a return to their proper place in society.[60] Nevertheless, although its first masters and traditions were imported from Stonyhurst, it did attempt to imitate the public schools more closely than its northern progenitor in order to undo the perception that Stonyhurst and the Jesuits were harsh and un-English. What is beyond question is that Beaumont's magnificent setting in what was originally part of Windsor Great Park and its proximity to London enabled it to chart instant success. Within a year it had fifty boys, three years later one hundred, and after another four years a hundred and fifty; and Newman was noting how it had cut into the Oratory School's clientele and made it 'thin'. One reason it did so was that Beaumont also took young boys, and shortly after opening a matron was engaged to care for them, although in 1868 it appears that there was something of a reaction against Beaumont, because they no longer had a matron and in consequence some boys had been neglected.[61]

Despite – or perhaps because of – the competition between the colleges, little heed was paid to improvements elsewhere until the sub-commission investigating Catholic higher education published its findings, based on responses to its questionnaire: the data was analysed in a *Special Report* by each of the five sub-commissioners and in a single *General Report*. This penetrating survey on the state of Catholic education momentarily deflected the attention of Catholics from the closed world of Catholic education to the national stage. The *Special Report* of the Jesuit Edward Purbrick asserted that Catholic establishments were 'infinitely superior' to non-Catholic ones in 'morality' (by which he meant chastity, not general moral development), and that they secured a higher average standard of knowledge in a wider range of subjects; but, the report added, the eldest and cleverest at each did not

---

[60.] P. Levi, *Beaumont, 1861–1961* (London: A. Deutsch, 1961), p. 16.
[61.] An additional cause of the Jesuits' success was their facility in attracting some of the most promising converts; more than one hundred entered the Society of Jesus, and during the 1860s, 1870s and 1880s the most prominent Jesuits in English education were all converts.

compare. Schools like Eton, Rugby, Cheltenham and Wellington were far superior in three respects: in scholarship; in composition or literary power; and 'in expansion of mind, earnestness of purpose, definiteness of aim'. Purbrick attributed the shortcomings to a variety of factors: the smaller number of pupils at Catholic schools; 'the very mixed character of our boys, who are drawn from the lower as well as the higher classes of society, from abroad as well as from England'; the advanced age and backwardness of incoming boys; the paucity of opportunity for comparison with the best non-Catholic schools; the absence of the stimulus that a university would provide; the absence of school prizes and scholarships; and – most tellingly – 'the terrible *vis inertiae* of comfortable, self-satisfied, mediocre, unambitious traditions'. Speaking his mind, Purbrick noted the 'pretty universal sense of intellectual inferiority' among the Catholic aristocracy, and agreed with fellow-converts as to the causes: apathy; ignorance of the extent of the deficiency; a fear of appearing to hold views opposed to those of the ecclesiastical authorities; fear of hurting their alma maters; and a dread of 'incurring displeasure, or becoming marked men' if they ventured to suggest a Catholic college at Oxford or Cambridge.[62]

Thirteen of the 100 responses to the questionnaires came from those connected with the Oratory School: from staff, current (Newman, St John and Pope) and past (Hopkins, Kelke and Moody), from parents and promoters (Allies, Bethell, Poole, S.N. Stokes, Thynne, F.R. Ward and Wegg-Prosser) – all of them converts. The shortcomings identified were much the same as those observed fifteen years previously, when the idea of the Oratory School was first mooted: the utterly inadequate payment of teachers; the listlessness and apathy of Catholics entering manhood; their deficiency in culture, limited powers of expression and ill-ease in society; their propensity to social frivolity and lack of any real spirit of work. The latter was particularly prevalent among the many Catholics who entered the army as a way of idling away their time, without any intention of making it their profession. St John and William Kelke (a

---

[62.] E.J. Purbrick, *Special Report* (Roehampton: privately published, 1872), pp. 8–9, 12.

master in 1867/68) struck an innovatory note by recommending the establishment at the leading Catholic schools of a Modern Side, as at Cheltenham and Harrow, which enabled boys to be prepared for Sandhurst and Woolwich in much the same way as the classical side prepared them for university.

The *Special Report* of Northcote, the president of Oscott, grappled with the key issue: the colleges' 'desperate struggle to fulfil the fourfold office of a Preparatory School, a Grammar School, a College, and a University'.[63] Northcote listed ten establishments catering for upper-class boarding education: besides Stonyhurst, Ushaw, Oscott, Edgbaston, Beaumont, Downside, Ware and Prior Park, he added St George's Croydon and St Lawrence's Ramsgate. Stonyhurst and Ushaw together accounted for almost half the 1200 boys concerned, aged between eight and eighteen; the rest, with an average of seventy-five boys each, were not large enough to offer a first-class education, since classes were either too small or too few. Northcote made the challenging suggestion that the number of upper schools be reduced to four. On reading this, Newman wrote to Northcote acknowledging that the Oratory School, though established to match the great Protestant public schools, had actually contributed to the problem by adding yet another small school to the list; and he offered to fit in with Northcote's plan, if 'judged to be best for the interests of Catholic education in England'.[64] The three conditions Newman stipulated were that the reorganisation should be carried out by 'the Bishops, *in union* with the principal clergy and the *laity*'; that all the schools would have to participate; and that the ownership of property would have to be respected.[65] In Newman's opinion it was for the Oratory School's own comfort that it should be either a public school or a preparatory school, as it was at present too broken up with different ages (there were sixty boys aged between eight and eighteen); but he suspected he would be alone among the Oratorians in preferring that it become just a preparatory school. Whatever happened to Northcote's plan, Newman thought the intrinsic

[63.] J.S. Northcote, *Special Report* (London: privately published, 1872), p. 19.

[64.] Newman to Northcote, 9 April 1872, *L&D* XXVI, p. 62.

[65.] Newman to St John, 10 April 1872, *L&D* XXVI, p. 63.

difficulty of numbers would eventually force them to make this choice, unless duty to the common good did so first.

Nothing became of the idea, and each school had to battle on as best it could. Six years later Northcote reopened the matter with Newman, pointing out that Oscott and the Oratory School were trying to occupy precisely the same ground; the special rivalry between them was a drain on finances and personnel, so that neither could break even, and Oscott swallowed up the services of ten or eleven priests which the diocese could scarcely afford to spare. Newman played down their special rivalry; he thought Beaumont a closer rival, as it had even managed to attract sons of several Oratory School promoters such as J.M. Capes, Monsell and Scott-Murray. What Newman *was* able to offer Northcote was a rather drastic, but practical, solution to assuage their shared anxieties: he proposed that all the schools should join together in a 'lock out' or cartel, raise their fees, and stand by each other!

Although attempts to create a top school in London had only a minor impact on the market for boarding provision elsewhere, on account of the location, it is instructive to observe what happened there. In 1863 Manning had opened St Charles's College, under the supervision of the Oblates of St Charles and the direction of his nephew William Manning. It claimed to pursue the English public school system: established to educate the capital's upper classes, with an absence of espionage and an emphasis on trust, with special attention given to the development of character, management by sixth-form prefects, all conducted amidst an unobtrusive religious influence – but of course this was sales pitch aimed at the emerging Catholic middle classes. The preponderance of converts among the Oblates helped it attract boys intended for the professions, and by 1876 it had 130 pupils, including church boys. It had by then moved from Bayswater to an eleven-acre site and grand buildings in St Charles's Square, at a cost of £40,000, and a further £1300 was lavished on outdoor facilities which included the latest fad, an asphalt skating-ring.[66]

[66.] No well-known old Catholic or convert names appear on the midsummer exam classifications of 1871 (Arundel Castle archive, MD.2145), and cross-reference with the Oratory School roll

A Jesuit plan for a London school had been blocked by Manning, but in 1873 Capel opened Kensington Catholic Public School, which claimed to cater exclusively for sons of gentlemen, though it had a Modern as well as a Classical Side and day-boys as well as boarders. Fees were the same as the Oratory School: eighty guineas, some twenty guineas more than the highest rate at St Charles's. By 1879 Kensington had seventy-four boys, mainly sons of soldiers, doctors and lawyers, but after an unsuccessful launch of a joint-stock company to expand numbers to 400 it had accumulated debts of £28,000 and was forced to close. When the bishops had previously offered Capel the rectorship of the Catholic University College it had been on condition that he gave up the school, but he had refused, arguing that the school was essential to guarantee to the college a supply of aristocratic as well as middle-class students.[67] The interesting development that can be noticed in the promotional literature of Kensington and St Charles's is that both claimed to be public schools. This may indicate that, at least in London, Catholic attitudes to them were changing, or – more likely – that it had become fashionable to borrow public school terminology in order to benefit from its associated kudos.

In 1872 St John retired as headmaster of the Oratory School and was replaced by the twenty-nine-year-old John Norris. Entry numbers fell sharply in the first two years of his thirty-nine-year reign, but they soon recovered. Being the only cradle Catholic among the Oratorians and the only one without an Oxbridge background, he must have seemed a surprising choice, yet he soon proved to be a natural schoolmaster and a good disciplinarian. But the loss of Mrs Wootten in January

---

indicates only one transfer (from Edgbaston to Bayswater). These facts strongly suggest that the two establishments catered for different publics. St Charles's College existed until 1905 when it became a training college for women teachers.

[67.] It seems likely that Kensington would have provided the Oratory School with stronger competition than St Charles's, but in the absence of any records (Newman makes no reference to it in his correspondence), it can only be surmised that the overlap between their clienteles was minimal.

1876 triggered another drop, and the lean years – with numbers remaining at about fifty – continued, this time until 1885. This failure to recover the second time can be attributed to the opening in August 1877 of what became the Oratory School's greatest rival, William Petre's school at Woburn Park.

The monopoly of Catholic boarding education by the religious orders and the hierarchy was only seriously challenged twice in the nineteenth century: by the foundations of Newman and Monsignor Petre. The eldest son of the twelfth baron Petre was born into one of the most distinguished old Catholic families, and had been educated at Stonyhurst, Downside, Oscott, and the Jesuit seminary St Beuno's. His foundation at Weybridge, in Surrey, followed three years on the staff at Downside, where he had attempted to reform the Catholic system from within. Personally he was not in favour of the public school system, and shrank from the idea of a Catholic Eton; his version of a Catholic liberal education entailed radical changes to the curriculum and regime of the public school model. It is doubtful whether Woburn would have survived him, as it smacked of personal eccentricity and novelty and relied for its success on Petre's remarkable rapport with teenagers and social standing. Its 'boy parliament', invested with real power to legislate for the school community, proved to be a constant source of trouble with parents, who feared mutiny; the masters – mainly non-Catholics – quickly became frustrated with a teaching role shorn of pastoral and disciplinary content.

The differing conceptions of a liberal education of Newman and Petre cannot be accounted for solely by the time-lag between the foundations. Petre's stress on natural science and on educating the aesthetic faculties diverged from the narrower classics-dominated curriculum of the traditional public schools that the Oratory School matched more closely. In contrast to the highly-structured standard school day – nine or ten hours of lessons and prep, punctuated with recreation time – Petre proposed 'a reasonable ease', time for private reading, reflection and the evolution of the literary faculties.[68] He felt that classical studies concentrated too much on language, to the detriment of appreciation of litera-

---

[68]. W.J. Petre, *Remarks on the Present Condition of Catholic Liberal Education* (London: Burns & Oates, 1877), p. 11.

ture, and while mathematics was the ideal subject for developing mental discipline, he considered the most suitable area of knowledge to be natural science, especially biology and physiology. He despised the culture of competitive exams, asserting that 'a reflective habit of mind should be the grand prize of a liberal education';[69] besides objecting to the London University exam system, because it encouraged cramming and a limited mental growth, Petre criticised the resulting mutual competition between the colleges, as each sought fame from the published exam results. He also criticised the harmful effects of the Jesuit surveillance system on the development of character. More generally he thought Catholic schools were too like boy-barracks rather than homes; instead, school authorities ought to yield 'to the just and loud demands of parents that their boys must be thoughtfully, gently, individually, intelligently cared for, must have what of comfort their social position may afford and their prospects warrant'.[70] Petre held up to Catholics two examples of good practice from the Clarendon Report, the Eton dame system and the Harrow system of house-tutorship: both systems of subdivision provided 'advantages of personal and individual influence, combined with minute and intelligent but elastic surveillance, and domesticity of life'.[71] His own educational ideal of twenty to thirty boys living under one housemaster was in operation at Woburn, and he also imitated aspects of the dame system as he employed a matron to look after the younger boys.

Despite some very obvious differences there was much in common between the foundations of Newman and Petre. As lay schools, both foundations aimed to prepare boys for life in the world, with an emphasis on integration in, rather than exclusion from, Protestant society; this was a task that required paying the salaries necessary to attract good lay schoolmasters.[72] Both Newman and Petre chose a curriculum based on a liberal rather than commercial education, and catered for parents who sought

---

69. W.J. Petre, *The Problem of Catholic Liberal Education* (London: Burns & Oates, 1877), p. 20.

70. *Remarks*, p. 19.

71. W.J. Petre, 'Large or small schools', *Dublin Review* 31, July 1878, p. 105.

72. Petre openly blamed ecclesiastics for choosing to invest in sumptuous buildings instead of paying the market rate for 'professors and tutors of first-rate and matured ability'.

for their sons a preparation for a professional career. Both schools recognised the drawbacks of admitting foreign boys and mixing classes: Newman's solution was to apply caution and to decide *ad casum*, while Petre's policy was to allow no exceptions. Petre's wish to minimise surveillance by stressing trust and personal influence was exactly what Newman had aimed at, and it was chiefly this shared characteristic which set the two schools apart from others. Both offered a generous liberty and incorporated the prefect system, though Petre went further with his enlightened but risky innovations of a flexible school timetable and self-governance by the boys. Petre believed that English boys had 'a manly self-respect', and he favoured the individual independence that would allow them to develop habits of natural virtue: 'Edgbaston was founded, I believe, with the express purpose of instituting [such] a reform', Petre wrote in his only reference to the Oratory School.[73]

Approached by a long tree-lined drive, Woburn School was situated in attractive parkland where, from a hill crowned with a Grecian chapel and a picturesque 'Gothick' ruin, there was a fine view of the Thames valley. The school advertised itself as teaching all subjects required for competitive examination, and had a dedicated Modern side. Though Petre hoped to attract 'parents who lead a life of greater occupation than the aristocracy',[74] social polish was required too; an elaborate dress code stipulated that boys leaving the grounds were required to carry top-hat, umbrella and gloves. Within a few years Petre managed to attract many old Catholic and convert families, despite being easily the most expensive Catholic school, with fees of £90 for those under twelve and £120 for those above. Woburn had to face similar difficulties to the Oratory School, and outside its circle there was 'persistent and deep-rooted opposition to the new educational venture from the established interests, and especially from the Jesuits'.[75] Yet Petre was not as isolated as

---

[73.] W.J. Petre, *Catholic Systems of School Discipline* (London: Burns & Oates, 1878), p. 43n.

[74.] W.J. Petre, *The Position and Prospects of Catholic Liberal Education* (London: Burns and Oates, 1878), p. 18.

[75.] V.A. McClelland, 'The liberal training of England's Catholic youth: William Joseph Petre (1847–93) and educational reform', *Victorian Studies* 15, 1972, p. 275.

Newman had been: somehow, despite the fact that eighteen Woburn boys went on to Oxford, he managed to persuade Manning to visit Woburn and give it his support and blessing.

By 1881 Oratory School numbers had fallen to forty-seven and financial disaster loomed. But Woburn, despite its high fees and despite having almost a hundred pupils, was losing money even faster; in 1884 Lord Petre refused to allow his son to squander any more of the family fortune on the venture and it closed. Later that same year, ironically, the father died and the son succeeded to the barony and the family estates, but by then Woburn Park had been sold off, and the attempt to re-establish the school the following year at Northwood Park on the Isle of Wight was abortive. The main beneficiary of Woburn's closure was the Oratory School, because, when the pupils dispersed, it took the lion's share. A measure of its revived fortunes in the years following can be gained from a comment of the Jesuit representing Stonyhurst at the first Catholic Headmasters' Conference in 1896: he reported that, 'even now it is certain that the Oratory School, Birmingham, has the reputation of providing better teachers than we in our Colleges, and hence the pick of the best classes of boys in this country'.[76]

'The most dangerous man in England'

In the opinion of one Newman expert, nothing demonstrated so effectively the gulf between bishops and laity, and between converts and their fellow-Catholics, as the clash over education.[77] The repercussions for the Oratory School were considerable, as the net effect was to polarise views in Catholic circles and to perpetuate the school's reputation as one for converts and 'radical' cradle Catholics. After the Darnell crisis, Newman began to steer it away from Liberal Catholic influence, but not without incurring further damage. The school was a key issue over which the paths of Acton and Newman

---

[76.] Colley to Provincial, 7 January 1896, *Letters & Notices* 122, January 1896, p. 296.
[77.] Newman, *On Consulting the Faithful in Matters of Doctrine*, ed. J. Coulson (London: G. Chapman, 1961), p. 15.

diverged, for Acton blamed Newman's unwillingness to back the Liberal Catholic journals on his desire to protect the school. The same could be said of Manning and Newman: the general issue over which Newman found his way parted with Manning's was education, the trigger being the omission of the Oratory School in Manning's *Dublin Review* article.

The buffeting suffered by the Oratory School in the 1860s was due to its precarious location amidst the turbulent cross-currents within the Catholic body; and particularly to its position in relation to the struggle for influence in education. When Manning was appointed to the see of Westminster in 1865, Newman sensed a new danger for the school: uncertainty that a large-scale reorganisation of Catholic education might be in the offing in which the school or Newman would be required to take part. He suspected that Manning was 'afraid of any influence I might exert on the rising generation of Catholics, and that he would break up or transform our school, if he could'.[78] His decision to do all in his power to save the school in the spring of 1867 was among other things an expression of his determination not to lose his foothold in education. It also served another purpose: the need to stand up to the 'formidable conspiracy, which is in action against the theological liberty of Catholics'.[79] If they were strong enough to silence Newman, no one else would be able to resist them, and 'a reign of terror has begun, a reign of denunciation, secret tribunals, and moral assassination.' The 'reign of terror' Newman referred to was the style of ecclesiastical governance which brooked no interference and swept aside all initiatives at variance with its own, and where 'one or two persons, such as Manning, seem to do everything'.[80] Acton, too, was alive to the threat; and he had foreseen that 'Newman's school, the future University (whether our own or at Oxford) and the whole interest of thought and science, are mixed up in our cause.'[81]

[78.] Newman to Monsell, 18 June 1865, *L&D* XXI, p. 499. As Newman explains in the same letter, this was one reason he held back from investing in the school.
[79.] Newman to Wallis, 23 April 1867, *L&D* XXIII, p. 187.
[80.] Newman to Monsell, 12 January 1865, *L&D* XXI, p. 383.
[81.] Acton to Simpson, 27 August 1862, *Correspondence of Acton and Simpson* III, p. 12.

The soundings taken by the bishops in 1864 (about Catholics going to university) had been clumsy; the questionnaire had been heavily biased and the fear or mistrust of an educated laity had been evident in such questions as: 'Ought the principle to be admitted that the laity should be more highly educated than their clergy [...]?'[82] Despite his reputation as an expert on university education, Newman had not been invited to express his views; the converts who had been asked to express their opinion were hand-picked and most of them urged Propaganda Fide to rule against Oxford and Cambridge. Newman's diagnosis was that the opposition came 'from unknown persons who mislead Propaganda, put the screw on the Bishops and would shut up our school if they could'.[83] Events leading up to the second warning, in 1867, also appeared heavy-handed. Simeon believed that 'Advantage had been taken of the ignorance of the Roman Congregation, and its prejudices have been worked upon by those who ought to have had a higher value for the education of which they are seeking to deprive us'; and he added that the English laity had been 'treacherously and basely dealt with'.[84] In Newman's opinion, it was the defects of English Catholic *secular* education that were not understood in Rome. He interpreted the opposition to his going to Oxford as that 'same dreadful jealousy of the laity, which has ruined things in Dublin. [...] Propaganda and our leading Bishops fear the natural influence of the laity: which would be the greatest, or (humanly speaking) is rather their only, defence against the world.'[85]

During discussion of Ffoulkes's Oxford hall scheme, Newman had advised friends 'that effective action must originate with the laity, parents with educational solicitudes, and so on'.[86] Then, after the bishops' meeting in 1864, he had encouraged friends to take up the Oxford question as 'It is the Laity's concern, not ours'.[87] 'Every thing must proceed from the laity',

82. *L&D* XXI, p. 510.
83. Newman to Gaisford, 16 December 1864, *L&D* XXI, p. 343.
84. Simeon to Newman, 3 December 1867, *L&D* XXIII, p. 380n.
85. Newman to Allies, 30 November 1864, *L&D* XXI, p. 327.
86. Arnold to Acton, 15 November 1863, *Letters of Arnold*, p. 137.
87. Newman to Gaisford, 16 December 1864, *L&D* XXI, p. 343.

he advised Monsell; 'it is spoilt if priests interfere.'[88] He hoped that the laity would put their case before the bishops without the need for an ecclesiastical go-between, and suggested to Monsell that a prominent layman could express it in an open letter to a Catholic nobleman. In the event, the Stafford Club's address – ostensibly directed to Newman himself – was aimed at the authorities in Rome. Talbot's reaction to it conveys the violence of the feelings it aroused in some quarters, for he denounced it as a manifestation of the absence of Catholic instincts in the English laity, of their insubordination and disloyalty to the Holy See, and of a dangerous spirit to be put down; and he warned Manning, 'if a check be not placed on the laity in England they will be rulers of the Catholic Church in England instead of the Holy See and the Episcopate'. Talbot considered the address a consequence of Newman 'having quietly encouraged young men going to the University, by means of his school'; yet the truly insidious feature of the episode was for him not the question of whether Newman should go to Oxford or not, but the attitude of the English laity.

They are beginning now to show the cloven hoof, which I have seen the existence of for a long time. They are only putting into practice the doctrine taught by Dr Newman in his article in the *Rambler*. They wish to govern the Church in England by public opinion [...] Dr Newman is the most dangerous man in England, and you will see that he will make use of the laity against your Grace. You must not be afraid of him. It will require much prudence, but you must be firm, as the Holy Father still places his confidence in you; but if you yield and do not fight the battle of the Holy See against the detestable spirit growing up in England, he will begin to regret Cardinal Wiseman, who knew how to keep the laity in order.[89]

The likes of Talbot did not have a monopoly on exaggerated

88. Newman to Monsell, 12 January 1865, *L&D* XXI, p. 384.
89. Talbot to Manning, 25 April 1867, E.S. Purcell, *Life of Cardinal Manning* II (London: Macmillan, 1896), pp. 317–18.

views. In an article in *The Rambler* entitled 'The Catholic Church in England in 1859' Simpson declared that, as a result of the bishops' policy, 'Religion is turned into administration, the clergy into theological police, and the body of thinking laymen into a mass of *suspects*, supposed to be brooding on nothing but revolution, and only kept together by motives of fear, and by external pressure of a clerical organisation'. He quoted from a leading old Catholic, Charles Weld, who complained to Simpson that

> there is no limit now to the clerical ambition in England to ignore the laity altogether with their services and their sufferings, and to reduce their flocks to a condition utterly exposed to absolute authority without any of the safeguards for individual liberty which elsewhere have been carefully protected. [...] The Bishops want to sit among us as Schoolmasters to dictate our political and social as well as ecclesiastical rules.[90]

The unfortunate outcome of the polarised and highly-charged atmosphere was that it became increasingly difficult to form a consensus on issues – such as education – which involved partnership between Church leaders and the laity: instead churchmen blocked lay participation, while laymen retaliated with exaggerated expressions of independence from the hierarchy and trespassed in church matters.

The public airings of the state of Catholic education in the periods 1848–50, 1859–61 and 1871–72 seemed to have led to little change, as the same deficiencies were dwelt upon yet again by Petre in 1877–78. The isolation of Newman and his school from mainstream educational practice might explain this, as would 'the terrible *vis inertiae* of comfortable, self-satisfied, mediocre, unambitious traditions' alluded to by both Purbrick and Petre. An additional factor was the influence on Catholic public opinion of W.G. Ward, who through the *Dublin Review* strongly opposed all those who recommended adopting public school practice. For Ward, 'the evils of a public school are inseparable from its very essence', while its goods were

---

[90.] *Downside Review* 84, April 1966, p. 185.

merely accidental, and depended entirely on the staff; and he buttressed his arguments with evidence from a wide range of sources: memories of his own school-days at Winchester; the writings of Allies, Arnold, Ferrar, Hughes, Newman, Oxenham and Simpson; and the Clarendon Report. He argued that celibate superiors were best able to secure paternal supervision, that shared education was a blessing for lay boys, and that Catholic schools should be small and few so as to promote individual attention; and he ridiculed the argument (as he saw it) that premature initiation in vice at school was a suitable preparation for the struggles of life. The conclusion he reached was that Catholic colleges and Protestant public schools stand out 'in most pointed mutual contrast' – 'A "Catholic Eton" is (to our mind) a contradiction in terms.'[91] It was a line he held consistently for fifteen years, and the climate of opinion it helped to sustain played its part in restricting the growth of the Oratory School.

Two decades later, Catholic opinions about Protestant education had mellowed, largely on account of the moral and disciplinary improvements at the public schools. It was in this climate that the policy on attendance at Oxford and Cambridge was reversed. These factors paved the way for the eventual adoption of the public school model by the colleges run by religious orders. Though Newman had realised he was unlikely to witness this development in his lifetime, he seems never to have faltered in his conviction that the step would eventually be taken.

[91.] W.G. Ward, 'Catholic colleges and Protestant schools', *Dublin Review* 31, October 1878, p. 315.

Chapter 7

Framing the Picture

The previous chapters have been devoted to examining the origins and early life of the Oratory School. Four looked at the foundation story at close quarters; the last one placed the school within the broader context of English Catholic education. This final chapter is an attempt to indicate a few framing elements to the story, making use of the perspective lent by the passage of time. To frame the picture, then, and to set it off, it is helpful to view it against four background themes: the separation of two educational traditions; the reform of the system of Catholic education; the fresh approaches inspired by the intellectual converts; and Newman's contribution to education.

Two traditions

Although the public school tradition (as usually understood) went back little beyond the reign of Victoria, the distinguished educationalist Michael Sadler argued that its main inspiration was Winchester, with additional input from three other 'ancient channels': Eton, Westminster and the Roman Catholic tradition in England.[1] Taking this line of reasoning further, Edward Pereira, the Oratory School's fourth headmaster, interpreted the fourth 'ancient channel', the Roman Catholic tradition, as the inheritance of medieval traditions and customs

[1.] M. Sadler, Speech day, *The Sedberghian* 42, July 1921, pp. 141–42.

preserved in the Catholic colleges – specifically, those which emphasised moral responsibility as well as intellectual achievement. Thus according to Pereira, whichever way it was traced back – via the ancient public schools or through the English Catholic colleges founded abroad – the blueprint of the Oratory School derived ultimately from a Catholic tradition.[2] In founding the Catholic University in Dublin, Newman had created a 'fusion of the university structures of Louvain and the collegiate components of Oxford, of the continental and English systems' (though there is no doubt that Newman preferred Oxford);[3] in similar fashion, he began the Oratory School by building on best public school practice. Effectively, in both his university and school foundations Newman sought to combine two traditions, and to do so by re-forming what had been preserved in the national tradition.

In founding a school for boys 'not destined to the ecclesiastical state',[4] the promoters broke away from the system of shared education: indeed, a measure of the scheme's novelty was the conviction among many old Catholics that it was doomed to failure because it was based on the merging of what they were convinced were two incompatible traditions – the continental college and the English public school. Chichester thought the difference between them was fundamental: the former was based on a 'belief in the greater importance of the life to come', while the latter rested on 'the idea of turning out men of the world for the world'.[5] For Newman the two were eminently compatible, though clearly not at the same level: 'The end of [...] a Catholic University or of any university is "liberal education"; though its ultimate end may be Catholicism'[6] – or in the words of a modern critic, 'the end of education is learning how to think, and [...] the ultimate end of education is to think like the saints'.[7] And just as Newman had argued for the harmony of

---

[2.] F.J. Grimshaw, 'The Oratory School', *The Tablet*, 2 May 1959, p. 428.
[3.] Ker, 'Newman the teacher', *Newman and Education*, ed. M. Davies (Rugeley: Spode House, 1980), p. 38.
[4.] Newman, draft manifesto, n.d., BOA.
[5.] Chichester, *Schools*, p. 12.
[6.] 'Circular and correspondence', July 1852, quoted in G. Rutler, 'Newman's idea of a Catholic university', *Newman Today*, ed. S.L. Jaki (San Francisco: Ignatius Press, 1989), p. 97.
[7.] Rutler, 'Newman's idea of a Catholic university', p. 106.

lecture theatre and college or hall of residence, and against secular studies by day and religion by night, so he envisaged school activity inside and outside the classroom as functioning in harmony. Indeed, the balance between the two was crucial: just as overemphasis on the religious dimension at the Catholic University in Dublin threatened to make it too like a seminary, so stress on the public school dimension had tended to make the Oratory School, under Darnell, too secular. That Newman recognised the ultimate supremacy of holiness over intellectual attainment is evident from his words of consolation to the mother of Francis Ward, who died just three years after leaving the Oratory School: 'what was your mission [. . .] except to bring him to heaven? That was your very work, – not to gain him a long life and a happy one, but to educate him for his God.'[8]

In recent debates about Catholic educational policy, Newman would certainly have sided with the holistic notion of a school against dualist tendencies which endorse the separation of the secular and religious: for Newman, the separation of intellectual and moral influence was *the* evil of the age. The 'dual function' school, seen as a solution to the dilemma of a Catholic education in the face of the demands of a liberal society, would have been unthinkable to Newman or to his convert friends.[9] But Newman was no less aware of the opposing but equally dangerous tendency, present in Newman's time as now, to stress the 'Catholic' dimension at the expense of true education. Mervyn Davies has argued that Newman, in Christianising education, respected its inner autonomy; he understood the connaturality of education and religion by recognising that 'Knowledge is one thing, virtue is another'.[10]

8. Newman to Mrs F.R. Ward, 22 September 1866, *L&D* XXII, p. 292.
9. Those who maintain that there is a fundamental dualism in Catholic education, contend that secular and religious education can be distinguished and separated, practically as well as conceptually. James Arthur argues that this separation has paved the way for various aberrations and runs counter to Church teaching, which proposes a harmonious synthesis between religious faith and culture (J. Arthur, *The Ebbing Tide: Policy and Principles of Catholic Education* (Leominster: Gracewing, 1995), pp. 81–82, 227–28, 231–35).
10. M. Davies, 'Newman and education: some questions for today', *Newman and Education*, pp. 6–8 (which quotes from the *Idea of a University*, p. 120).

His harmonious synthesis of the secular and religious in education – 'to fit men for this world while it trained them for another'[11] – would therefore appear to undo Chichester's false dichotomy.

Yet for Chichester, matters did not rest solely with an incompatibility of aims; he also claimed an *educational* superiority for the collegiate tradition over the public school tradition. Like W.G. Ward (and like the advocates of the private school system), he strongly favoured a regime with close supervision and strict discipline. The separate argument about the merits of a narrow curriculum over a broad one – depth versus breadth – was deemed less important than the disciplinary one; besides, the argument was inconclusive, and indeed remains disputed a century and a half later. For the likes of Chichester and Ward, the early troubles at the Oratory School and the sudden extinction of Woburn seemed to confirm their view that a Catholic public school was an impossibility. For us, the Darnell affair demonstrates something very different: that the establishment of a Catholic public school was no simple task.

On account of the special circumstances surrounding the foundation of the Oratory School, it is easy to categorise the school incorrectly. In the same way as Newman's model university was an idealised Oxford imbued with a Catholic spirit, so his notion of a model school for sons of the upper and professional classes was an idealised public school, purified of its failings and raised up by the same Catholic spirit.[12] Yet Newman felt at liberty to adopt or reject any particular public school practice, and his decisions sometimes disconcerted his friends and associates, men like Acton and Darnell who had their own preconceived ideas of what a Catholic public school should be.

[11.] *Historical Sketches* III, p. 152.

[12.] In similar fashion Woodard accepted the public school as his model in which to combine high educational and religious standards – though the leading school historian T.W. Bamford has argued that the idea of a 'Tractarian Eton' was illusory because the Tractarians opposed the Church–State principle of Arnold (T.W. Bamford, *The Rise of the Public Schools: a Study of Boys' Public Boarding Schools in England and Wales from 1837 to the Present Day* (London: Nelson, 1967), pp. 43–46).

The 1860s and the 1870s were decades of reform for public schools, even though change was strongly resisted by the oldest foundations. Being a new foundation, the Oratory School was unencumbered with tradition and, on account of its close parental involvement, well placed to address the demands of the day. The school was actually ahead of the reforms, in part because its very existence was the result of a call from parents, but also because it benefited from Newman's vision. (Although Petre also felt able to carry out reforms at Woburn unimpeded by the brake of Catholic collegiate traditions, he did not benefit from parental input in the same way.) The major public schools and the Catholic colleges gravitated towards the new enlightened ideal – an educational *via media* – from opposite directions; the tightening up of discipline at the public schools in the 1860s and 1870s, and the gradual loosening up at the Catholic colleges over a much longer period, illustrate one aspect of this process. But in other areas the process was not symmetrical. Thus, as regards attitudes to modesty and privacy, the numerous changes to dormitory arrangements at the public schools were not paralleled at the Catholic colleges, where reforms of this nature were not needed.

Given the reputation of public school life, it is understandable that the majority of old Catholics viewed Newman's experiment with a mixture of caution and concern. Their perplexity was undoubtedly heightened by the division of opinion among the converts themselves: some gleefully regaled native Catholics with horror stories illustrating the worst deficiencies of a public school education, while others (like Scott-Murray and Lord Thynne) romanticised their schooldays at Eton or elsewhere. These conflicting impressions may explain why, three decades after the Oratory School opened, Petre could still observe the complete disagreement among Catholics over how to combine 'the advantages of full mental culture with the humility and steadiness of a religious spirit'.[13] Evidently, despite the Oratory School's example, the problem of combining the two had not been resolved to general satisfaction.

Besides being subjected to retrospective distortion in both

13. Petre, *Remarks*, p. 4.

directions, another risk of taking school memories at face value
was that they quickly ceased to reflect the contemporary
reality. The public school stories circulated by the likes of
Chichester and Ward ensured that Catholic misgivings were
kept alive, and undoubtedly delayed the adoption of the public
school model by Catholic educators; but by the late 1870s these
stories had only the most tenuous link with contemporary
reality. The eventual acceptance of the model in the 1900s
came about largely as a result of the growing alignment of the
two systems, due in no small part to the improved image (and
reality) of the public schools.[14]

One interesting difference between the Anglican and Catholic
boarding-school systems is illustrated by the fluctuating fortunes
of the Oratory School: without an obvious 'Catholic Eton', there
was no recognised pecking order in the Catholic system, hence
the ease with which schools like the Oratory School, Beaumont
and Woburn could quickly become popular with the higher
reaches of society – and lose favour equally quickly. In the period
1840–1930 as many as seven different establishments were
regarded as the 'Catholic Eton': Stonyhurst, Oscott, the Oratory
School, Beaumont, Woburn, Downside and Ampleforth. If, on
the other hand, the Oratory School is considered as part of the
public school system, then it is clear that it broke one of the
conventional patterns: the Darnell crisis was an exception to the
rule that crises occurring in nineteenth-century boarding foundations invariably resulted in a closer identification with the
public school model. Exceptionally, the Oratory School moved
away from it in the direction of the Catholic collegiate model –
illustrating once again the precarious position it occupied
between the two educational systems.

'A hornet's nest'

When Newman undertook the task of overseeing the foundation of the Oratory School in 1858, he was heavily constrained

[14.] Other factors were also important: the recognition of parental
demands by the Catholic colleges; the opening of Oxford and
Cambridge to Catholics; and the gradual integration of Catholics
into society.

by circumstances. Four years later, as a safeguard against the secularising tendencies that had led to the Darnell crisis, he was forced to adopt measures that brought the school closer in several respects to the colleges; the time was not ripe for an 'independent school' (though it is tantalising to speculate what this would have entailed). The school's shift towards the college system was greater than it need have been, due largely to the influence of Bellasis and especially of Hope-Scott; it was the latter who pressed for the introduction of certain collegiate characteristics such as direct control by the Oratory as a body and supervision of the boys outside lessons by Oratorians.

Beneath the immediate issue there lay a fundamental question, which was perhaps never answered or even explicitly posed: what should be the Oratory's attitude to educating the children of the wealthy? Newman distinguished the school from other Oratorian works, insisting that it must be self-sufficient, and must be supported by those whom it was primarily intended to serve. He allowed himself and the other Oratorians to lend money to the school, but insisted on interest payments being met – despite the handicap this meant for the school. The Oratorians who worked part-time for the school received part of their board in return for their contribution; those who were involved full-time received a proper salary. To Newman's mind, justice demanded as much. Hope-Scott saw the matter otherwise: he viewed the education of sons of the upper and professional classes as a charitable enterprise, which implied that the Oratorians should forfeit their remuneration. A school run along these lines effectively subsidised the education of the well-to-do, a pattern that was replicated in all the colleges run by religious for this social group in the nineteenth century.[15] In the secular colleges, the *quid pro quo* was that fees from lay boys supported church boys, though once they were

[15.] The Taunton Report reveals that the nine masters and four ushers at Stonyhurst were effectively unpaid, receiving only their maintenance; their notional salary of £40 per annum went to support the theology students who would eventually replace them. This enabled Stonyhurst to maintain low fees: 40 guineas for boys under twelve; 50 guineas for those above; and 60 guineas for boys in Rhetoric, the highest class.

able to do without this support they could, and did, revert to becoming pure seminaries (as Oscott did in 1889). The Oratory School was handicapped, therefore, by the fact that it was competing in a market that was not only saturated but also heavily subsidised. Well into the second half of the twentieth century, English Catholic public schools were the almost exclusive preserve of religious orders, and it is probable that the degree of subsidy they gave provided a major deterrence to the foundation of lay-run establishments. Despite all this, and although the financial pressures at Edgbaston were considerable, Newman withstood Hope-Scott's arguments to cease paying the Oratorians; and he ensured that the Oratory continued to hold back from providing financial subsidies, that it maintained a high fee level, and that it employed lay masters, paying them as best it could.

Newman's original proposal for the school stipulated the involvement of just two Oratorians; and he envisaged that it should move into the country and into lay hands within twenty years. Several promoters had originally rejected the siting of the school next to the Oratory for the very reason that it seemed to reduce it to a Catholic college; and certainly the location of the school amidst a rapidly spreading industrial conurbation severely frustrated its public school ambitions. Insufficient resources and prolonged uncertainties after the Darnell crisis meant that it was unable to construct really imposing buildings or to acquire adequate neighbouring land to substitute for a rural setting; in fact, difficulties over renting playing fields that were both inexpensive and close by dogged the school authorities until the school moved to Caversham in 1922. This disability gave schools like Beaumont and Woburn a significant advantage, but the problem was insoluble so long as the Oratorian connection remained. The problem of location was not confined to the Oratory School, of course: similar concerns over the perceived disadvantages of a city site challenged the authorities at the five major schools in London. Four of them relocated: Charterhouse in 1872, St Paul's in 1884, Christ's Hospital in 1902 and Merchant Taylors' in 1933. Westminster was the only one that stayed put.

Back in 1848 Capes had identified a major weakness of the Catholic colleges as 'the confusion of the ecclesiastic and the lay

student in one indiscriminate body'.[16] Thirty years later the
problem remained the same, as Petre pointed out:

> Our colleges have hitherto existed for the support,
> primarily, of various forms of ecclesiastical interest; and,
> situated as Catholics have been until recently, I am
> strongly of opinion that the anomalous state of things
> educational, is but the correlative of the anomaly of our
> hitherto social and civil condition.[17]

In Petre's view the Jesuits, the Benedictines and the secular
clergy were all unwilling to run establishments primarily
intended to serve the needs of laymen or to provide a liberal
education. What was needed, he contended, was another
school which was unhampered by the needs of a corporate
body and which was truly 'public' in serving public interests;
and just a single school would be sufficient for Catholics of the
class who could afford Harrow or Rugby. Since a compromise
between the colleges was unrealistic, on account of their incompatible aims and what he described as their 'pitted commercial
interests',[18] this reforming school needed to be on a secular or
independent basis. No doubt Petre would have modified his
views after the changes at Beaumont, Downside and
Ampleforth at the beginning of the twentieth century, as they
answered his criticisms by their whole-hearted commitment to
school education. The success these schools enjoyed is
undoubtedly because they addressed the system's main defect –
and did so by adopting the public school model.

Petre claimed there was a link between the policy of keeping
teaching out of the hands of laymen and the 'the *prevailing
mediocrity of Catholic teachers*' in the colleges.[19] The system of
student–teachers was unsatisfactory, because the clerical
students were simply too young; for Petre, teaching was work
for a man in his maturity, not for early manhood or failing
years. Where permitted in the secular colleges, lay schoolmas-

---

[16.] Capes, 'Catholic and Protestant collegiate education', *The Rambler*,
December 1848, p. 236.
[17.] Petre, *Position and Prospects*, p. 17.
[18.] Petre, *Remarks*, p. 25.
[19.] Petre, *Position and Prospects*, p. 22.

ters were at a distinct disadvantage to the clerics, as they were poorly paid and had little scope for responsibility. These factors contributed to the parlous state of the profession of schoolmaster among Catholics, a problem that affected even the Oratory School, where the need for lay schoolmasters was alleviated only by the steady flow of fresh converts.

As Petre included among the supposedly self-serving motives of the colleges (particularly those of the religious) the emphasis on assuring a supply of vocations, it is interesting to consider whether he would have applied this criticism to the Oratory School. The idea of a school as a feeder for the Oratory had been in Newman's mind in 1849:

> I think you will find no order or congregation but finds a school necessary to feed the order. The Benedictines profess this to be the only reason of their school at Downside, *by which they do not gain*. Stonyhurst has fed the Society. The Rosminians have begun a school. The Passionists, who have no school, have no novices. Looking to the future, it is a question whether we can keep up the Congregation without a school in some shape or other.[20]

This consideration is entirely absent from his correspondence in 1857–59, though it is noteworthy that by 1883 no fewer than seven of the twelve Birmingham Fathers had come to the Oratory via the school, having been either masters or boys there; three other ex-pupils joined in the years immediately following, and another three joined the London Oratory. However, these gains were achieved with fewer of the compromising characteristics mentioned by Petre; above all because of the school's abiding emphasis on preparation for the world, but also because of the understanding at the Oratory that only those interested in teaching would undertake it – as borne out by Newman's remark in 1862 that 'we should be dished and ruined' if St John's health failed.[21]

There is no doubt, however, that the Oratory itself was compromised to a significant extent by its commitment to the

[20.] Newman to Faber, 23 November 1849, *L&D* XIII, p. 305.
[21.] Newman to Miss Ryder, 22 July 1862, *L&D* XX, p. 239.

school. Faber had a point when he argued that turning school-master was more than just another pastoral work, and that undertaking a boarding school would divert from and modify St Philip Neri's simple idea of the Oratory, for the school and the Birmingham Oratory became so interdependent after the crisis that Newman had to admit: 'To put an end to the school would be almost to put an end to the Oratory'.[22] Nevertheless Newman's actions were clearly justifiable on the grounds that conditions in mid-nineteenth-century England called for some accommodation of the Oratorian Rule. Unlike the London Oratorians, Newman judged the condition of 'grave necessity', which would permit him to undertake the school, did in fact exist on account of the dire need of his fellow converts.

It is significant in this context that when two Oratorians decided to take over a Catholic grammar school in Birmingham in 1887, Newman registered his displeasure. He had it recorded in the minute book that the arrangement had been made without his full consent and knowledge; that he did not want it to be broadcast 'that the new School was established by us as a Congregation – it being the work of two zealous Fathers of the Congregation only'; and that he would allow no Congregation money to be spent on it.[23] And he invoked the Rule which restricted Oratorian activities lest it detract from the Oratory's primary work.[24]

It would be interesting to know what Newman made of Petre and Woburn, but very little can be gleaned from the *Letters and Diaries*. The single direct reference to Petre and his school – 'I don't fear Mr Petre – though for a time he may embarrass us'[25] – seems to indicate that Newman was satisfied with his own vision. The story has survived of how Petre once tried to gain Newman's support in his campaign against the educational

---

[22.] Newman to the Duke of Norfolk, 23 January 1882, *L&D* XXX, p. 54.

[23.] Birmingham Congregation minute book, 11 September 1887, *L&D* XXXI, p. 229n.

[24.] The inevitable occurred four years after Newman's death, when the Oratory undertook full financial responsibility for St Philip's Grammar School.

[25.] Newman to the Duke of Norfolk, 23 January 1882, *L&D* XXX, p. 54.

methods of the religious orders. He visited Edgbaston and spoke at great length on the subject while Newman listened in complete silence. When he had finished, Newman simply changed the subject and asked Petre whether he had come by the North-Western or Great Western line, and proceeded to compare their respective merits![26]A major difficulty at both the Edgbaston and Woburn foundations was that of merging two educational traditions using people who possessed an intimate knowledge of only one of the two strands; it was a problem that was almost intrinsic to the enterprise. The lack of familiarity of Darnell and his masters with religious instruction and training at Catholic establishments was mirrored by the absence of safe-guards at Woburn for preventing a possible slide into licence and anarchy. The chief founders of the Oratory School, however, were familiar with both traditions: Newman had stayed at Oscott and toured the Catholic colleges, while Bellasis and Hope-Scott had first-hand knowledge of Catholic educa-tion both in England and on the European mainland. By contrast, Petre had no experience of public school life, and he betrayed his ignorance in his idealised notion of its ways.

In one crucial respect – the financial basis – it was Petre's school, not Newman's, which conformed to the collegiate type: once its subsidy was cut, Woburn died, since it relied on Petre's largesse in much the same way as the colleges relied on their benefactors. Reference has already been made to the major benefactions at the colleges before the Oratory School was founded, but an indication of the scale of other, roughly contemporaneous benefactions helps put the developments at Edgbaston into context. At Ampleforth a gift of £12,000 from a Benedictine was used to rebuild the college completely in the period 1859–61. Beaumont was purchased using £16,500 from a Jesuit (who gave a further £42,000 to the Society later). Stonyhurst moved into grand new buildings in the 1880s with the help of £60,000 from the rector's own patrimony. By contrast, Newman considered that affluent parents should shoulder the financial burden of schooling; the Oratorian loans were merely a temporary – though necessary – concession on

[26.] W.F.P. Stockley, *Newman, Education and Ireland* (London: Sands, 1933), pp. 154–55.

account of adverse circumstances. Newman's correspondence shows he was keenly aware of the financial difficulties elsewhere: William Sewell failed at Radley with debts approaching £50,000, and fled the country to avoid debtors; Thomas Stevens amassed debts of £100,000 in setting up Bradfield, despite using all his patrimony, and went bankrupt. Newman continued to insist that the Oratory School be self-sufficient, and although it never fully paid its way, by 1883 the average annual loss from the beginning was only £100. McClelland's contention that the Oratory School merely contributed to a dilution of teaching capacity in the Catholic body, while continuing the process of lavishing huge sums on boys' schools,[27] is patently absurd for a foundation that arguably contributed more than any other to reforming Catholic boarding education, and at a fraction of the cost of setting up any of the other Catholic boarding establishments.

The vehemence of the opposition to the Oratory School was a reflection on Catholic attitudes to education. Pointing out that the education of the laity was not the exclusive province of church authorities, Petre called for a 'fair division of function and of interest'.[28] But the interests were not amenable to calls from eccentric outsiders; later on, chastened by his experiences, he declared: 'Catholic education is a hornet's nest'.[29]

Fifty years later, after wholesale changes in the methods of management and discipline at the colleges, Lord Howard described the new order as 'the result of the abandonment of the foreign system to which we had become accustomed in the schools of the Continent'.[30] He claimed that the change gave the schools a more English character and enabled the pupils to participate better in English life, and that it had reversed the trend of Catholics sending their sons to non-Catholic public schools. But not all historians of Catholic education have seen the adoption of the public school model as inevitable or even desirable. Some have lamented the colleges giving up their

[27.] McClelland, 'A Catholic Eton', pp. 14–15.
[28.] Petre, *Catholic Systems*, p. 6.
[29.] Quoted in McClelland, 'Liberal training', p. 265.
[30.] FitzAlan, Viscount [E. Howard], 'Catholics in public life', *Catholic Emancipation, 1829 to 1929: Essays by Various Authors* (London: Longmans, Green & Co., 1929), p. 152.

more balanced and practical curriculum; others have regretted the surrender of their traditional character to the more secular example of the Protestant public school, with 'its sad consequence in their modern barrenness as a religious force in England'.[31]

'A middle station'

The integration of the Catholic community into English society was greatly assisted by the activity of converts, but it was a slower process than it might have been because of their isolation. In her study of mid-century converts, Pauline Adams notes that the absence of an equivalent group among cradle Catholics to the body of university-educated, professional, middle-class converts meant that this group was thrown back on its own society and that it retained its distinctive convert identity longer than its upper-class counterpart.[32] The Oratory itself was an object of suspicion for old Catholics on account of its nearly undiluted convert composition, and the school was in a similar predicament; more than half the eighty-two boys admitted in the first four years were sons of converts, and over the next decade the proportion was at least a quarter. The convert association partly explains the school's prolonged isolation within Catholic circles and hence its limited effect on other establishments.

The three-way bid for influence in Catholic education witnessed the eventual consolidation of episcopal control at the expense of input from the laity and religious orders. Only in the provision of boarding education for the well-to-do was episcopal control challenged, and here the religious had the upper hand – a position which turned into a virtual monopoly once the ecclesiastical colleges became pure seminaries. The sole survivor of lay initiative was the Oratory School; and it is doubtful whether even this would have survived but for Newman's protective presence. In a broader context, the school represented a stark exception to

---

[31.] Sire, *Gentlemen Philosophers*, p. 165.

[32.] P.A. Adams, 'Converts to the Roman Catholic Church in England, circa 1830–1870', B.Litt., Oxford, 1977, pp. 5–6.

the steady attenuation of lay initiative in the second half of the nineteenth century. At the close of the century, a bishop would pronounce that there were five provinces 'in which a layman may be called upon to help in the good cause of religion': priest, board, club, press and purse. Education was not an area he was called to work in; it was a matter 'which, naturally, no layman can undertake to solve'.[33] It was a caricature of the role of the laity in the Church in two senses, for it belittled the scope of the laity and it implied that initiative was the clergy's prerogative. The school foundation had been the focus of a rare concentration of convert experience, talent and energy, which Newman attempted to harness, yet he met with stiff opposition. It is difficult to resist the argument of Adams that ecclesiastical leaders failed to turn the convert inheritance to proper advantage, partly because they were unused to handling an educated laity, and that they thereby squandered an unrepeatable opportunity.[34] However, this argument is weakened by the presence of notable converts among the ruling faction; indeed, Newman complained that 'the converts have behaved to *me* much worse than old Catholics'. [35]

Accusations made at the time (and since) that the Oratory School was devised to exclude episcopal oversight are wide of the mark. Rather than a suppression of due ecclesiastical authority, the foundation represented an assertion of the rights of parents to contribute to arrangements for the education of their offspring. The converts had not inherited the attitude prevalent among cradle Catholics of the period, of underplaying their role in the Church and relying on the hierarchy to resolve their difficulties. The Protestant schools, where the majority of the promoters had been educated, functioned independently of church structures – and indeed laboured under the contrary problem, of being vulnerable to confusion in religious teaching and practice, as a result of the far more tenuous episcopal oversight (as well as the absence of a Catholic magisterium). The jurisdiction of Anglican bishops for licensing masters at Church of England endowed schools was abolished in 1869; thereafter it was only in schools such as those of the

---

[33] J.C. Hedley, *The Public Spirit of the Catholic Laity* (London: CTS, 1899), pp. 7–8.

[34] Adams, 'Converts', p. 6.

[35] Newman's diary, 21 January 1863, *AW*, p. 257.

Woodard foundation that there were measures to safeguard religious orthodoxy – measures which led to a steady stream of ecclesiastical vocations from both masters and boys.

Possessing a remarkably balanced view of their role in the Church, converts such as Bellasis and Hope-Scott supplied something desperately lacking in the Catholic body. On the one hand, they did not adopt an attitude of helplessness or meek submission to Church authorities in the face of problems in which they had a right to engage and a claim to competence; in particular, they were conscious of their rights regarding the education of their children. On the other hand, they appreciated the scope of ecclesiastical jurisdiction in matters relating to Church doctrine, sacraments and government, and recognised the Church's competence and role in education. In short, they were blessed with an ability to distinguish more clearly than many cradle Catholics the respective spheres of action of the hierarchy and laity. Newman's appreciation of the respective roles of laity and pastors was very advanced for his time: his insight was encapsulated in his dynamic rule – 'Nothing great or living can be done except when men are self governed and independent: this is quite consistent with a full maintenance of ecclesiastical supremacy'.[36] This flew in the face of the apparent policy 'all over Europe [...] to keep the laity at arms-length', which Newman predicted would only result in antagonism 'between the hierarchy and the educated classes',[37] and the risk of a thwarted laity turning anticlerical or the educated classes slipping into religious indifference.

Several lay convert friends of Newman shared his balanced understanding of the need for 'a middle station at which clergy and laity can meet, so as to learn to understand and yield to each other – and from which, as from a common ground, they may act in union upon an age, which is running headlong into infidelity'.[38] Unhindered by a misplaced passivity in relations with the hierarchy, they were able to breathe fresh life into the Catholic body. The injection of a sizeable convert element into the Church created an opportunity for progress; once

[36.] Newman to Ornsby, 2 December 1864, *L&D* XXI, p. 331.
[37.] Newman to Fottrell, 10 December 1873, *L&D* XXVI, p. 394.
[38.] *Ibid.* Here Newman refers to the role the Catholic University can perform.

absorbed their freshness risked being lost in an atmosphere of continual emphasis on submission to Church authorities. As the school story shows, cooperation with Newman entailed working together on a collaborative enterprise. Several minor crises prior to May 1859 were provoked by Newman's declining to proceed until the parental body matched his commitment. These painful pauses had a salutary effect: Newman had to hold himself back from a tendency to push ahead in his eagerness to make himself useful to the Church, while the promoters were forced to make substantial commitments. It was a process of education by which Newman gradually led parents to an awareness of their responsibility; spelling out his demands to those closest to him, he effectively delegated to them the task of transmitting them to others.

When the Oratory School opened, parents were heavily involved: in financial commitments beyond the mere payment of fees; in promoting the school and finding pupils; and in resolving problems concerning the buildings, the curriculum and even the appointment of staff. Understandably the degree of commitment among the collaborators varied according to taste, talent and available time. While the involvement of the leading promoter Bellasis was uppermost, the single greatest commitment was a common one, that of generously entrusting their sons to a risk-laden venture, conscious that the real advantages would not accrue in the early years. However, the claim that the school was a joint foundation does require qualification so as to avoid overstatement. The professional, family and other commitments of parents on the one hand, and the complex nature and technical know-how in organising a school on the other, provide the parameters for such collaboration. The evidence indicates that Newman pitched his demands in such a way as to bring out the fullest cooperation that could be expected; he did not allow his friends to remain as spectators, because parental cooperation was a principle on which Newman would not yield. In this he provided a striking contrast to the prevailing climate at the colleges, which was characterised by an 'unworthy antagonism between heads of schools and parents'.[39]

[39.] Chichester, *Schools*, p. 109.

In harnessing parental enthusiasm for the school, not everything proceeded to plan. One of the promoters' handicaps was
a tendency to take religious fervour for granted and to under-
estimate the need of systems and structures for times when
there was less goodwill. Some of their letters betray a certain
naiveté about the measures required to guarantee the school's
Catholic character (a defect that was healed by experience). In
addition, more than once Newman encountered the reluctance
of the laity to provide financial support; if they did show interest and gave money for immediate objects (the poor, the
training of priests), they seemed to care little about higher
education, literature or the education of the laity. The lack of
lay commitment, manifested financially, frustrated the lofty
aspirations of the school founders – although in defence of the
laity it should be noted that the demands on their resources at
the time were immense.

In her analysis of letters from parents to a public school
headmaster in the period 1929–50, Christine Heward identifies
three broad areas of parental concern: educational matters,
social structure and the male role.[40] If desires for the emancipation of Catholics and preparation for a life of usefulness may
be identified with the latter two, then the parental letters used
in this study of the Oratory School conform closely to Heward's
pattern. Nevertheless there is a further theme, which subsumes
the others into a single whole: the Christian perspective which
views education in its wider religious dimension, as a means to
perfect social structures and to prepare the young for a life of
service in the world. The story of the foundation provides a
rich example of the extent of growing parental interest and
influence in a sphere of life that had traditionally been out of
bounds for them. The claim that the school was a prototype
parental foundation is undoubtedly true in the sphere of
Catholic education, but a more challenging consideration is
whether the claim transcends its denominational setting and is
credible in the national context – though its verification lies
beyond the possibilities of this work.

Mention should be made of the Liberal Catholics who moved

40. C. Heward, *Making a Man of Him: Parents and their Sons' Education at
an English Public School, 1929–50* (London: Routledge, 1988), pp.
ix–x.

in Acton's circle, for they were inclined to exaggerate the scope of their freedom, with lamentable consequences: interference in ecclesiastical affairs and a soft-peddling, or even denial, of the hierarchy's legitimate role. Their effect on the school, whether directly or through association with Newman, was considerable; they inspired attitudes of independence which dispensed with oversight – including Newman's – and thus contributed to the Darnell crisis. Damage to the school's name was the price Newman was forced to pay for dealing with this talented but reckless party, and it was further tarnished by the fate of prominent Liberal Catholics: J.M. Capes returned to the Church of England in 1870, though by 1882 he had become a Catholic again; Ffoulkes rejoined the Anglican Church for good; Döllinger refused to accept the definition of Papal Infallibility and was excommunicated in 1871; Acton, though never formally outside the pale of the Church, rejected its jurisdiction; Arnold returned to the Anglican Church, but underwent a second conversion in 1876. Besides Arnold, two other ex-masters left the Church: Henry Challis in 1873, five years after his brief spell at the school, and Edward Ransford, Darnell's first assistant.

Relatively little has been said about the effect on the school's fortunes of its association with Bellasis and Hope-Scott. Despite the absence of evidence, it is clear that they helped to assuage the fears of many parents of the dangers of a worldly or half-baked Catholicism at the school. According to a priest friend, Bellasis 'felt an instinctive repugnance to the lukewarmness and indifference of so-called Liberal Catholics', and warned his children not to act or talk like one;[41] and although he lobbied for access to Oxford and Cambridge, he loyally accepted the official discouragement in 1865, with the sacrifice it involved. The bishops, and particularly Manning, sought Hope-Scott's counsel as a leading Catholic layman, and his untiring efforts and generosity for Catholic causes made him universally respected. Both Bellasis and Hope-Scott were on excellent terms with Bishop Grant and other Church leaders, and moved easily in old Catholic circles; unlike Acton they were convinced that a reconciliation between Newman and those

[41.] Bellasis, *Memorials*, p. 204.

opposing him was possible. It is strange that they were apparently unable to do more to mediate for Newman and the school, but at least, thanks to the survival of their correspondence, recognition can be accorded them for their prominent role in the survival, as well as the establishment, of the Oratory School.

Newman: theology in action

With the gradual separation of Church and secular powers there has come about an increased understanding of the tasks proper to each. The respective roles of the laity and hierarchy were brought into sharper focus at the Second Vatican Council (1962–65),[42] but Newman is one of those credited with the formulation of a 'theology of the laity' *avant la lettre*, though not in any systematic fashion. Richard Stork has pointed out that in the process of its development the usual pattern can be observed: the pastoral phenomenon comes first, before the theological formulation.[43] While most Newman specialists have emphasised his contribution to the articulation of this theology, this study of the Oratory School indicates the extent to which it both inspired, and arose from, the activity in which he was immersed. One small, but crucial insight of Newman's is contained in the draft school manifesto, which supplies a positive definition of the laity: the school was 'for youths whose duties are to lie in the world'. Attempts to define the laity in the

---

[42.] The Dogmatic Constitution on the Church *Lumen Gentium* (nos 31, 37) affirmed that it belongs to the laity, by reason of their special vocation, to seek the kingdom of God by engaging in temporal affairs and directing them according to God's will. 'They live in the world, that is, they are engaged in each and every work and business of the earth and in the ordinary circumstances of social and family life which, as it were, constitute their very existence.' The Constitution exhorted Church pastors to recognise the contributions and charisms which each of the faithful brings to the common task, the salvific mission of the Church in the world, and in particular to recognise and promote the dignity and responsibility of the laity.

[43.] R.A.P. Stork, 'John Henry Newman and the laity', S.T.D., Lateran University Rome, 1966, pp. 12–13.

past had usually lapsed into negative definitions, and indeed an example of this occurs in the very same document: 'a school for the education of boys, not destined to the ecclesiastical state'.

Newman's elevation to the cardinalate effectively confirmed both his orthodoxy and the wisdom of his policy in meeting the trends of the time: embracing what was wholesome in progress and reforms, while challenging the secular principles espoused by reformers. In an ecclesial context, the highly charged atmosphere of rigid conservatism among religious leaders and fear of lay interference tended to reduce the laity to 'a state of permanent tutelage'.[44] Newman helped steer the laity along a mid-course between the excesses of the time and sought to form truly lay Catholic minds; in contrast to his bishop's 'horror of laymen', Newman hoped they could 'be made in this age the strength of the Church'.[45] Newman's mindset was evident when he urged his lay friends involved in the school to defend opinions and claim rights, to lobby and act: by encouraging and assisting the school initiative he fostered freedom of lay action within the bounds of ecclesiastical jurisdiction. This evidence tends to confirm Stork's claim that Newman's most fundamental contribution to the doctrine on the laity was 'his insistence on the need for the laity to assert their freedom and to realise their responsibility'.[46]

McClelland has described Newman's Christianity as existing in a water-tight compartment cut off from the world around him, and dismissed the notion that Newman's liberal education could lead to the 'training of good members of society' and 'fitness for the world'.[47] But the facts about the school speak for themselves. The promoters and school parents sought both a liberal education and a genuine preparation for life's challenges. Then as now, Newman is rightly acclaimed for his contribution to meeting the challenge of an authentic Christian presence in the world. His emphasis on down-to-earth training for duties in the world is vividly illustrated by his insistence on

---

44. Trevor, *Light in Winter*, p. 455.
45. Newman to J.M. Capes, 10 April 1851, *L&D* XIV, p. 252.
46. Stork, 'Newman and the laity', p. 297.
47. McClelland, *Cardinal Manning* (London: OUP, 1962), p. 22; *English Roman Catholics*, p. 108.

such a lay education, even for those pondering a vocation to the priesthood. Mrs Wootten understood the point, and she once told the Duchess of Norfolk that Newman 'by simple gentle easy ways will form his boys for useful manhood'.[48] It was precisely the promoters and Newman (and, later, Petre) who identified the absence of an appropriate preparation at the colleges, and who acted to remedy the deficiency. For all his intellectual qualities, Newman could be as streetwise as he was cerebral: 'Today a pupil, tomorrow a member of the great world: today confined to the Lives of the Saints, tomorrow thrown upon Babel'.[49]

The portrayal of Newman as someone strongly motivated by class-exclusiveness and bent on collaboration only with the upper classes in his various educational ventures is simply not supported by the evidence. While Newman did not seek to challenge the social structures of his age, it should not be forgotten that through the Oratory he oversaw a number of initiatives to alleviate pressing social needs in Birmingham. The accusation takes no account either of the Oratorian Brief or of Newman's great intellectual gifts; and it also overlooks the fact that the education of 'privileged' youth was no soft option. At Oxford Newman battled against secular and liberal tendencies; in Dublin he encountered clerical tendencies; at the school he contended against both. At the Catholic University he had to conciliate the gentry, who distrusted an enterprise with clerical sponsorship; at the Oratory School, which was lay-sponsored, he was exposed to clerical hostility. It seemed inevitable that Newman's educational work, precisely because he did not throw in his lot with the conventional and the powerful, should provoke antagonism and cause him anxiety and suffering.

Newman's autobiographical memoirs are useful in revealing his motives and setting his school activity on a larger canvas. In them he emphasises how he had 'seen great wants which had to be supplied among Catholics, especially as regards education', but from the authorities there was 'no consideration towards a person who was doing something towards that supply'.[50] 'From

48. Letter, n.d. [May 1861], Arundel Castle archive, C.581.
49. Newman, *Idea of a University*, p. 233.
50. 8 January 1860, *AW*, p. 251.

first to last, education, in this large sense of the word, has been my line', he recorded, but his efforts had given offence 'by insisting that there was room for improvement among Catholics'. They had annoyed Church authorities in Rome and

> especially at home, because I have set up a school, and so interfered with the vested rights [...] of this and that College or Seminary. Hence the keen sensitiveness of Dr Grant & the two Dr Browns, not to say the Cardinal, and the multitude of slanders which have been spread & are believed, about our boys and our treatment of them.[51]

Newman's range of reactions to pressures on the school – a willingness to give it up if necessary; a determination to preserve it for the common good; or a readiness to accommodate a sensible rearrangement of Catholic provision – reveals an underlying attitude of service to Catholic education and detachment from personal ambition. It was an attitude he shared with fellow converts in using whatever possibilities were at hand to further the cause of reforming Catholic culture and learning. Only once during the foundation – by assuming that the promoters would wish to assist the Catholic University – did Newman seriously misjudge the mood of his fellow converts; and this instance is all the more surprising, given his direct experience of the dearth of English interest in the university.

Newman's fellow-Oratorian Ignatius Ryder did not think he 'ever cared much for the child or the boy except in idea, but the young man he loved and yielded him all the honours of manhood ungrudgingly'.[52] Had Ryder been privy to Newman's termly reports, or attended the boys' 'characters', he might have altered his opinion. Newman's warm sympathy for boys was reflected in his choice of the school motto, *Salve cor sacram Philippi juventutis amans* ('Hail holy heart of Philip, lover of youth'). It stands in marked contrast to the attitude of even such a famous headmaster as Arnold of Rugby, who sought to get over the 'odious' state of boyhood as quickly as possible,

---

[51.] 21 January 1863, *AW*, p. 259.
[52.] W. Ward, *Cardinal Newman* II (London: Longmans, Green & Co., 1912), p. 356.

because he was unable to comprehend the boy-state and its accompanying naughtiness between childhood and manhood. The adoption of the dame-system by Newman was as much a matter of his own personal preference as it was a reflection of the widespread loss of favour of harsh regimes and desire to secure the comfort and care of little boys. Newman told a niece who kept a boarding house for her husband (a master at Bedford School) that 'we have here quite enough experience of trouble in our own school here, to know how much those ladies sacrifice who devote themselves to the welfare and comfort of thoughtless boys'.[53] Viewed in the wider context, he believed that 'It is one of the best points of this unhappy age, that it has made so many openings for the activity of women'.[54]

Is it possible to summarise Newman's overall contribution to school education? Although his impact was confined to the Catholic domain, he has been compared favourably with famous Victorian headmasters on account of three important contributions he made: in dispensing with authoritarianism 'without lowering spiritual, moral or intellectual standards'; in pressing lay teachers' claims for a greater share in the control and organisation of Catholic education; and in educating Catholics to take their place in a non-Catholic environment.[55] The school story confirms this verdict, but modifies it in two ways. In the first place it shows how Newman's work was severely constrained by circumstances, and therefore less radical and greatly reduced in impact; and secondly it illustrates how his insights and reforms were remarkably wide-ranging and ahead of his times. It must be remembered that Newman's mark on Oxford education was made, not only by reforming of systems, but by personal influence, according to his principle that 'The heart is commonly reached, not through the reason, but through the imagination, by means of direct impressions, by the testimony of facts and events, by history, by description. Persons influence us, voices melt us, looks subdue us, deeds inflame us'.[56] Likewise Newman's

---

[53.] Newman to Mrs Mozley, 27 February 1885, *L&D* XXXI, p. 36.
[54.] Newman to Mrs Mozley, 26 February 1884, *L&D* XXX, p. 316.
[55.] Jackson, 'Newman', pp. 231–32.
[56.] Newman, 'The Tamworth Reading Room', *Discussions and Arguments*, p. 293.

contribution to school education, though less telling than his contribution to education at university level, can be measured not so much in terms of new arrangements as by a variety of indirect means. Three insights into the human condition underpinned his foundation at Edgbaston: his conviction that the school's mission was best viewed as a joint undertaking with parents; his insistence that preparation for the world required an appropriate training; and his stress on the importance of trust between staff and boys.

Given Newman's prodigious gifts, it is natural to ask whether the Oratory School was a waste of his talents, and whether he expected to remain in charge of such a small school for so long. Certainly the burden came unexpectedly, but it was on account of loyalty to his friends that he felt that, once committed, 'we must in fairness to them work the experiment out'.[57] Not one to seek the limelight, Newman was content to oversee a pastoral mission he once described in the following words:

> Parents send their sons to school because they are in the way, because home instruction is expensive, in order that there may be method in their instruction, – that they may be submitted to discipline – that they may have the stimulus of emulation – and that they may be introduced into the society of their equals, both as a moral preparation for the world, and a formation of character, and also as a means of making acquaintances and friendships which may last through life.[58]

As to the task of creating a Catholic public school, it is fitting that the final word on Newman's ability to form one should lie with the Oratory School's most famous old boy, Hilaire Belloc:

> They [the boys] were taught to be as free – as self-reliant and as free – as any of the young Englishmen who were growing up around them in the great public schools; but with it all there was an atmosphere of healthy religion, an unconstrained frequency in the approaching of the

57. Newman to Flanagan, 25 February 1859, *L&D* XIX, p. 50.
58. Newman to Northcote, 23 February 1872, *L&D* XXVI, p. 26.

Sacraments, a sincere faith and a high code both of morals and of honour, which appeared so natural and so native to the place, that it would have been called spontaneous by anyone who did not know that the founding of the school, its influence, and its spirit were due to Cardinal Newman.[59]

[59.] 'John Henry Cardinal Newman', *The Lamp* 39, 1890, pp. 138–39.

Select Bibliography

Manuscript Sources

Ampleforth Abbey, Yorkshire
Grissell Papers (JX24–1)

Arundel Castle, West Sussex
Correspondence (C.556, C.557, C.581)
La Serre, H., 'Memoirs on the late Cardinal Newman and the Oratory School', n.d. (MD.2119)

Cambridge University library
Acton Papers

National University of Scotland, Edinburgh
Hope-Scott Papers

The Oratory of St Philip Neri, Birmingham
'Horarium for Oratory School boys' (A.14.9)
'One or two notes on Oratory School matters' (A.24.6)
'Papers about the Oratory School (chiefly financial)' (A.26.5)
'Papers about enlargement of the Oratory School, etc., 1860–63' (A.51.3)
'Oratory School, early reviews (mostly financial)' (B.1.3)
St John's diary, 1862 (B.2.5)
'Bellasis's album' (C.1.10)
Moody's diary, 1859–60 & 1862–66 (OS)
'Oratory School beginning, 1857–59' (OS)

Secretary's *Day Book*, 1861–78 (OS)
Oratory School financial summaries, 1860–74 (OS.3)
'1861-2, Darnell' (85.1–12)
School prospectuses and classification lists (Album 7)
Staff lists, prize lists, invitations to the school Latin play
    (Bellasis XIV)
Congregation Register of Decrees
Minute book of General and Deputy Congregations

The Oratory School, Woodcote
Mark book, 1873–88
School accounts ledger (1859–60, 1878–93)
School photograph albums
The Weekly Wasp (schoolboy magazine), 1868

Printed Sources

Acton, J., *Selections from the Correspondence of the First Lord Acton*,
    ed. J.N. Figgis and R.V. Laurence, London: Longmans, 1917
——, *The Correspondence of Lord Acton and Richard Simpson*, 3
    vols., ed. J.L. Altholz and D. McElrath, Cambridge: CUP,
    1971–75
The Amoeba (school magazine of Woburn Park) [Downside
    Abbey]
Arnold, T., *Passages in a Wandering Life*, London: Edward
    Arnold, 1900
——, *Letters of Thomas Arnold the Younger, 1850–1900*, ed. J.
    Bertram, London: OUP, 1980

Barry, W., *Memories and Opinions*, London: G.P. Putnams's &
    Sons, 1926
[Bellasis, E.], *A Contribution towards Oratory School Annals: the Year
    1858*, London: privately printed, 1887 [BOA, N.L.D.2.1]
[——], *Extracts from a School Boy's Diary, 1864–65*, London:
    privately printed, 1887 [BOA, N.L.D.2.1]
[——], *Further Extracts from a School Boy's Diary, 1866–70*,
    London: privately printed, 1889 [BOA, N.L.D.2.1]
——, *Memorials of Mr Serjeant Bellasis, 1800–1873*, London:
    Burns & Oates, 1893; 1895

'an old boy' [Belloc, H.], 'John Henry Cardinal Newman', *The Lamp* 39, 1890, pp. 137–39

Boland J.P., 'School-days under Cardinal Newman', *Homage to Newman, 1845–1945*, ed. G. Wheeler, Gloucester: British Publishing Co., 1945, pp. 39–40

Brownlow, W.R.B., *Memoir of Sir James Marshall*, London: Burns & Oates, 1890

Brownson, O., 'Capes's four years' experience', *Brownson's Quarterly Review* 20, July 1850 (reprinted in *The Works of Orestes Brownson* XX, New York: AMS Press, 1966, pp. 1–22)

[Capes, J.M.], 'Catholic and Protestant collegiate education', *The Rambler*, December 1848, pp. 235–41

[——], 'The duties of journalists: Catholic and Protestant education', *The Rambler*, January 1849, pp. 325–31

Carteret-Bisson, F.S. de, *Our Schools and Colleges*, London: Simplain, Marshall & Co., [1884]

Charlton, B., *The Recollections of a Northumbrian Lady, 1815–1866: being the Memoirs of Barbara Charlton*, ed. L.E.O. Charlton, Stocksfield: Spredden Press, 1949; 1989

Chichester, C.R., *Schools*, London: Burns & Oates, 1882

Clarendon Commission (*Report of Her Majesty's Commissioners appointed to inquire into the Revenues and Management of certain Colleges and Schools, and the Studies pursued and Instruction given therein*), British Parliamentary Papers, 1864, XX, 4 vols.

Döllinger, J.J.I., *Lord Acton Briefwechsel, 1820–90*, 4 vols., ed. V. Conzemius, Munich: Beck, 1963

FitzAlan, Viscount [E. Howard], 'Catholics in public life', *Catholic Emancipation, 1829 to 1929: Essays by Various Authors*, London: Longmans, Green & Co., 1929, pp. 141–58

Gorman, W.G., *Converts to Rome: a Biographical List of the more notable Converts to the Catholic Church in the United Kingdom during the last Sixty Years*, London: Sands & Co., 1910

Hinds, T.M., *Oratory School Register, 1859–1919*, privately printed, 1966 [Oratory School, Woodcote]

Hopkins, G.M., *The Letters of Gerard Manley Hopkins to Robert*

Bridges, ed. C.C. Abbott, London: OUP, 1935
——, *Further Letters of Gerard Manley Hopkins, including his Correspondence with Coventry Patmore*, ed. C.C. Abbott, London: OUP, 1938; 1956
——, *The Journals and Papers of Gerard Manley Hopkins*, ed. H. House & G. Storey, London: OUP, 1959
Hutton, P., Northcote, J.S., Purbrick, E., Sweeney, J.N. and Wilkinson, F. (eds), *Higher Catholic Education: General Report of the Sub-commission*, London: privately printed, 1872

Manning, H.E., 'The works and the wants of the Catholic Church in England', *Dublin Review* 1, 1863, pp.139–69 (reprinted in Manning, *Miscellanies* I, London: Burns & Oates, 1877, pp. 27–71)

Newman, J.H., 'On consulting the faithful in matters of doctrine', *The Rambler*, July 1859, pp. 198–230 (reprinted as *On Consulting the Faithful in Matters of Doctrine*, ed. J. Coulson, London: G. Chapman, 1961)
'H.O.' [——], 'Seminaries of the Catholic Church', *The Rambler*, September 1860, pp. 398–401 (reprinted in *L&D* XIX, pp. 554–57)
——, *An Essay in aid of a Grammar of Assent*, London: Longmans, Green & Co., 1870; 1898
——, *Sermons Preached on Various Occasions*, London: Longmans, Green & Co., 1870; 1898
——, *Historical Sketches* III, London: Longmans, Green & Co., 1872; 1909
'Catholicus' [——], 'The Tamworth Reading Room', letters to *The Times*, February 1841 (reprinted in *Discussions and Arguments on Various Subjects*, London: Longmans, Green & Co., 1872; 1891, pp. 254–305)
——, *The Idea of a University: Defined and Illustrated*, London: Longmans, Green & Co., 1873; 1907
——, *My Campaign in Ireland, Part 1: Catholic University Reports and other Papers*, ed. W. Neville, Aberdeen [Ireland]: A. King & Co., 1896
——, *Addresses to Cardinal Newman with His Replies*, ed. W.P. Neville, London: Longmans, Green & Co., 1905
——, *John Henry Newman: Autobiographical Writings*, ed. H.

Tristam, London: Sheed & Ward, 1956

——, *Newman the Oratorian: His Unpublished Oratory Papers*, ed. P. Murray, Dublin: Gill & Macmillan, 1969

——, *The Letters and Diaries of John Henry Newman* 31 vols., ed. C.S. Dessain *et al.*, London: T. Nelson, 1961–72; Oxford: Clarendon Press, 1973–2005

Northcote, J.S., *Higher Catholic Education: Special Report by the President of St Mary's College, Oscott, upon the Evidence Supplied to the Sub-commission*, London: privately printed, 1872

'A.M.D.G.' [Oakeley, F.], 'English public schools and colleges in Catholic times', *The Rambler*, September 1861, pp. 346–60

The Oratory School Magazine, 1891– [Oratory School, Woodcote]

'Our public schools and universities before the Reformation', *The Rambler*, November 1861, pp. 119–24

'X.Y.Z.' [Oxenham, H.O.], 'Catholic education', *The Rambler*, July 1860, pp. 248–53 (reprinted in *L&D* XIX, pp. 551–54); November 1860, pp. 100–17 (partly reprinted in *L&D* XIX, pp. 558–60)

Paul, C.K., *Memories*, London: Kegan Paul & Co., 1899

'Personal reminiscences of a Catholic Eton', *Journal of Education* 374, September 1900, pp. 555–57

Petre, W.J., *Remarks on the Present Position of Catholic Liberal Education*, London: Burns & Oates, 1877

——, *The Problem of Catholic Liberal Education*, London: Burns & Oates, 1877

——, *The Position and Prospects of Catholic Liberal Education*, London: Burns & Oates, 1878

——, *Catholic Systems of School Discipline*, London: Burns & Oates, 1878

——, 'Large or small schools', *Dublin Review* 31, July 1878, pp. 98–105

Purbrick, E.J., *Special Report on the Answers Received by the Sub-commission on Higher Catholic Education*, Roehampton: privately printed, 1872

'St Charles' College, Bayswater', *Westminster Gazette*, February 1876 (reprinted in F.J. Kirk, *Reminiscences of an Oblate of St Charles*, London: Burns & Oates, 1905, pp. 72–78)

Simpson, R., 'The Catholic Church in England in 1859', *Downside Review* 84, April 1966, pp. 171–92

The Synods in English: being the Text of the four Synods of Westminster, ed. R.E. Guy, Stratford-on-Avon: St Gregory's Press, 1886

Taunton Commission (*Report of the Commissioners appointed by Her Majesty to inquire into the Education given in Schools in England, not comprised within Her Majesty's two recent Commissions on Popular Education and on Public Schools*), British Parliamentary Papers, 1867–68, XXVIII, 21 vols.

Ward, W.G., letter to the editor, *The Rambler*, February 1849, pp. 446–57
——, 'Catholic education', *The Rambler*, January 1861, pp. 237–73
——, letter to editor, *The Rambler*, May 1861, pp. 100–17
——, 'Public school education', *Dublin Review* 5, July 1865, pp. 1–43
——, 'Catholic college education in England', *Dublin Review* 31, April 1878, pp. 327–59
——, 'Catholic college discipline', *Dublin Review* 31, July 1878, pp. 87–97
——, 'Catholic colleges and Protestant schools', *Dublin Review* 31, October 1878, pp. 279–318
——, book review of 'The new departure in Catholic liberal education', *Dublin Review* 31, December 1878, pp. 487–90
Wilkinson, F., *Addendum to the Report of the Sub-commission on Catholic Higher Education*, privately printed, 1872

Secondary Sources

Adams, P.A., 'Converts to the Roman Catholic Church in England, circa 1830–1870', B.Litt., Oxford, 1977
Addington, R., *The Idea of the Oratory*, London: Burns & Oates, 1966
Aldrich, R., *An Introduction to the History of Education*, London: Hodder & Stoughton, 1982
Allies, M.H., *Thomas William Allies*, London: Burns & Oates, 1907

Allitt, P., *Catholic Converts: British and American Converts Turn to Rome*, Ithaca: Cornell University Press, 1997

Altholz, J.L., *The Liberal Catholic Movement in England: the 'Rambler' and its Contributors, 1848–1864*, Montreal: Palm Publishers, 1962

Bamford, T.W., *The Rise of the Public Schools: a Study of Boys' Public Boarding Schools in England and Wales from 1837 to the Present Day*, London: Nelson, 1967

——, 'Public school masters: a nineteenth-century profession', *History of Education* 8, 1973, pp. 29–47

Barnes, A.S., *The Catholic Schools of England*, London: Williams & Norgate, 1926

Barr, C., *Paul Cullen, John Henry Newman, and the Catholic University of Ireland, 1845–1865*, Gracewing: Leominster, 2003

Basset, B., *The English Jesuits from Campion to Martindale*, London: Burns & Oates, 1967

Battersby, W.J., 'Secondary education for boys', ed. G.A. Beck, *The English Catholics*, pp. 322–36

Beales, A.C.F., 'The struggle for the schools', ed. G.A. Beck, *The English Catholics*, pp. 365-409

——, *Education under Penalty: English Catholic Education from the Reformation to the Fall of James II, 1547–1689*, London: Athlone Press, 1963

Beck, G.A. (ed.), *The English Catholics, 1850–1950: Essays to Commemorate the Centenary of the Restoration of the Hierarchy of England and Wales*, London: Burns & Oates, 1950

Belloc-Lowdnes, M., *The Young Hilaire Belloc*, New York: Kennedy & Sons, 1956

Bergonzi, B., *A Victorian Wanderer: the Life of Thomas Arnold the Younger*, New York: OUP, 2003

Bryant, M., *The London Experience of Secondary Education*, London: Athlone Press, 1986

Buscot, W., *The History of Cotton College at Sedgley Park, 1763–1873: at Cotton, 1873–*, London: Burns, Oates & Washbourne, 1940

Butler, C., 'Newman and modern education', *Downside Review* 70, 1952, pp. 259–74

Butler, E.C., *The Life and Times of Bishop Ullathorne, 1806–1889*, 2 vols., London: Burns, Oates & Washbourne, 1926

Caparrini, B.R., 'A Catholic public school in the making: Beaumont College during the rectorate of the Reverend Joseph M. Bampton, SJ (1901–1908). His implementation of the 'Captain' system of discipline', *Paedogogica Historica* 39, December 2003, pp. 737-57

Card, T., *Eton Renewed: a History from 1860 to the Present Day*, London: John Murray, 1994

——, *Eton Established: a History from 1440 to 1860*, London: John Murray, 2001

Champ, J.F., *Oscott*, Birmingham: Archdiocese of Birmingham Historical Commission, 1987

Chandos, J., *Boys Together: English Public Schools, 1800–1864*, London: Hutchinson, 1984

Chavasse, P., 'Newman and the laity', *Newman Today*, ed. S.L. Jaki, San Francisco: Ignatius Press, 1989, pp. 49–78

Coulson, J., 'Newman's idea of an educated laity', *Theology and the University: an Ecumenical Investigation*, ed J. Coulson, Baltimore: Helicon Press, 1964, pp. 47–63

Cramer, A., *Ampleforth: the Story of St Lawrence's Abbey and College*, Ampleforth Abbey, 2001

Culler, A.D., *The Imperial Intellect: a Study of Newman's Educational Ideal*, New Haven: Yale University Press, 1955

Davies, M., 'Newman and education: some questions for today', *Newman and Education*, ed. M. Davies, Rugeley: Spode House, 1980, pp. 4–20

Devas, F., *The History of St Stanislaus' College, Beaumont, 1861–1911: a Record of Fifty Years*, Old Windsor: privately printed, 1911

Evennett, H.O., *The Catholic Schools of England and Wales*, Cambridge: CUP, 1944

——, 'Catholics and the universities, 1850–1950', ed. G.A. Beck, *The English Catholics*, pp. 291–321

Foster, S., 'Monsignor Lord William Joseph Petre (1847–93): a pillar of Downside', *Recusant History* 22, 1994–95, pp. 88–101

Gathorne-Hardy, J., *The Public School Phenomenon, 597–1997*, London: Hodder & Stoughton, 1977

Gilley, S., *Newman and His Age*, London: Darton, Longman & Todd, 1990

Gruggen, G. & Keating J., *Stonyhurst: its Past History and Life in the Present*, London: Kegan Paul & Co., 1901

Heeney, B., *Mission to the Middle Classes: the Woodard Schools, 1848–1891*, London: SPCK, 1969

Hibbert, C., *No Ordinary Place: Radley College and the Public School System, 1847–1997*, London: John Murray, 1997

Hill, R., *Lord Acton*, New Haven: Yale University Press, 2000

Holland, M.G., *The British Catholic Press and the Education Controversy, 1847–1865*, London: Garland, 1987

Holmes, J.D., *More Roman than Rome: English Catholicism in the Nineteenth Century*, London: Burns & Oates, 1978

Honey, J.R. de S., *Tom Brown's Universe: the Development of the Victorian Public School*, London: Millington, 1977

Horwood, T., 'The rise and fall of the Catholic University College, Kensington, 1868–1882', *Journal of Ecclesiastical History* 54 no.2, April 2003, pp. 302–18

Jackson, J., 'John Henry Newman: the origins and application of his educational ideas', Ph.D., Leicester [?], 1968 [BOA]

James, L., *A Forgotten Genius: Sewell, of St Columba's and Radley*, London: Faber & Faber, 1945

Ker, I.T., 'Newman the Teacher', *Newman and Education*, ed. M. Davies, Rugley: Spode House, 1980, pp. 32–41

——, *John Henry Newman: a Biography*, Oxford: Clarendon Press, 1988

——, *The Achievement of John Henry Newman*, London: Collins, 1990

Leinster-Mackay, D.P., *The Rise of the English Prep School*, London: Falmer, 1984

——, 'Private or public schools: the educational debate in *laissez-faire* England', *Journal of Educational Administration and History* 15 no. 2, July 1983, pp. 1–6

Levi, P., *Beaumont, 1861–1961*, London: A. Deutsch, 1961

MacDougall, H.A., *The Acton–Newman Relations: the Dilemma of*

Christian Liberalism, New York: Fordham University Press, 1962

Mack, E.C., *Public Schools and British Opinion since 1860: the Relationship between Contemporary Ideas and the Evolution of an English Institution*, New York: Columbia University Press, 1941

Mangan, J.A., *Athleticism in the Victorian and Edwardian Public School*, Cambridge: CUP, 1981

Marett-Crosby, A., *A School of the Lord's Service: a History of Ampleforth*, London: James & James, 2002

Martin, B.W., *John Henry Newman: His Life and Work*, London: Chatto & Windus, 1982

Martin, R.B., *Gerard Manley Hopkins: a very Private Life*, London: Harper Collins, 1991

McClelland, V.A., *Cardinal Manning: His Public Life and Influence, 1865–1892*, London: OUP, 1962

——, 'The liberal training of England's Catholic youth: William Joseph Petre (1847–93) and educational reform', *Victorian Studies* 15, 1972, pp. 257–77

——, *English Roman Catholics and Higher Education, 1830–1903*, Oxford: Clarendon Press, 1973

——, *The Liberal Education of England's Youth: Idea and Reality*, Hull: University of Hull, 1979

——, 'A Catholic Eton: by hook or by crook? John Henry Newman and the establishment of the Oratory School', *Aspects of Education* 22, 1980, pp. 3–17

——, 'School or cloister? An English educational dilemma, 1794–1889', *Paedagogica Historica* 20, 1980, pp. 108–28

——, '*Sensus fidelium*: the developing concept of Roman Catholic voluntary effort in education in England and Wales', *Christianity and Educational Provision in International Perspective*, ed. C. Brock and W. Tulasiewicz, London: Routledge, 1988, pp. 61–88

——, 'Tractarian intellectualism and the silent heritage: 1840–50', *Oscott College, 1838–1988: a Volume of Commemorative Essays*, ed. J.F. Champ, privately printed, 1988, pp. 83–92

——, 'Authority and freedom: John Henry Newman and the formation of Youth', *In History and in Education: Essays Presented to Peter Gordon*, ed. R. Aldrich, London: Woburn Press, 1996, pp. 58–73

McGrath, F., *Newman's University: Idea and Reality*, London: Longmans, Green & Co., 1951

Mohnen, W.G., 'Voruniversitäre Erziehung bei John Henry Newman, dargestellt am Beispeil der Oratory School' (Pre-university education in the eyes of John Henry Newman, as represented by the example of the Oratory School), Ph.D., Teachers High School of the Rhineland, Cologne, 1978

Muir, T.E., *Stonyhurst College 1593–1993*, London: James & James, 1992

Mulcahy, D.G., 'Personal influence, discipline, and liberal education in Cardinal Newman's Idea of a University', *Newman-Studien* 11, 1980, pp. 150–58

Nash, A., *Newman's Idea of a School*, Woodcote: Oratory School Association, 1990

Newsome, D., *Godliness and Good Learning: Four Studies on a Victorian Ideal*, London: John Murray, 1961

——, *The Convert Cardinals: John Henry Newman and Henry Edward Manning*, London: John Murray, 1993

——, *The Victorian World Picture*, London: John Murray, 1997

Norman, E., *The English Catholic Church in the Nineteenth Century*, Oxford: Clarendon Press, 1984

The Oratory School, Caversham, Reading: its History, Development and Present-day Activities, Gloucester: British Publishing Co., [1938]

Ornsby, R., *Memoirs of James Robert Hope-Scott*, 2 vols., London: John Murray, 1884

Pereiro, J., *Cardinal Manning: an Intellectual Biography*, Oxford: Clarendon Press, 1998

Pollen, A., *John Hungerford Pollen, 1820–1902*, London: John Murray, 1912

Rees, D. (ed.), *Monks of England: the Benedictines in England from Augustine to the Present Day*, London: SPCK, 1997

Roach, J., *A History of Secondary Education in England, 1800–1870*, London: Longmans, 1986

Roberts, F., *A History of Sedgley Park and Cotton College*, Preston: privately printed, 1985

Rothblatt, S., 'An Oxonian "idea" of a university: J.H. Newman and "well-being"', *The History of the University of Oxford* VI, ed. M.G. Brock and M.C. Curthoys, Oxford: OUP, 1997, pp. 287–305

Rutler, G.W., 'Newman's idea of a Catholic university', *Newman Today*, ed. S.L. Jaki, San Francisco: Ignatius Press, 1989, pp. 95–120

Sabben-Clare, J.P., *Winchester College: After 600 Years, 1382–1982*, Southampton: Paul Cave, 1981

St Quintin, G., *The History of Glenalmond: the Story of a Hundred Years*, Edinburgh: Constable, 1956

Shrimpton, P.A., 'John Henry Newman and the Oratory School, 1857–72: the foundation of a Catholic public school by converts from the Oxford Movement', Ph.D., London, 2000

Shrosbree, C., *Public Schools and Private Education: the Clarendon Commission 1861–64 and the Public Schools Act*, Manchester: Manchester University Press, 1988

Simon, B. and Bradley, I. (eds), *The Victorian Public School*, Dublin: Gill & Macmillan, 1975

Sire, H.J.A., *Gentlemen Philosophers: Catholic Higher Studies at Liège and Stonyhurst College, 1774–1916*, Worthing: Churchman, 1988

Speaight, R., *The Life of Hilaire Belloc*, London: Hollis & Carter, 1957

Stork, R.A.P., 'John Henry Newman and the laity', S.T.D., Lateran University, Rome, 1966

Sugg, J., *Ever Yours Affly: John Henry Newman and his Female Circle*, Leominster: Gracewing, 1996

Tinkel, A.J., 'Cardinal Newman's school: a history of The Oratory School', paper read to the History of Reading Society, 15 September 2004

Trevor, M., *Newman: the Pillar of the Cloud*, London: Macmillan, 1962

——, *Newman: Light in Winter*, London: Macmillan, 1962

——, *The Arnolds: Thomas Arnold and his Family*, London: Bodley Head, 1973

Tristram, H., *Newman and His Friends*, London: John Lane, 1933

——, *Cardinal Newman and the Church of the Birmingham Oratory: a History and a Guide*, Gloucester: British Publishing Co., 1962

——, 'The school-days of Cardinal Newman', *Cornhill Magazine* 58, June 1925, pp. 666–77

——, 'Cardinal Newman and the function of education', *Blackfriars* 9, 1928, pp. 478–94

[——], 'The Oratory School', *OPM* 133–80, January 1932 – December 1935

——, 'London University and Catholic education', *Dublin Review* 199, October 1936, pp. 269–82

Tyerman, C., *A History of Harrow School*, Oxford: OUP, 2000

Upton, A.J., 'Oscott College and Catholic education in the nineteenth century: a comparison with the English public school', M.Ed., Birmingham, 1981

Van Zeller, H., *Downside By and Large: a Double Fugue in Praise of Things Lasting and Gregorian*, London: Sheed & Ward, 1954

Ward, B., *History of St Edmund's College, Old Hall*, London: Kegan Paul & Co., 1893

——, *The Dawn of the Catholic Revival in England, 1781–1803*, 2 vols., London: Longmans, Green & Co., 1909

——, *The Sequel to Catholic Emancipation: the Story of the English Catholics continued down to the Re-establishment of their Hierarchy in 1850*, 2 vols., London: Longmans, Green & Co., 1915

Ward, W., *The Life of John Henry, Cardinal Newman*, 2 vols., London: Longmans, Green & Co., 1912

Index

The connection of individuals to the Oratory School is indicated in italics: co-founder, dame, headmaster, master, parent, Prefect of houses, promoter, pupil, or spiritual director. References to illustrations are given in bold.

CPSIA information can be obtained at www.ICGtesting.com
Printed in the USA
BVOW03s0220220615

405571BV00001B/26/P